Amer
Govt

THE
AIR FORCE
MAFIA

THE
AIR FORCE
MAFIA

PETER N. JAMES

ARLINGTON HOUSE·PUBLISHERS
NEW ROCHELLE, N. Y.

Library of Congress Cataloging in Publication Data

James, Peter N   1940-
   The Air Force Mafia.

   1.   United States. Air Force. Foreign Technology
Division. 2.   Intelligence service--United States.
3. Aerospace industries--United States. I. Title.
UG633.J26   358.4'13'4320973   74-23872
ISBN 0-87000-289-9

To my loving wife
Diane

For being at my side throughout the ordeal
For laboring at great personal sacrifice to keep us afloat
For typing an endless number of drafts
For typing the final
For your constructive criticism and overall contribution to
        this work
For standing by your principles

                              your husband,
                                    Peter

Contents

BOOK I
The Indictment

BOOK II
The Odyssey

"Don't shoot from the hip . . . line up the ducks first."—advice given to the author by Palm Beach Shores multi-billionaire John D. MacArthur.

THE
AIR FORCE
MAFIA

In the News

- *The Palm Beach Post* (West Palm Beach, Florida, October 20, 1971):

Last Oct. 4, at 8:10 A.M., Peter James, an engineer with intimate knowledge of both Russian and American space programs, told his Pratt & Whitney Aircraft superiors he was going ahead with a book (about the incompetence and Mafia-like tactics of espionage agents affiliated with the Air Force Foreign Technology Division). . . .

At 2:30 P.M. the same day the assistant project engineer was given an "option" by company officials—resign or be fired.

James, who had worked for the company for nine years, said he would not resign.

At 2:45 P.M., James signed his corporate debriefing form, visited the payroll and retirement sections, turned over his "secret" level badge to a security officer and for the last time drove out the gate of the huge rocket and jet engine development center on Beeline Highway near West Palm Beach. . . .

The company declined to comment on James' ouster.

- *The Miami Herald* (Miami, Florida, April 2, 1972):

Pratt & Whitney officials at first declined to comment on James' charges. Then, a company official said: "There is absolutely no con-

13

nection between the reason Mr. James is no longer employed by Pratt & Whitney and his announced intention to write a book."

• *The Palm Beach Post* (September 30, 1973):

Peter James is a writer who lives in Palm Beach Shores. He worked for nine years at Pratt & Whitney in Palm Beach County until he was fired in 1971 for violating company rules, according to the corporation.

It was part of his job at Pratt & Whitney to do work for the Air Force (Foreign) Technology Division, which James says operates inefficiently, expensively and often illegally.

The story of the division, as told by Peter James in *The Post* today and this week, is somewhere between a soap opera and a real-life spy chiller.

James has documentation for most of what he says, but some facts were hard to verify from other sources. The Central Intelligence Agency, as usual, isn't talking. The Air Force, as usual, isn't talking. And Pratt & Whitney chooses to keep its comments to a minimum.

Although he explains inner-workings of U.S. spy efforts, James says these articles contain no material it would be illegal for him to publish.—The Editors

• *The Dayton Daily News* (Dayton, Ohio, September 30, 1973):

At present, the Air Force is investigating James' thus-far unproven allegations of death threats, harassment, falsification of intelligence documents, spying on American citizens and other unethical and illegal activities. . . . Pratt & Whitney officials told *The Daily News* that James was fired for violation of company rules, not for security reasons.

A company spokesman said he could not respond point by point to questions about James without getting involved with classified information.

Col. George R. Weinbrenner, commander of the Foreign Technology Division, which gathers scientific and technical information on foreign aerospace developments, referred questions about James to Air Force headquarters in Washington, D. C.

Officials there gave this response: "The Air Force is aware of James' allegations and is investigating. It would be inappropriate to comment on them while the investigation is in progress."

Privately, a high Air Force official dismissed the charges as those of a "disgruntled employee" and expressed the belief that there is "nothing to it."

Whether truth or the figment of an active imagination, the story unfolded by James makes fascinating reading.

- *The Palm Beach Post* (October 2, 1973):

When he worked as a space systems analyst for Pratt & Whitney in the late 1960s and early 1970s, Peter James made intelligence assessments of information collected by the Foreign Technology Division. Over the years he concluded that many operations of the division were illegal.

Attempts by *The Post* to obtain comments from Pratt & Whitney resulted in the company's allowing us to submit written questions. A spokesman replied:

> "In past years we have performed analytical work under contract to the Air Force Foreign Technology Division. But we know of no threats or coercive actions against either the company or Mr. James by anyone in the Air Force.
>
> "Mr. James was dismissed by Pratt & Whitney on Oct. 4, 1971, for violation of company rules and not for any security reasons.
>
> "Because a point-by-point rebuttal would require us to divulge classified or proprietary information we cannot respond to your other questions."

- *The Palm Beach Post* (an editorial, October 5, 1973):

Peter James, who both collected information for the Central Intelligence Agency and analyzed data collected by the Air Force Foreign Technology Division, has told a James Bondish story of spying that ought to spur both interest and action from Congress.

The spy story, just concluded in serial form in *The Post*, brings home—in fact, right up to the Pratt & Whitney gates—the alarming infiltration of the military into American companies, research establishments, universities and other institutions. . . . It is little wonder that the Air Force doesn't want to see its spy program exposed in book form when serial form already is cause for hard concern and investigation by Congress.

- *Letter dated October 24, 1973, to Peter James from Senator William Proxmire (D.-Wis.):*

Dear Mr. James:

I appreciate having the five part exposé you wrote for *The Palm Beach Post* on the Air Force Foreign Technology Division.

It is a most interesting exposition and I shall give it my careful and prompt attention. If you should have any further documentation, I would be most pleased to receive it.

Sincerely,
William Proxmire, U.S.S.

- *Air Force response to Senator William Proxmire dated December 11, 1973:*

Dear Senator Proxmire:

This is in response to your letter of October 31 to the Air Force Chief of Staff concerning alleged improper activities by the Foreign Technology Division (FTD), Wright-Patterson AFB, Ohio, in the conduct of intelligence collection and analysis.

This matter has been investigated by the Air Force Office of Special Investigations (AFOSI). As you are aware, Mr. Peter N. James, who made the allegations, provided AFOSI with a lengthy sworn statement, supported by numerous documentary exhibits which he believes lend credence to his allegations. Based on this sworn statement, numerous military and civilian FTD employees and officials named by Mr. James, or who were identified as having been familiar with the many facets of the allegations, were interviewed. These interviews support Mr. James' facts insofar as dates of international meetings, identities of FTD attendees, etc., are concerned. The interviews do not, however, appear to substantiate his allegations against FTD of improper administrative conduct, intelligence collection malpractice, threats or harassment. The investigation did not reveal any evidence, other than Mr. James' statement, to substantiate his claim of an alleged FTD-inspired conspiracy to threaten or harass Mr. James and his wife in Brussels, Belgium in September 1971. Various personnel specifically identified by Mr. James as having been present at that time were interviewed. All denied any knowledge of alleged threats or harassment.

. . . We trust this information will be useful.

Sincerely,
Joseph J. F. Clark
Associate Director
Legislative Liaison
Department of the Air Force

- *The Hillsdale Daily News* (Hillsdale, Michigan, February 4, 1974):

A former space and military intelligence engineer accused top-level United States officials of perpetrating a conspiracy to commit what could be defined as treason during his speech at Hillsdale College Sunday.

Peter N. James, 33, a native of Florida, didn't use the word "treason," but when the term was used to describe his subject he didn't disclaim it either. His speech, entitled, "Systems Analysis of Detente," was part of a Center For Constructive Alternatives (CCA) symposium on communism to run through Friday.

. . . James' thesis holds that the United States government knowledgeably and purposefully committed this nation to an agreement with the Soviet Union which contains the seeds of this country's destruction, and further conspired to withhold information revealing the perfidious action from the United States public.

It is James' professed intention to break the silence on the alleged treachery, despite the loss of his job, threats on his life by government intelligence agents and the formidable prospects of taking on the entire executive branch of the national government, he said.

In doing so, James is admittedly skirting the letter of the law by revealing the numbers of classified government documents—documents he says he prepared himself—which contain the substantiation of his charges.

• *The Washington Post* (Washington, D. C., March 14, 1974):

For six years aerospace engineer Peter N. James, 33, lived in a twilight world of technological spying.

He was a CIA informant on Soviet rocket technology as well as a Pratt & Whitney Aircraft propulsion engineer who traveled to international scientific conferences in such places as Athens, Madrid, Belgrade, Venice, and Paris. There James would mingle with Soviet scientists and then covertly report to his CIA contact what he had learned.

His work earned him letters of commendation from the Air Force, from his employers and from the CIA as well.

James has now come in from the cold, at the price both of his job and his dual role as a CIA informant. And he has given Congress, Air Force investigators, the FBI, and CIA an extraordinary story of cloak-and-dagger harassment by an obscure military intelligence agency —the Air Force's Foreign Technology Division.

After investigating the James affair, contained in a 29-page sworn statement plus exhibits given to the Air Force Office of Special Investigations, Sen. William Proxmire (D-Wis.) called yesterday for abolition of the Foreign Technology Division. . . . Defense

Secretary James R. Schlesinger told Proxmire during a hearing last week that he would look into the allegations.

- *Los Angeles Herald-Examiner* (Los Angeles, California, March 15, 1974):

WASHINGTON (AP)—Sen. William Proxmire, D-Wis., Thursday called for the abolition of a little-known Air Force spying operation after hearing reports the agency intrudes into the defense industry and is accused of threatening a CIA informant.

- *Aerospace Daily* (March 15, 1974):

Both Proxmire and James, who plans to publish a book on his experiences . . . charged that pressure was brought against companies and individuals to gather information on foreign military developments. Proxmire called for abolition of the Foreign Technology Div., based at Wright-Patterson AFB, Ohio. . . .

Proxmire, in calling for an end to FTD activities, charges that "They recruit employees of defense firms and enter into contracts with these firms in order to obtain data about foreign scientific and technical developments. As such, they duplicate the intelligence operations of other organizations and provide no unique capability."

What Proxmire is apparently either unaware of or chooses to ignore is the fact that this type of intelligence operation is widely practiced by industrial nations of the world. The Soviets, and other Eastern European nations, regularly send large delegations to gather information on new defense or technology developments. . . .

There is concern in both the military and industry that Proxmire, aided by a man who admittedly wants to sell a book, may do damage to what is considered to be a routine method of gathering intelligence, which is carried out by industry people and military attachés alike.

- *Dayton Daily News* (March 17, 1974):

WASHINGTON—The Pentagon has signaled to Sen. William Proxmire (D-Wis.) an apparent willingness to severely restrict the activities of a worldwide Air Force intelligence operation headquartered at Wright-Patterson Air Force Base.

The restrictions would ostensibly be economy moves, aimed at eliminating overlap of activities of the Air Force's Foreign Technology Division (FTD) with the intelligence-gathering work of the

Central Intelligence Agency, the Defense Intelligence Agency and the U.S. State Department.

FTD would retain its Wright-Patterson work force, which would concentrate in the future strictly on the analysis, production and dissemination of foreign aerospace scientific and technical intelligence information collected by other agencies.

Senator Proxmire, however, said this week that he wants the Pentagon to go further, and completely abolish the FTD, a unit of the Air Force Systems Command, which is headquartered at Andrews Air Force base near Washington.

The Pentagon's proposal comes in direct response to complaints aired last autumn by Peter N. James of Palm Beach, Florida, an engineer fired in 1971 by Pratt & Whitney Aircraft Corp.

• *The Palm Beach Post* (March 19, 1974):

James called the Pentagon's proposal "a step in the right direction," but said the planned cutback won't go far enough.

"When the full story of the Foreign Technology Division and its operations is made public, it will become readily apparent that the FTD can be disbanded and the more qualified analysts and agents can be absorbed into the Central Intelligence Agency and Defense Intelligence Agency," James said.

Note to the Reader

IN A LETTER dated January 20, 1974, Senator William Proxmire asked me to review the Air Force's reply to his office and to provide him with whatever response I thought was necessary. On February 11, 1974, I signed a contract with Arlington House Publishers to write *The Air Force Mafia* and notified Senator Proxmire and other interested parties of my decision; this book is my response to the Air Force.

I hope this work shocks both liberals and conservatives and all law-abiding American taxpayers who have had their fill of irresponsible and incompetent government officials and spokesmen who have secretly abused the authority entrusted to them for short-term personal gains.

This work should not be construed as a vicious attack against the United States Air Force—an organization I deeply respect and one which greatly contributes to our national security—but an attempt to expose an uncontrolled cancerous outfit which has seized the machinery of the Air Force Systems Command and used the good name of the Air Force to achieve unethical and illegal objectives that run contrary to American democratic principles and tradition. It is my hope that the long-term benefits derived from the work within will far outweigh the short-term outrage and denunciation that will surely follow its release into the public domain.

I assume full responsibility for its content and I have written this manuscript with the understanding that the First Amendment to the Constitution is a privilege one should exercise responsibly without jeopardizing the national security of the United States or violating the rights of others; it is also a privilege afforded to Americans "to petition the government for a redress of grievances."

Prologue

The Air Force Mafia—A Bird's Eye View

IN BUILDING 828 of Wright-Patterson Air Force Base near Dayton, Ohio, there exists a hush-hush operation of spies who answer to no one but the United States Air Force, who spy on their fellow citizens and whose operations are so illegal and unethical that they are known privately as the Air Force Mafia.

This uncontrolled espionage network reaches into the pockets of every American, violates the constitutional rights of U.S. citizens, has adversely affected the designs of U.S. weapons systems, and sometimes impedes the intelligence gathering activities of duly constituted agencies such as the Central Intelligence Agency (CIA). Its power is so awesome that the management of Pratt & Whitney Aircraft, a multi-million dollar aerospace firm dependent on Air Force contracts, lied publicly in 1973, apparently to protect the firm's interests vis-à-vis the Air Force and to preclude further disclosures concerning Pratt & Whitney's involvement with espionage agents from Building 828.

Behind the doors of Building 828 are stories of ineptness, failure, and conspiracy. In the name of national security these intelligence agents and their cohorts have threatened American citizens who have gotten in their way.

I know, because I have been in Building 828 as Pratt & Whitney's foreign technology expert and I have worked with this Air Force outfit, officially known as the Air Force Foreign Technology Division. After almost three years of association with the division, called FTD by its agents, I attempted to break relations with it because I did not wish to participate in what has been described by knowledgeable insiders as a "national intelligence scandal."

In 1971, my superiors in Pratt & Whitney ordered me to cooperate with the agents in Building 828 in spite of my written request of October 1970 to be phased out of any further dealings with them. After I attempted to expose the Air Force Mafia to other branches of the United States government, my wife and I were harassed and threatened by Air Force Mafia espionage agents and I was subsequently fired in October 1971 by Pratt & Whitney Aircraft management. At the time of my firing, only a handful of individuals, including upper Pratt & Whitney Aircraft management, knew that I had an excellent reputation in classified circles analyzing intelligence for the Air Force and collecting intelligence for the CIA, and this was not simply a case of an employee violating company rules, as the company alleged. The story went beyond the gates of the huge Pratt & Whitney jet and rocket engine development complex in Palm Beach County, and it transcended questionable U.S. intelligence operations both at home and abroad.

With Senator Sam Ervin's Watergate Committee having brought before the American people the cast of characters involved in the Watergate break-in, the "White House horrors," and the Watergate cover-up; with Special Prosecutor Leon Jaworski having methodically indicted and brought to trial many of these men; and with Chairman Peter Rodino's House Judiciary Committee having brought to light more questionable dealings in the Executive Branch of government, the public has been bombarded with what would appear to be the tail end of the so-called scandal. Not so; what is missing in the thousands of pages of testimony is the story of the Air Force Mafia which, like the White House plumbers and other members of the President's special intelligence unit, operated in secret. Despite all the talk and outward signs of cooperation during these hearings, the U.S. intelligence establishment has been sitting on a time bomb. The Air Force Mafia story is another mosaic of the Watergate saga, when men almost stole a nation under the guise of national security.

For all practical purposes, the Foreign Technology Division can be thought of as being an intelligence arm of the prestigious Air Force Systems Command, but it is not officially considered to be a part of the United States intelligence community, and it therefore is not subject to control by the United States Intelligence Board, which reports to the President and oversees U.S. intelligence operations. In fact, a majority of Americans has not even heard of the Air Force Foreign Technology Division, whereas the CIA is known to all and is synonymous with spying.

Without controls by government bodies, ambitious intelligence officers within the Foreign Technology Division (FTD) were able in the late 1960s to extend their power and influence and eventually overstep the bounds of their assigned intelligence role. As Pratt & Whitney's foreign technology expert, I had to deal with the agents in Building 828 and I saw their power grow. Here is what I found before I was fired by Pratt & Whitney Aircraft:

• In a secret agreement with the Department of State, FTD is authorized to conduct extravagant intelligence missions using U.S. embassies in most foreign capitals as their bases of operations. To steal Soviet secrets and under the guise of national security, FTD agents have been granted the authority by Uncle Sam to coerce, intimidate, and blackmail American citizens. American embassy employees have collaborated with FTD agents to intimidate further the citizens who have been targeted. Because of an agreement between FTD and American embassies, complaints filed by American citizens do not reach the appropriate authorities in the States, and efforts are made to cover up incidents which at a later date might prove to be embarrassing to FTD or the embassy.

• Foreign Technology Division agents have infiltrated American companies, research establishments, universities, and other institutions in an effort to influence the conduct of research and the flow of technical intelligence used to justify the design or development of future military weapons systems. The infiltration of American institutions by the Foreign Technology Division usually occurs as an outgrowth of some legitimate intelligence purpose, which is later exploited by FTD agents; the legitimate arrangement permits FTD operatives to get their foot in the door, so to speak. After an FTD agent establishes contact with an American scientist or engineer who appears sympathetic to the goals of the officers in Building 828, the agent may ask the American about his firm's secret projects, or the agent may enlist the American to spy on his colleagues or cultivate more contacts in his firm for the division.

Communications between Foreign Technology Division agents and new recruits bypass official government-company channels and make use of private home addresses and secret post office box numbers. Thus, higher echelon officers within the Air Force Systems Command and Air Force Headquarters in Washington are purposely eliminated from the decision-making process and they therefore exert no control over the planning and execution of some FTD intelligence operations. Likewise, the security chiefs of government contractors are bypassed and they therefore are not privy to the covert dealings between their employees and FTD agents.

The infiltration within Pratt & Whitney Aircraft reached the stage where one high-level manager was transmitting company jet engine secrets to FTD agents who were known to be friendly with the General Electric Engine Group in Cincinnati, Ohio—Pratt & Whitney's main jet engine competitor. Corporate security investigators failed to learn the details of FTD's involvement with Pratt & Whitney engineers because of an elaborate cover-up at the highest levels.

• In an attempt to influence Air Force intelligence assessments on Russian weapons systems, so that it could sway decision-makers in the Pentagon and Congress, the Foreign Technology Division threatened to terminate relations with Pratt & Whitney Aircraft unless its foreign technology expert in the company's headquarters in East Hartford, Connecticut, was replaced as the liaison representative with the division. The division's threat was made both verbally and in the form of a memorandum, which was sent to the Pratt & Whitney Aircraft field representative for Wright-Patterson Air Force Base. The memorandum was delivered several weeks before the Air Force was to announce the award of the multi-million dollar F-15 air superiority fighter engine contract that Pratt & Whitney was vying for.

• The Directorate of Foreign Technology of the Air Force Aeronautical Systems Division (another spy unit) in collaboration with its mentor, the larger Foreign Technology Division in Building 828, had a private working agreement during the late 1960s with McDonnell Douglas, the aerospace firm in St. Louis, Missouri. Because of a working relationship with Air Force intelligence officers, McDonnell Douglas design engineers were given intelligence information on Russia's most advanced operational fighter aircraft, the MiG 25, which has been recently deployed in the Middle East and by the Warsaw Pact countries; under the covert arrangement, this intelligence was not necessarily made available to McDonnell's competitors, North American Rockwell Corporation (currently called Rockwell International Corporation) and Fairchild-Hiller Corporation, because there exists little control over the private dealings between lower echelon Air Force intelligence officers and private government contractors. McDonnell Douglas used the secret intelligence it was provided on the MiG 25 and in December 1969, the Air Force Aeronautical System Division awarded the firm a hotly contested $1.1 billion contract to develop the F-15, this nation's most advanced air superiority fighter aircraft. The F-15 has a striking resemblance to the MiG 25.

Because there are no congressional controls over private arrangements between government contractors and the military intelligence services, the American taxpayer is unwittingly subsidizing costly and unfair competitions that permit the executive branch of government and the military services to determine unscrupulously in advance who will be awarded defense contracts. This loophole, unknown to many congressmen, leaves open the possibilities of graft, kickbacks, and an assortment of other illegal activities in which billions of dollars in contracts and the jobs of hundreds of thousands of decent Americans ride on the whims of a few power-hungry men.

• To protect the integrity of intelligence reports prepared by the military intelligence services, Air Force Mafia agents are ordered frequently to debrief and discredit the sources of raw intelligence reports (i.e., intelligence reports from the field that have yet to be analyzed and incorporated into what are called finished intelligence reports) that differ greatly with the on-the-record positions of the Defense Intelligence Agency (DIA) or the Foreign Technology Division.

Air Force Mafia agents are known to submit doctored debriefing reports which discredit for life reliable government intelligence sources. These self-serving inflammatory reports are filed throughout the intelligence community and the damage to America's intelligence effort because of this practice is immeasurable.

Defectors with a language problem have been unwittingly used by Air Force Mafia agents during debriefing sessions to verify fraudulent or what are sometimes called, "indefensible" intelligence reports.

• Foreign Technology Division intelligence officers and their cohorts fabricate intelligence information and doctor finished intelligence reports. When FTD reports are known to be wrong, no responsible efforts are made to correct them because of job security or other self-serving reasons. The erroneous information, however, is often incorporated into the design specifications of future U.S. weapons systems or is used by private government contractors in studies of weapons systems that have yet to be proposed to the government.

• The quality of intelligence reports prepared by the Foreign Technology Division and/or the Defense Intelligence Agency, which relies heavily on analysts from Building 828, has been privately or publicly criticized by experts affiliated with the Florida and Connecticut branches of Pratt & Whitney Aircraft, General Electric in Cincinnati, the Air Force Aero Propulsion Laboratory at Wright-Patterson Air Force Base, the Air Force Rocket Propulsion Laboratory at Edwards, California, the Office of the Director of Defense Research and Engineering, the President's National Aeronautics and Space Council, the President's Defense Blue Ribbon Panel, the Central Intelligence Agency, and other sectors of our government. In spite of this fact, twenty to thirty billion dollars is spent *annually* by the Defense Department on the development and procurement of weapons systems originally justified on the basis of intelligence reports prepared by FTD and the military intelligence services.

• Some intelligence assessments prepared by "insecure and technically deficient" analysts within Building 828 are mere quotes out of Russian textbooks which have been approved for release outside the Soviet Union by the KGB, the Soviet intelligence service. Plagiarized excerpts are usually classified secret to perpetuate the fraud that FTD analysts have methodically reviewed thousands of pages of highly secret intelligence from the field from perhaps a top-notch agent in Russia so that the reader would draw the conclusion that the report represents the best that the U.S. intelligence establishment has to offer, and the report therefore is the "last word" on the subject.

Several translated Russian textbooks, inadvertently forwarded to Pratt & Whitney by FTD officers, had lead sentences of paragraphs changed in pencil to give the appearance that the analyst had analyzed the material. The changes appeared to have been prepared for a typist so that the new wording could be woven into the body of a finished intelligence report. In another case, an FTD agent candidly admitted to me that their analysts often throw what is termed "garbage" into an intelligence report—to pad the report—just to meet a deadline and save their jobs. The garbage method of analysis has resulted in gross errors by the military services in assessing the design characteristics of Russian rocket engines built during the 1960s.

• To determine the scope of the division's fraudulent reporting methods, I planted an erroneous story about Soviet work on a high speed bomber with a U.S. government agent in Germany during 1970. In March of 1971, while critiquing a Defense Intelligence Agency (DIA) report at the request of Foreign Technology Division agents, I ran across the story I planted in Germany. It was classified secret and interspersed with other information to support a fraudulent thesis that the Air Force Mafia was supporting concerning Soviet work on advanced bombers for the 1980 time period; an honest and thorough intelligence report would have qualified the information and indicated how it was acquired. Instead, the report, which was written mainly by FTD analysts, left the reader with the impression that a leading Russian defense official was the source of the intelligence.

As mentioned earlier, the Foreign Technology Division exerts ultimate control over its espionage operations by making secret agreements with corporate employees without the knowledge of corporate managers or security officials. Sometimes, rather than subverting the intent of a legitimate agreement, the Air Force Mafia may reach a secret agreement first, and then seek to legitimize it by proposing through legal government-corporate channels an arrangement with the employee's firm, thereby making corporate officials believe that they are assisting Uncle Sam in a very worthwhile cause such as evaluating foreign technical publications for the Air Force. The details of the employee's real involvement with FTD are known only between the employee and the division, and the problem is compounded because the employee does not know how deeply he is committed until it is too late to back out. The Air Force Mafia reveals very little of its operations to anyone, let alone a recruit who has not proven himself. Additionally, a corporate employee who signs a secret contract with FTD is bound for life to protect the secrecy of the Air Force Mafia's operations.

The Foreign Technology Division has had years of experience in trapping American engineers and scientists to achieve unethical objectives, and its methods have become more subtle with time. When I first became involved with FTD as Pratt & Whitney's foreign technology expert, an intelligence officer sent a letter to my home saying that the division would pay for a European vacation if I wished to go. In the letter he said, "I just happened to hear about a conference in Rome that might be of interest to you." The officer was offering me a government-paid trip without the knowledge of my employer, Pratt & Whitney. He even wrote part of a report called an abstract, which he thought I could submit at the meeting. He said: "Just for my own entertainment, I wrote up an abstract that might be accepted by the meeting sponsors. Feel free to rewrite into your own words. The abstract should arrive at the address below by 30 November 1969." The officer also asked me to "be sure

29

to make your corporate affiliation clear in the abstract submission letter. I'll be able to help with the actual paper [report] later if you so desire." In essence, the officer expected Pratt & Whitney's name to appear on the report as a cover for FTD, since he was willing to "help" write the report later. I did not accept the offer for numerous ethical reasons.

Persons who have simultaneously collected and analyzed intelligence, as I did for the CIA and the Air Force, would have grasped immediately the hidden significance of the secret proposal. As a rule, Russian scientists attending the meeting would be expected to approach the authors of FTD-sponsored presentations to discuss the paper in more depth. If I were part of the FTD team, then FTD agents would debrief me afterward and prepare a raw intelligence report. Ideally their report would contain an objective unevaluated summary of what I had learned from the Russians. This is not always the case and some reports are doctored. By controlling both papers (subject matter) presented at international meetings and the content of the debriefing reports, the military is in effect assured of favorable intelligence assessments which support its cause. Thus, armed with controlled intelligence information for dissemination to Congress and their civilian chiefs in the Defense Department, who in most cases are not even remotely familiar with how intelligence assessments are prepared, the Air Force Mafia, playing the role of a silent partner, in reality controls and may dictate the design, development, and procurement of military hardware without any outward sign of an irregularity.

One popular pastime in Building 828 is to promote the development of scramjet engines (i.e., very advanced jet engines that will some day power military aircraft that can travel better than twice as fast as current interceptor aircraft) by claiming superior work by the Soviets in this area. The Building 828 scramjet campaign is supported by the submission of abstracts at international meetings which have been ghost-written by FTD officers, such as the one mailed to my home.

The security departments of government contractors have had only fair success in uncovering agreements between their employees and the Foreign Technology Division. An aerospace engineer from a West Coast firm was fired when it was learned that he was secretly under contract with FTD to analyze Russian technical translations at a rate of $10 per hour. But Pratt & Whitney's full involvement with the division was concealed from corporate and government investigators in what has been termed in civilian intelligence circles as a "Fahrenheit 451 exercise"—the destruction of politically explosive documents that were embarrassing to both the company and government. This episode is discussed in later sections because it also had an adverse effect on the SALT I Agreement signed by President Nixon and General Secretary Leonid Brezhnev in Moscow in May 1972. SALT I was a nuclear sellout of the first order as far as the United States was concerned, and the information contained in the destroyed intelligence reports and other government documents identified a Russian capability as early as 1970 which was secretly ignored by the Executive Office when SALT I was signed, thereby permitting the Soviets to subvert the intent of the SALT I agreement.

Other American corporations and universities which have dealings with officials from the division are:

Aerojet General Corp.
Atlantic Research Corp.
General Electric Co.
Grumman Aerospace Corp.
Howmet Corp.
Lockheed Aircraft Corp.
Marquardt Corp.
McDonnell Douglas Corp.
Purdue University
Rocketdyne (Division of Rockwell International Corp.)
Thiokol Chemical Corp.
University of Utah
University of Washington

Some employees from those organizations and others are believed to have participated in intelligence operations without informing their superiors. The others are:

The Boeing Company
Illinois Institute of Technology
International Business Machines Corp.
General Dynamics Corp.
Raytheon Corp.
Stanford University
TRW Systems Group
University of Connecticut
Virginia Polytechnic Institute and State University

Agreements between companies and the Foreign Technology Division—usually to evaluate Russian technical translations to assist Uncle Sam—have been subverted by FTD agents to recruit, intimidate, or coerce employees into accepting spy missions at home or abroad, or to support fraudulent intelligence assessments.

An example of intimidation is what happened to Pratt & Whitney's foreign technology expert in Connecticut. The expert differed with FTD in the assessment of Russian jet engines. His assessments indicated that in some areas the Russians were not as advanced as FTD wanted the Defense Department to believe. An officer wrote to the company and said that FTD would break relations with Pratt & Whitney—this meant that the company would not receive its share of government intelligence reports on Russian weapons systems—if it would not replace the expert. The demand placed the company in an awkward position because the division would continue to supply government intelligence reports to General Electric and other jet engine competitors. In a decision which caused repercussions between the Connecticut and Florida branches of Pratt & Whitney, company headquarters in Connecticut told the Air Force that the request was improper and that Pratt & Whitney had no intention of replacing the employee. The Florida branch wanted to capitulate to the Air Force because it was the Florida management's policy to do anything to please the Air Force. When the company headquarters' decision reached the division, Air Force Mafia agents retaliated by placing the conscientious foreign technology expert under surveillance. The agents escalated their campaign to discredit him, and this included ransacking his motel room with the hopes of finding something incriminating. The Foreign Technology Division then began dealing with Pratt & Whitney's Florida branch, where the managers were more responsive to FTD's wishes.

Congressional leaders and the public have been led to believe that the military intelligence services are doing an effective job and require a large budget to protect our national security. In recent years this thesis has been spearheaded by a number of anti-CIA books such as *The CIA: The Myth and the Madness*, by Patrick McGarvy; *The Secret Team: The CIA and its Allies in Control of the World*, by L. Fletcher Prouty; and *The CIA and the Cult of Intelligence*, by Victor Marchetti and John Marks. These publications, coupled with the Watergate disclosures, have conditioned the public into believing that spying and scandal are synonymous with the CIA. The truth is that the military intelligence services are not doing an effective job; they do not require a massive budget as they allege; and spying and scandals are inherent throughout the intelligence establishment, and this includes the military intelligence services and the FBI. Furthermore, the CIA's known budget is only about 15 percent of the total U.S. intelligence budget, whereas the military intelligence services consume over 80 percent of the intelligence budget, now estimated to exceed six billion dollars. Of this amount, as much as 90 percent of the military intelligence budget has been expended in the past on collection operations such as covert programs and electronic surveillance (i.e., spy-in-the-sky satellites, intelligence ships, etc.), and about 10 percent on analyzing the intelligence collected. This disproportionate ratio—about nine to one—is reflected by the massive amount of raw intelligence reports that are unseen by analysts' eyes and by the comparative poor quality of finished intelligence reports prepared by the Foreign Technology Division and the Defense Intelligence Agency. In short, a fortune in U.S. tax dollars is spent on collecting intelligence that is never analyzed.

Because the Foreign Technology Division is part of the Air Force Systems Command and not officially part of the U.S. intelligence establishment, FTD's intelligence budget is not included in the congressionally approved intelligence budget of the military intelligence services. For this reason, there have been few, if any, meaningful inquiries into FTD's intelligence programs and operations over the years.

The Foreign Technology Division's cost of translating and editing a single Russian textbook ranges between 5,000 and 50,000 dollars. A study I conducted at Pratt & Whitney of Russian textbooks translated by FTD at a cost of about one million dollars showed that less than 1 percent were of any value, and in those cases, the translations were helpful only in establishing Russian technical trends which could have been ascertained more cheaply by other means.

Air Force Mafia agents are routinely flown to foreign capitals to spy on Russians attending international events. In some cases the ratio of U.S. agents to Russian participants is three to one, and it is not uncommon to find Mafia agents masquerading in absurd Enrico Fellinian disguises while tailing high-level Russian scientists. On some occasions teams of agents have been dispatched to foreign cities in which no Russians have shown up. These agents have remained abroad with no targets to spy on for days at the government's expense.

FTD agents were once authorized to fly across the United States to debrief me at Pratt & Whitney in Florida, but I refused to accept them for reasons discussed in subsequent chapters. Several months later, however, these agents would not walk 100 yards to debrief me when I was in Building 828 after I had consented to see them as a personal favor for another agent. The Foreign Technology Division's fiscal concern over U.S. tax dollars is exemplified by the fact that two division agents flew to Penn State University just to say good-bye to a source, while two others missed a junket to New Orleans to find out whether another source would consider talking with them; their junket was thwarted because a conscientious CIA intelligence officer suggested that they walk their fingers through the telephone book first.

If members of the Congressional Armed Services and Appropriations Committees were to subpoena officials of the CIA, the Foreign Technology Division, and the Defense Intelligence Agency and ask for raw intelligence reports prepared by each organization, they would find that as a rule the CIA's coverage of foreign events was not only better than the military intelligence services, but the CIA costs the taxpayer considerably less. By reviewing the results of the U.S. government's massive overseas intelligence collection operations, it can be shown that the military intelligence services' operations are not cost-effective and in many cases they are outright wasteful.

An in-depth investigation of the Foreign Technology Division would bring out more than cost skeletons. It would show ineptitude and flagrant disregard for the U.S. Constitution, and, as in the Watergate fiasco, it would show that there are arms of the U.S. government which answer to no one, mock the American system, and violate the rights of American citizens.

Some of the aforementioned material was contained in a five-part copyrighted series I authored that was published in the *Palm Beach Post* during the latter part of 1973. In the chapters that follow I wish to take the reader on an odyssey behind secret doors and into the depths of the espionage jungle and tell a story of foreign intrigue and conspiracy—a story of what happens when persons attempt to blow the lid off a national intelligence scandal, and what others are willing to do to keep the lid on. Documentation, photographs, and other supporting material to corroborate the general thrust of what I have to say, are provided in the Appendix. I regret that I do not have in my possession documentation to corroborate everything I say, but this would be an impossible task. In some instances I have protected the identities of sources of information and espionage agents, but many of these persons have been identified privately in statements I have made under oath to agents of the Air Force Office of Special Investigations; these statements have been subsequently transmitted to Congressman F. Edward Hebert (D-La.), chairman of the House Armed Services Committee, and Senator William Proxmire (D.-Wis.). In one instance I have changed the sequence of an event to protect from disclosure the location of an Air Force secret intelligence complex.

Book I
The Indictment

1

April 25, 1968: It was 7:10 A.M. when Stan Zelazek, the sprightly Pratt & Whitney Aircraft marketing engineer, met me in the waiting lounge of Palm Beach International Airport. We had an appointment with Major William Morris of the Foreign Technology Division at Wright-Patterson Air Force Base later in the afternoon to discuss the company's recent agreement with the Air Force in the area of foreign technology.

Our jet took off on schedule and within minutes we were flying over Pratt & Whitney's Florida Research and Development Center, a fenced-in jet and rocket engine development complex spread over 7,000 acres of swamp and muck just north of the Florida Everglades. Pratt & Whitney was my first and only home after I graduated from Cleveland's Case Institute of Technology in 1962, and I was quite satisfied working in the company's systems analysis department as a space systems analyst. From the elevation of the Boeing 727, I could see the main building and jet engine test stands amid deep green pines, fresh water ponds, and alligator-infested canals. After seeing man's twentieth century invasion into nature's tranquil ecological paradise from above, I sympathized with the wildlife and their short-lived rebellion against the ear-shattering tests of the company's engines which sometimes could be heard on the east coast of Palm Beach County, fifteen miles away. Having given up on the human race to solve their problems, a restless raccoon took matters into his own hands one late evening and gnawed away at the company's test instrumentation; the following day's engine test ended in dismal failure and company project managers were forced to explain sheepishly to the government that its default on the test was really due to the nocturnal activities of a sleepless black-eyed bandit rather than human error. A few more engine failures of this nature and the white-helmeted engineers who invaded their domain would soon have to leave it.

As the jet climbed higher I got a glimpse of our Chevrolet parked in the company's west parking lot; my wife Diane was in her office either preparing a summary of a military crash report or listing the mundane components of the company's jet engines for her bosses in the service department. Twenty yards from her desk was an innocuous letter in my filing cabinet—a simple sheet of paper which would slowly draw the company into an entangled web of secrecy, espionage, and manipulation, and into a myopic nightmare that seemed as irreversible and illogical as the Vietnam War. It was a letter dated February 1, 1968, and written on official Air Force stationery. Authored by Mr. Nicholas Post, a high-level civilian with the Foreign Technology Division, it proposed that the company participate in an exchange of information with the division. According to the proposal, FTD would send the company translations of foreign technical literature and classified technical intelligence reports (spy reports) in return for the company's expert opinion of the material sent, to be summarized in an annual report. The company accepted Post's proposal in a letter to Major William Morris, group leader in the technology branch of FTD, and promised to deliver its first annual report on foreign rocket technology to FTD in 1969. My attendance at international space conferences in Athens, Madrid, and Belgrade led my superiors to select me to coordinate the program. Thus, Stan Zelazek and I were flying north to Dayton and in my briefcase were personal photographs I had taken of a Russian space exhibit in Belgrade, Yugoslavia. We were told that Major Morris and Col. Lee R. Standifer of FTD would brief us on Soviet space technology during our one-day stay to get us "on board."

We touched down shortly after 2:00 P.M. in Dayton, Ohio, and were met by paunchy Fred Polhemus, the fast-talking Pratt & Whitney field representative for Wright-Patterson Air Force Base. Polhemus, a friend of former Florida State Senator Scott Kelly (who ran unsuccessfully for governor in Florida) spirited us to the air base, named after the aviation pioneers Orville and Wilbur Wright and Lt. Frank Patterson, a Dayton pilot killed in a 1918 plane crash. The base, adjacent to Fairborn, Ohio, and about eight miles northeast of Dayton, looked impressive with its rows of B-52 Strategic Air Command bombers ready to go into action if needed. Polhemus handled the visitation and car parking clearance forms as officers from the Air Force Logistics Command signed in guest visitors ahead of us.

"Building 828 is where we go," Polhemus said, showing our vehicle pass to a nonchalant guard in Area A. He pulled into a parking lot before a two-story U-shaped building resembling the aluminum door firms of the Palm Beaches with the exception that above the door fixtures was the sphinx-like insignia of the Foreign Technology Division and on the center face of the structure were the words: "Foreign Technology Division AFSC." This was the supersecret intelligence arm of the Air Force Systems Command, but unlike the CIA headquarters building in Langley, Virginia, sheltered from the Washington parkway by a serene wooded area, Building 828 is situated but a few feet from the main thoroughfare on the base, separated by a cracked concrete sidewalk and a roped-off lawn.

On the other side of the swinging glass doors, however, it was another story: two armed guards behind a desk manned a control station equipped with closed circuit television displays, telephones, and a security alarm system. The FTD receptionist checked our company identification badges, and after some confusion over the visitation clearances forwarded by the Pratt & Whitney security department, Major William Morris greeted us in his khaki, open collar, short-sleeve shirt. With red visitor's identification badges on our lapels, the three of us followed the cordial major through a turnstile in the lobby under the watchful eyes of the two guards, down a narrow corridor monitored by closed circuit television cameras, up a flight of stairs, past a steel door that the major opened with a key, and through a maze of compartmentalized offices separated by opaque petitions high enough so that officers in one compartment couldn't see what their colleagues in the adjacent compartments were working on, but low enough so that conversations and an occasional horselaugh could be heard without one having to strain. The major's desk was in the corner of the secured department. I had expected to see an office lavishly furnished with an executive desk, glass top, and carpet; I found instead an old desk flooded with papers and bright red and blue Defense Department secret reports. The bookcases were crammed with Russian textbooks and looseleaf notes. With a beaming smile Major Morris introduced us to his assistants: Capt. Harold Gale, Lt. David Pfeifle, another lieutenant whose name escaped me, and two civilians.

The major gave us an informal briefing on the status of rocket technology in the Warsaw Pact countries by reading excerpts from the draft of his group's latest intelligence product—a secret report about an inch thick containing an analysis of Russian publications and spy reports.

"Where do you get most of your intelligence?" I asked.

The major smiled and volunteered, "That's something we don't talk about."

I presented the Belgrade photographs to the major, and as he leafed through them with the captain and two lieutenants breathing down his neck, James Bartley, one of the civilians, leaned over and whispered: "Pete, have you been contacted by anyone from our government after attending these conferences?"

I shook my head. "No, I haven't. Why do you ask?"

"It's not important."

It was really none of his business and it would have been improper for me to disclose that I had indeed been contacted by the CIA after returning from each international meeting. In fact, I had briefed Justin F. Gleichauf, chief of the CIA Miami field office, of what I had learned from my Russian contacts and I had prepared special intelligence reports for the CIA with the knowledge and approval of Pratt & Whitney's security department.

Major Morris commented about the rocket thrusters in a photo, but he was interrupted by Lieutenant Pfeifle. "Now we know why you took that shot, Pete! Look at that Yugoslav broad next to Cosmos 144, will ya!"

Before he got carried away with his superlatives, I interjected, "That's no Yugoslav broad. That's my wife!" The embarrassed lieutenant blushed and folded his arms, having stuck his foot in his mouth before his superiors.

Our meeting broke up at 5:40 P.M.—they put in overtime on our behalf—and I got the distinct impression that the super-secrecy of Building 828 had to be related to something more than just an Air Force project to evaluate Russian textbooks and spy reports. Polhemus drove Zelazek and me to the Ramada Inn in Dayton so we could freshen up for dinner before returning to the base for Colonel Standifer's briefing. Zelazek, a company man all the way, was concerned over the fact that engineers from Rocketdyne, a division of Rockwell International and Pratt & Whitney's primary competitor in the rocket engine field, had their own desks in Building 828 and were assisting the Foreign Technology Division in evaluating

Russian rocket technology. The engineers' salaries were being paid by Rocketdyne in California, a government contractor, yet their work assignments were dictated by FTD intelligence officers. It was a weird arrangement and it indicated that FTD and Rocketdyne had something going on the side. What bothered Zelazek, however, was that Major Morris and Captain Gale had asked us to forward proprietary data (i.e., company secrets) on rocket engines to FTD with the understanding that it would be protected from disclosure to the company's competitors. The major requested the data because during this period Pratt & Whitney was developing an advanced rocket engine and his group needed the information to compare it with Soviet rocket technology, and thus, upgrade the reliability of its intelligence assessments. Zelazek pointed out that the Rocketdyne engineers' desks were no more than ten feet from the FTD officers' desks, and though it was the major's intent to protect the data we chose to send, it was doubtful that the data could indeed be protected. Besides, when people work together in such buddy-buddy close surroundings for years, it is a fact of life that few secrets are really kept from each other.

Fred Polhemus took us to his favorite restaurant, in which you could eat all you wanted for about four dollars—Fred was unquestionably the gourmet of Pratt & Whitney's field representatives—and then drove us back to the base, where a staunch-faced security officer stood outside the entrance of the briefing room as a desk officer checked our security clearances at a nearby table. There were about one hundred people in the room when we arrived, including Major Morris' assistant, Capt. Harold Gale, an officer in his late twenties or early thirties with a joker-like smile who looked as if he could be a stickler if he wanted to.

Colonel Standifer's low-keyed secret-level briefing took the better part of an hour, and perhaps for the first time I realized that in the intelligence business, unless you are on the inside, you must either accept the results of an intelligence briefing or you may choose not to accept it, but you have absolutely no means of corroborating or disclaiming anything that is said, since the information needed for your personal examination is classified and unavailable. It was as if the intelligence arm of the U.S. government, an elite secret club, composed of men who allegedly know the facts and who can use their position to influence our domestic and foreign policy, were really the official instrument of propaganda. This was my first intelligence briefing and I saw this parallel: U.S. government officials relied on the intelligence establishment for their information in much the same manner that Soviet citizens relied on *Pravda*—it was interesting.

41

Captain Gale invited us to join him and Colonel Standifer for drinks at the Officer's Club on the base, a short distance from Building 828. I was hoping to learn more about FTD and what they expected from the company, but with a band blaring for the satisfaction of several officers and their dates and with the conversation drifting from the "shaking boobs" of a girl on the dance floor to the hope of Colonel Standifer that a recession would hit the country so he could purchase a farm at a cheap price after he retired, I learned very little. The colonel did make a cryptic remark later in the evening which was puzzling. Shortly after the cocktail waitress poured another round of drinks, he asked me, "Have they assigned you a slot yet?"

"A slot?" I asked.

The colonel held up his hand and replied, "Forget I asked you. It's not important." Standifer had apparently spilled the beans on a secret FTD program, but I couldn't make any sense out of it.

Our gathering broke up before midnight in the windswept parking lot. Captain Gale sauntered over to our car. "Major Morris asked me to monitor the Pratt & Whitney program for him."

I did not fully comprehend the significance of Gale's comment at the time, but as it turned out, I would never see Major Morris again, because several months later he transferred out of the Foreign Technology Division. Thus, Captain Gale was to become the focal point for the execution of the company's letter agreement with FTD. With Polhemus and Zelazek in the car waiting for me, Gale continued: "I'll filter out what you don't need." In essence, Gale would use his discretion to determine what intelligence data to send the company. This is a security practice termed "need-to-know," aimed at preventing unauthorized disclosure of sensitive information to persons who do not need the information to execute their assignment.

"If anything comes across your desk that looks half-way interesting, we'd appreciate receiving a copy," I said, climbing into the car.

Gale laughed. "You and about twelve other guys!"

"Twelve other guys?" He returned my query with a Cheshire cat smile and watched us as we drove off.

The next morning Zelazek and I boarded a jet to Palm Beach, by way of Atlanta, and in the afternoon we made a verbal report to H. Norm Cotter, the soft-spoken authoritative head of the systems analysis department in the Florida Research and Development Center. It was my conclusion that the benefits derived from the company's foreign technology program would be directly proportional to the effort we wished to expend and how much we could learn about FTD's secret projects. Somehow, we had to cut through the bureaucratic red tape and diplomatic "no comment" answers and obtain foreign data that would truly assist the company. This meant that I had to assert myself and gain FTD's confidence. It also appeared that I had to don the hat of a private investigator to learn what deals were being made between FTD and Pratt & Whitney's competitors. What did Colonel Standifer mean when he asked me: "Have they assigned you a slot yet?" And who was Captain Gale referring to when he said, "You and about twelve other guys!" It was disturbing to think that Pratt & Whitney was a major government jet engine contractor, yet no company official knew anything substantive about Building 828. I could not say that about our competitors. There were a lot of questions that needed answering.

2

I sent FTD excerpts from three of my company trip reports covering meetings with Russian scientists and espionage agents on the European scene. In return, Pratt & Whitney received from FTD a deluge of unclassified Russian technical translations. The program was officially off the ground.

Almost all Russian reports I received measured an eighth of an inch thick for an article translation, to over three inches thick for a textbook translation. Some reports were stamped "Official Use Only," which meant that their distribution was limited to government personnel and their contractors such as Pratt & Whitney. Distribution of other FTD unclassified reports was unlimited and these reports were being sold to the public by the Department of Commerce Clearinghouse.

In addition to the translations, FTD sent stacks of five- by eight-inch cards which they called *TIPS cards;* these were mainly excerpts or summaries of Russian reports. If a particular card contained worthwhile information, Captain Gale wanted me to notify him, especially if I thought that the report merited full translation. There were two types of translations that FTD could offer. They called the first type a *machine translation,* which uses a special computer to translate Russian Cyrillic letters into English. They called the second an *edited machine translation*, because the machine's output is edited by Air Force language specialists to correct ambiguities resulting from missing words or because the computer's vocabulary is limited.

I was overwhelmed with the amount of technical publications made available to the West because it was my impression that the Russians did almost everything in secret. Due to a special agreement between the two governments, the United States and the Soviet Union had for years exchanged hundreds of thousands of unclassified technical publications, and since the Air Force was limited in manpower, it needed outside assistance to evaluate the material. And this is where Pratt & Whitney Aircraft fit in. We were part of an Air Force foreign literature exploitation program, and someone in FTD had apparently convinced the Air Force Systems Command headquarters that this was a worthwhile effort.

Though Pratt & Whitney was now officially part of the exploitation program, FTD officers were still going to great lengths to conceal the scope of their involvement with other companies. They weren't volunteering any information and many of my telephone queries were answered with the terse rebuttal, "You don't have the need to know."

After examining Russian textbooks and publications for about a month, I could not believe that the translation program was the real reason FTD had approached Pratt & Whitney Aircraft. Much of the material FTD sent was junk, and it was obvious that Russian security specialists had carefully screened the publications before releasing them to the West. From outward appearances it seemed that hundreds of American intelligence specialists were tied up evaluating worthless publications, when their time could be better spent evaluating hard intelligence, such as spy reports from the field.

In July 1968, about five months after the foreign technology program began, FTD sent Pratt & Whitney secret reports prepared by both the Foreign Technology Division *and* the Defense Intelligence Agency (DIA). This appeared to be a new twist; the Foreign Technology Division is part of the Air Force Systems Command and is not accountable to the United States Intelligence Board, but the reports indicated that DIA—the intelligence arm of the Defense Department and a member of the United States Intelligence Board—had final approval over some FTD assessments. The organization and interrelationships of the intelligence agencies were purposely never made clear to us at Pratt & Whitney. I wanted to get together with Captain Gale and have him explain their chain of command, but I was told by my superiors not to press the issue because it might offend the Air Force.

In addition to finished intelligence reports, which were the Defense Department's assessment of Russian capability based on the evaluation of Russian publications and raw intelligence (spy reports from the field), FTD forwarded five- by eight-inch cards stamped "Secret—No Foreign Dissemination." These cards contained summaries of raw intelligence acquired by spies throughout the world, and in many cases, though the intelligence appeared harmless, the cards were classified to protect sources and their access to intelligence at a later date. The "No Foreign Dissemination" marking meant that the data could be seen only by Americans with a Department of Defense security clearance (i.e., our NATO allies were prohibited from seeing the reports). In other cases the cards were marked: "Secret—No Foreign Dissemination, Except UK and Canada." Depending on the classification markings, exceptions were also made for West Germany, New Zealand, Australia, France, and other countries. What caught my attention, however, was that in addition to sending me information collected about the Soviet Union, FTD had sent classified intelligence about West Germany, Israel, and other friendly countries, indicating that the scope of its operations was worldwide and not limited to the Communist bloc countries. Why we were spying on our allies was another question.

Because I was collecting intelligence for the CIA and analyzing intelligence for the Air Force, I quickly realized that I held a unique position in the establishment. As a general rule, the United States intelligence community is compartmentalized into collectors of intelligence—these are the so-called "spooks"—and analyzers of intelligence—the white collar analysts who sit behind desks in secret government hideaways evaluating intelligence collected by spooks. For security reasons, an analyst is not told who collected the intelligence he evaluates, and a spook is not told what happens to the intelligence he collected. Spooks and analysts are rigidly compartmentalized, and it is the government's policy to control the travel itineraries of its analysts so that they will not encounter members of the Eastern bloc. In fact, some intelligence specialists have never met a Russian and others are prohibited from leaving the continental United States even after they have retired. Unlike my government counterparts, I had yet to sign a secrecy oath with any intelligence organization. My connections with the Foreign Technology Division were based on an informal letter agreement with Pratt & Whitney, and my dealings with the CIA were based on a verbal understanding. Thus, by mid-July 1968, I found myself wearing three hats: space systems analyst for Pratt & Whitney; intelligence analyst for the Air Force; and collector of intelligence for the CIA.

August 1, 1968: I summarized seven secret Defense Intelligence Agency reports on Russian propulsion technology in a memorandum distributed to the men of "mahogany row," a select group of Pratt & Whitney managers whose offices overlooked the man-made pond and pine woods in front of the Center. Richard Coar, the engineering manager who accepted FTD's proposal to evaluate foreign technology for the Air Force, was included on the distribution list. For many managers, this was their first exposure to classified intelligence on Russian weapons, and the intelligence memorandum whet their appetites for more information.

The Foreign Technology Division rose to the occasion and on August 7, 1968, it sent a team of intelligence experts to the Florida Research and Development Center to brief the company on Russia's rocket propulsion effort. The head of the team was Lt. Col. William Trigg, chief of the Foreign Technology Division's branch at Edwards Air Force Base in California. In what was a dazzling performance, the gray-haired colonel and his entourage put on quite a show; they snowed us with new revelations and pronouncements of coming events based on FTD's most reliable intelligence, but in many instances, it was hard to get a handle on what they actually said. Generally speaking, almost everyone was impressed. I was surprised about what FTD did *not* know about the Russian effort compared to what I thought it should have known, and it made me wonder whether the facts presented by the Trigg troupe were really facts or mere speculations based on the evaluation of incomplete intelligence. This was a significant point because aerospace managers who attend these kinds of briefings are the men responsible for formulating new technical directives, aimed mostly at countering the Soviet threat.

Shortly after the Russian invasion of Czechoslovakia in August 1968, the Foreign Technology Division notified the company that a classified propulsion conference was being held at the Air Force Space and Missiles Systems Organization in California. The purpose of the meeting, officially termed the "FTD Propulsion Symposium," was to brief persons evaluating foreign translations for FTD. The announcement identified by name and organization members of the FTD evaluation team. Scrawled in print on one page of the announcement was a message to the manager of the Hacienda International Hotel in El Segundo, California, asking that reservations be made for the individuals listed. It was mind-boggling! The super-secrecy of the Building 828 complex at Wright-

Patterson Air Force Base defied description, and internally it rivaled the best of Ian Fleming's Spectre complexes, but FTD intelligence officers had no compunction over mailing to an unauthorized person, in this case a hotel manager, one of the biggest bonanzas for a Russian agent: the list of men evaluating Russian propulsion technology for the United States Air Force. The irony was further compounded by a stern warning in the announcement:

> It is a well known fact that Communist countries are engaged in a concerted espionage effort directed toward obtaining the military, scientific, and technical knowledge possessed by the United States and certain other Western countries.
>
> In FTD, we are engaged in the evaluation of foreign aerospace scientific and technical information and material so as to reduce the possibility of technological surprise. . . . Because we in FTD do possess and have access to information of value to the Soviet espionage system, we must be fully aware that we are potential targets of the Soviet agent.

Besides the eleven firms and universities that were being represented, I learned that the Library of Congress and the F. W. Dodge Company, a division of McGraw-Hill publishers, were also connected to the FTD operation. Foreign technology contracts existed between the F. W. Dodge Company and American firms, with FTD playing the role of the silent observer. Lowell E. Ruby, my immediate technical supervisor, represented Pratt & Whitney at the El Segundo meeting.

About a week later I telephoned the Pratt & Whitney Aircraft foreign technology expert in the corporate headquarters in East Hartford, Connecticut, and privately expressed reservations over the FTD translation program because the documents they had sent me were almost all lengthy political diatribes by Communist propaganda artists who injected Vladimir Lenin and the history and glory of the Bolshevik Revolution into the heart of just about every obsolete publication they were willing to release to the West. The East Hartford expert, whom Diane called *the Eagle*, gave me the name of a contact in Building 828 and suggested I ask permission to visit *the secret facility*. I followed his advice, and after an exchange of letters with FTD, I was given the okay to visit "Project Have Stork," which according to the Eagle would unlock more of FTD's secrets.

3

November 11, 1968: The wind was gusting and the coconut palms of Palm Beach International Airport swayed to and fro, illuminated only by the lights of the terminal building. My technical supervisor Lowell Ruby and I boarded a jet this evening for a secret destination, known only to the corporate traffic and security departments. Ruby, who resembles former Secretary of Commerce Maurice Stans, though on the shorter side, was promoted to project engineer as a result of his work in the company's rocket engine programs. With silver-gray hair and a deep Florida tan, something he prided and worked on during weekend fishing excursions with his son, Ruby should have been the director of sales and marketing for the Florida Research and Development Center, because he was not only qualified, but he had a way with people which projected sincerity, something that the company lacked in its dealings with the government. The distinguished project engineer was in a snake pit in Florida, however, and his talents were being wasted; the jealous managers who ritualistically stabbed him in the back whenever they could didn't help his situation any. Ruby had developed an ulcer in his duodenum, and it was probably this condition that contributed to his amiable and docile personality in recent years, though I'm sure his rivals—the pseudo-psychologists of the research center—interpreted this as a sign of weakness on his part. I had been assigned to work under Ruby after I joined Pratt & Whitney and it was a pleasure working for him.

We checked into a small motel just before midnight and were greeted in the lobby by the Eagle, the foreign technology expert from corporate headquarters in East Hartford, Connecticut. He did not look like an espionage agent, and the Eagle was the type of man one tended to forget after being introduced to. I had met him once before—he gave a one-day briefing on Russian jet engines technology at the Florida Research and Development Center shortly after we agreed to assist FTD—and besides his subtle humor and introverted personality, I remembered the Eagle best during the Florida visit because he wore a hat in the scorching sun to protect a bald spot. The Eagle briefed Ruby and me of his involvement with FTD, and at times it appeared as if he wanted to tell us something. He withdrew repeatedly into a shell, however, apparently uncertain whether he could take us into his confidence, and it was best to leave well enough alone. Being an intelligence expert, he knew that an indiscretion on his part—such as disclosing classified or sensitive information to another party in a restaurant—could cost him his job or Pratt & Whitney unnecessary problems with the Air Force Office of Special Investigations, a unit in Washington whose duty it is to protect our national secrets. There was no telling who was monitoring our conversation, if anyone, but the Eagle was taking no chances.

As prearranged, the three of us were met the next morning in the parking lot of a Howard Johnson's restaurant by two Air Force Foreign Technology Division intelligence specialists. To conceal the clandestine nature of their visit, both were dressed as civilians. The first was Capt. Harold Gale—the last time I met him was in the parking lot of the Officer's Club at Wright-Patterson Air Force Base —and the other was Lt. David Pfeifle, who I met in Building 828 during the same visit. They greeted us in guarded language.

"We'll drive and you follow," Gale said, addressing the Eagle.

At 9:15 A.M. two cars pulled onto the crowded highway and made their way across town in bumper-to-bumper traffic to the parking lot of a large building I first mistook for a medical center. Its lobby resembled that of a modern library. The officers escorted us through a network of hallways, elevators, security checkpoints and unmarked steel doors. A stairwell from the last security checkpoint led to a maze of conference rooms, where white-shirted intelligence analysts and shapely secretaries were working feverishly.

"Welcome to Project Have Stork!" a balding executive in his late

50

forties said, grasping Lowell Ruby's hand. This was the director of the secret facility and Project Have Stork was a code name.

Unknown to pedestrians in the street and citizens who visited the building for other reasons, Project Have Stork and Project Have Eagle, another code name that had me baffled in Florida, were secret FTD programs coordinated from the secret facility; a section of this complex housed raw intelligence reports prepared by the CIA, Defense Intelligence Agency (DIA), the Air Force Foreign Technology Division, and other branches of the U.S. Intelligence establishment. The intelligence covered Soviet personalities, facilities, weapons systems, science, technology . . . you name it; it was there. Many of the technical classified reports had been written by men such as my CIA contact, Justin Gleichauf, who would debrief agents, defectors, informers, and other persons having contact with the Eastern bloc. The facility appeared to be a gold mine for foreign intelligence, and there was no question that an agent "in place," a spy for the Soviet Union, for example, could do irreparable damage to the nation.

In addition to a substantive cross-reference filing system, a special library in another annex of the facility housed practically every significant "open literature" Eastern bloc publication—material available to the man-in-the-street in Eastern European countries—and it had translating services available for on-the-spot translations of significant publications. The director showed us analysts' rooms no larger than eight by ten feet where we could work during our visit. One room contained a red-covered three-inch thick index volume identifying the subject matter filed in the facility's massive retrieval system. The director's assistant gave us a convoluted briefing of how intelligence was analyzed at Project Have Stork, but his use of code names, intelligence jargon, and "no comment" answers to our queries raised more questions than he answered. The "paper mill" described by the assistant director indicated that U.S. military intelligence analysts spent more time fighting the bureaucratic jungle that their administrative superiors had created than analyzing the intelligence collected. I thought it was interesting that the director would not elaborate on FTD's "collection operations," a term the officers similarly used to allude to FTD's worldwide espionage operations.

To check the scope of the facility's retrieval system, I requested information on the Belgrade International Astronautical Federation Congress I attended in 1967 to determine whether my input to the CIA was filed here. It was: Gleichauf had copied my personal notes and submitted them to the CIA headquarters in Langley, Virginia, where they were processed. I recognized almost all of my pet phrases, including the accidental misspelling of a Russian name. There was nothing on the cards that could identify me as the source of information, which is what Gleichauf had promised. This indicated that the CIA indeed protected its intelligence sources, even from other U.S. government intelligence specialists. From an analyst's viewpoint, this may not have been all that good.

The reports protected sources of information so well that it was impossible to determine how reliable or competent a source was. If Dr. Wernher von Braun, for example, were to report on a particular Soviet rocket development, it was a certainty that one could place a great deal of confidence in what he had to say. But if the source were an unreliable rocket scientist whose report contrasted with the von Braun report, the cards would force an intelligence analyst to weigh both reports equally.

The secretarial staff supplied us with classified cards on Russian technical developments, while Captain Gale and Lieutenant Pfeifle sat in the corner engrossed in a Russian textbook, periodically screening our technical intelligence requests to ensure that we did not order secret documents that had no bearing on the company's programs. To check out the reliability of the intelligence filed in the facility, I requested biographical information on Russian scientists I knew on a first name basis—men I had socialized with on more than one occasion—and I found that the verbal descriptions of Russian scientists in our intelligence files were erroneous. I had photographs of the personalities concerned and there was no resemblance to the photographs and the descriptions on file. This is one reason why field intelligence reports are termed "raw" intelligence, because they have yet to be evaluated in relation to their consistencies and inconsistencies and what is known to be true, what is unknown, and what is known to be false.

To give me another perspective, I imagined that I was an American citizen with no science or intelligence background who had accidentally stumbled into the secret facility and I asked myself: what would this person think about the operation? My first thought is that one would notice the volumes and volumes of books and cards and draw the conclusion that someone had gone to great lengths to set up an enormous cross-filing system. The mysterious coded markings on the cards wouldn't make much sense, and the cards themselves would make uninteresting reading because of the technical jargon and frequent references to abstract names and foreigners. But it looked impressive, and since someone had gone to all this trouble to create the facility, one would assume that the secret work was important.

By the end of the day I felt uneasy: the raw intelligence on my desk might someday be used to justify a new weapon system or a shift in our military strategy vis-à-vis the Soviet Union, yet the cards failed to offer substantive information as to how the report was generated, under what circumstances, and what the general qualifications of the source were—this type of information is sometimes as important, if not more important, than the intelligence reported.

Whenever I asked the director about the background of the cards I received, he would reply: "You don't have a need-to-know." While there were legitimate national security reasons for his position, because some persons obviously had to be protected by nature of the sensitive positions they held, the policy of controlled ignorance—in fact, the authors of *all* raw classified reports were anonymous—left open the likelihood that unknown persons could spoon-feed intelligence analysts with incorrect information for an ulterior motive, such as justifying the development of a weapon system that couldn't stand on its own merits or stacking intelligence reports to support an unpopular foreign policy decision. I thought that this was a significant point because, like most Americans, I had assumed that the intelligence establishment was organized so that something like this couldn't happen. Obviously, this was not the case. The fact that FTD officers were reluctant to talk about the collection and dissemination of raw intelligence information, allegedly because of national security reasons, stimulated my curiosity even more.

After two red-eyed days at the secret facility, and with Russian names coming out of my ears, I returned to the Palm Beaches, greatly impressed with the scope and organization of the secret Air Force complex, but disturbed over what I considered to be an undisclosed weak link in our overall intelligence structure: unnamed intelligence specialists could slant raw intelligence reports to accommodate the whims of their superiors, and the evaluator of the information—the intelligence analyst—couldn't do anything about it. He had to have faith in the system, even if logic dictated otherwise. Besides my Pratt & Whitney responsibilities, I was now intrigued with the overall question of how the U.S. government collected and analyzed intelligence and how this process influenced U.S. foreign and domestic policy. And, of course, where did FTD fit in?

4

On December 4, 1968, the Air Force Foreign Technology Division presented another briefing at the Florida Research and Development Center. The new faces representing FTD included Col. Vincent Rethmann, who later retired to join the foreign technology group at McDonnell Douglas in St. Louis; Major Meyers, a jet engine specialist; and two civilian analysts named Tom Wills and Bob Zurschmeid (phonetic spelling). An engineer from the General Electric Company, whom I later came to know as "Fat Wally," assisted the Air Force by presenting his findings. Thirty-five Pratt & Whitney managers attended the secret-level briefing on Russian jet engine developments, including the Eagle and several of his colleagues from East Hartford. The briefing was worthwhile mainly because we learned that Fat Wally of General Electric had a close personal relationship with FTD officers, and it appeared that General Electric enjoyed an immense political advantage over Pratt & Whitney with the Air Force because of its long-term association with FTD. Thus, after less than one year association with FTD, there was no longer any doubt that both Rocketdyne and General Electric —the company's primary competitors in the rocket and jet engine fields—had long-standing relations with FTD, and there was no telling what Russian secrets had been passed to them by FTD over the years. It made me wonder how fair the engine competitions between these companies really were.

It was generally accepted throughout the aerospace industry that to win government contracts, marketing engineers would wine and dine prospective customers, and this included the use of professional call girls and secretaries who supplemented their meager earnings with wild nights on the town at both the contractor's and government's expense it all went under the heading of "promotion and public relations." The competition was vicious, and the accepted low morals, though allegedly confined to contract competitions, had its way of seeping into the fabric of the lower echelon employees as well. I heard of one aerospace firm on the West Coast whose "secret room" held more than Uncle Sam's secrets. This room was kept locked because of a super-sensitive secret program, but it also provided a vivacious secretary the privacy she needed to fulfill her sexual urges whenever any of the boys in the firm were willing. The joke was not that the girl performed well on company time, but that this never-discovered passion pit which was being subsidized by the taxpayer was so private that even the security guards didn't have a key to the room!

The FTD connection introduced a new element to the competition, though it was more subtle. They secretly controlled the dissemination of raw and finished intelligence reports on Russian weapons systems to aerospace contractors. This meant that unless I treated my FTD contacts with kid gloves, they could conceivably send substantive intelligence exclusively to Rocketdyne or General Electric. Our marketing and sales departments knew most of the tricks—in fact, they had one Air Force colonel's number; whenever he visited the Center a particular glib secretary who is considered to be a live wire usually escorted him during and after hours—but they were out in left field when it came to FTD.

Several days after the FTD briefing I received the classified cards I had ordered from the secret facility. With the arrival of this intelligence, the Pratt & Whitney foreign technology program took more of a clandestine twist. In early 1968, when the company first entered into the letter agreement with FTD, Lowell Ruby sent over two hundred memoranda throughout the engineering departments asking the various specialists for their cooperation in the foreign technology program. Almost all of the memoranda were ignored, though the backs of the notices made good scratch paper. The message did get out that I was analyzing unclassified translations for FTD. For security reasons, only a handful of persons out of the 6,000 employed at the Center knew that the classified cards in my filing cabinet were spy reports. Trying to keep this fact a secret from persons seated near me was a difficult task, because during the day the cards were spread all over my desk, and the bright red cover sheets we used at Pratt & Whitney to designate that secret documents had been removed from the filing cabinet were likewise strewn atop my desk.

By the end of 1968 I was known as "Mr. Foreign Technology" at the Florida Research and Development Center, and I was busy analyzing the raw intelligence I had selected at the secret facility. In the Center's cafeteria my colleagues would sometimes brush against me in the hamburger line, pretend to slip me a secret message, and then ask boisterously, "How's the spy business?" One engineer had a hang-up about the rubber soled suede shoes I wore and he would ask, "Been in Vienna lately?" Naturally, they were only joking, and none knew about my CIA connections, but I sometimes wondered whether their jokes would catch up with me if I ever ventured behind the Iron Curtain.

On January 28, 1969, Lieutenants David Pfeifle and Barry Penswick of FTD visited Pratt & Whitney to learn about the company's advanced rocket engine program. At the end of their stay Lieutenant Penswick asked to see Lowell Ruby on what he said was a private matter. Ruby was busy with other company business, so I told the two officers that they could either deal with me or call Ruby after they returned to the base.

"We'd rather not use the phone," Pfeifle said. Penswick nodded in my direction, apparently giving Pfeifle the green light to discuss it with me.

Pfeifle whispered, "Pete, could you give us a list of company engineers who attend specialty conferences?"

"Why do you need that?" I asked the nervous lieutenant. "Is this a personal request or official business?"

"Headquarters wants it."

"I'd have to get management's approval."

"How about a company organization chart?" Penswick asked. "That'd serve our purpose."

"I couldn't give you that either. Let me forward your request to Lowell [Ruby]."

"Keep it private, *please*."

The officers left the Center quietly, and I brought up their request with Norm Cotter, my department head, and Lowell Ruby. "What the hell do they want a list of names for?" Cotter asked indignantly.

"They wouldn't say," I replied.

"Well, they won't get it! It's none of their damn business! We can't have them [FTD] dealing with other engineers or we'll lose control of the data exchange." The normally cool H. Norm Cotter delegated Ruby to write a diplomatic "no" letter without alienating the Air Force. The original agreement between the Foreign Technology Division and the company specified that Lowell Ruby would be the manager of the company's foreign technology effort. Since Ruby had gotten bogged down with other company programs, I was delegated to coordinate the program with FTD and write the report; in fact, I was now spending all of my time on foreign technology and Ruby was spending less than 5 percent of his time on the program. Cotter was disturbed because FTD was supposed to coordinate its part of the program with either Ruby or me. Now, it appeared that the Foreign Technology Division wanted to work through other company engineers for a purpose that was not yet clear.

The comments by officers in Building 828 about "collection operations" and their mysterious "I know something you don't know" catlike expressions indicated that FTD was heavily involved in collecting intelligence abroad, and this was not only the CIA's responsibility. I had a gut feeling that FTD's agreement with Pratt & Whitney was related to something more than evaluating technical trash that it translated, and that the initial program was being used for getting its foot in the door. The Pfeifle-Penswick request may have been the key to a secret program in Building 828 that we were not aware of, and it may have been related to Colonel Standifer's comment during my first visit to FTD: "Have they assigned you a slot yet?"

February 6, 1969: About a week later, Lowell Ruby wrote to Captain Harold Gale and said that Lieutenant Pfeifle's request could not be honored because almost all Pratt & Whitney's engineers attended conferences. Ruby diplomatically asked Gale to coordinate all work performed for FTD with either me or himself. The company held its ground and I waited with anticipation the Foreign Technology Division's next move; it obviously wanted a list of names.

April 2, 1969: Captain Gale of FTD telephoned Lowell Ruby at the Center and said that the draft of my report on Russian rocket capability which I submitted the week earlier was one of the best it had received. The jubilant captain was very complimentary and said that his group would incorporate my work into its studies. I was congratulated by Ruby and Cotter after the captain's call and told that the primary objective of the foreign technology program —to please the United States Air Force—had been achieved. With my superiors patting themselves on the back, I returned to my desk to reassess the company's foreign technology program. The back slapping episode may have been justified, but I was left with the feeling that they had considered the foreign technology program to be nothing more than a public relations effort aimed at pleasing the United States Air Force. In marketing language, good relations with the Air Force meant more contracts, and that was the name of the game.

On April 30, 1969, Captain Harold Gale visited the Florida Research and Development Center to discuss my report and the possibility of coaxing Max Schilling and Marv Glickstein, two engineers from the applied research department, into evaluating advanced Russian rocket metals that FTD specialists had read about in Russian publications. Schilling, known as a shrewd lunch-hour bridge player, questioned the advanced state of Russian technology claimed by FTD, and, after a search of the company's records, found that Pratt & Whitney had tested similar metals about six years earlier. Schilling later verified his results in a succinct memorandum to Lowell Ruby. In effect, the Russian "advances" that FTD touted in its secret intelligence assessments on what the rocket industry calls brazing materials were erroneous; either FTD was completely out of touch with the U.S. aerospace industry or it may have been using the alleged Russian advances as a pretext for dealing with other company specialists for a still unclear purpose. The FTD assessments of Russian brazing materials also cast a shadow on its other assessments.

Captain Gale asked Lowell Ruby whether the company would be interested in hearing a briefing on Russian rocket technology. "We'll call it a technical discussion," he said to Ruby lightheartedly, apparently because an Air Force regulation stipulates that formal intelligence briefings must be approved beforehand.

Ruby jumped to his feet. "Sure, I'll pass the word around. Pete can reserve the conference room."

"Good," the captain said. "I'll need a list of attendees for the people back home—to show them Pratt & Whitney's interest in FTD. They'll love it." He grinned and glanced in my direction. There it was: the list again. Ruby asked me to contact the men on mahogany row and get the show on the road.

About sixty managers and engineers attended the impromptu "technical discussion" in the company's plush presentation room. I thought the briefing was an insult to the intelligence of almost everyone in the room, and I was not alone. Mild mannered Joe Silk, the retired Air Force colonel who was assisting Dr. R. A. Schmidtke, director of the applied research department in the

Center, left the presentation room shaking his head. "It was a waste of time," he muttered to an associate.

Other persons similarly felt this way, though none would dare say it to Captain Gale's face, respecting his rank and the fact that the company's livelihood depended on maintaining good relations with the Air Force. After all, FTD was still part of the Air Force, though at times I had doubts whether Air Force headquarters in Washington knew it.

I cornered Lowell Ruby at his desk while Captain Gale was engaged by several managers whose smiling faces—conditioned with years of experience to pump up with a barrage of platitudes the ego of anyone in a uniform because it is best for the company in the long run—would have shocked even their own secretaries.

"Lowell," I said. "I don't think the captain should be given any names." I studied Ruby's countenance as he examined the just-typed list of attendees to the "technical discussion." Ruby's boss, H. Norm Cotter, was against giving FTD any names, but he was not in his office, so the responsibility now rested on Ruby's shoulders. Captain Gale approached us smiling from ear to ear.

"I can't see where it would do any harm," Ruby answered quickly.

"Oh, you've typed out the list!" Gale said. He picked it up and grinned. "Pete, could you identify the specialties of some of these men? It'll give headquarters an idea who attended the discussion." Ruby adroitly avoided my eyes and shuffled papers on his desk, turning his back on us.

I identified about six of the attendees for Gale, dragging out the job description of each man, hoping that Ruby would interrupt me; he didn't.

Whereas Lieutenants Pfeifle and Penswick were unsuccessful in obtaining a list of company employees three months earlier, Captain Gale now had in his possession a list of company engineers who had attended a "technical discussion"—a list of Pratt & Whitney's best propulsion specialists; the cream of the crop.

5

In May and June of 1969, Diane and I vacationed in Europe and attended an international space conference in Venice and an air show in Paris. I had private meetings at these events with Russian scientists and some of their espionage agents. Of course, I was not alone.

Venice, Wednesday, May 7, 1969: Huddled by the Basilica of St. George on San Giorgio's Isle were seven American engineers conspicuously staring at the Russian delegation congregated before St. Mark's basin. The senior member of the group meandered up to me and cautiously asked, "Well, there they [the Russians] are. How do you break the ice?"

"Walk up and introduce yourself," I replied facetiously.

"You can't do that."

"Why not?"

"They might suspect something!" he exclaimed, returning to the group. This appeared to have been his first trip to an international conference. As we have always done, Diane and I introduced ourselves to the younger members of the Russian delegation. As she showed our newly made Russian friends photos of the Palm Beaches, Vasili Sarychev, whose thick black eyebrows resemble those of General Secretary Leonid Brezhnev, introduced us to the famous Academician Georgiy Petrov, director of the Institute of Space Research in Moscow. As we conversed with Petrov, a dark-haired American aerospace executive edged toward us. Petrov turned toward the executive to see if he wanted anything, but the executive quickly turned his head and glanced at his watch. Petrov and I continued our colloquy, and the man edged still closer, obviously eavesdropping. The academician, known in the Russian scientific community as an expert fisherman, walked me toward the boat landing to get a better look at the casting techniques of his Italian counterparts; the executive followed closely on our heels, ridiculously trying to act as a noninterested bystander. It was my hope that the super-sleuth wasn't affiliated with the U.S. intelligence establishment because in this case he could only contribute isolated bits of information, based on the fragments of the conversation he may have heard, and it appeared that he could do more damage than good to the intelligence community by turning in an erroneous report of what he thought Petrov told me. I terminated the discussion with Petrov a few minutes later and the sleuth returned to his colleagues near St. George's. The engineer who asked me, "how do you break the ice?" was among them.

Venice, Thursday, May 8, 1969: In the evening we attended the conference banquet at the Hotel Cipriani and shared a table with an Irish atheist, a gloating Englishman who criticized our involvement in Vietnam, and a conservative navy commander from California who had built his own bomb shelter to cheat death. After General Bernard Schriever's speech on orbital space stations, I was confronted by a coy American who had befriended me. "Have you learned anything from the Russians?" he asked.

"I'm getting good biographical data," I answered, "but nothing great."

"You've got a secret weapon we don't have," he said, eyeing Diane in her white lace pantsuit.

"Yes, she's quite an asset. The Russians loosen up around her."

"That's what I mean. Just biographical data, huh? Good luck." This was another indication that U.S. intelligence was operating in Venice.

Venice, Friday, May 9, 1969: I left Diane in the Hotel Monaco and stepped outside. On the way to St. Mark's landing I passed hundreds of gray pigeons flocked about an elderly woman who had her brushes and oil paints spread out on an outdoor cafe table facing the Grand Canal. Screaming children hovered over an old man who awed his youthful audience with plastic replicas of whistling dogs, as the owners of the sidewalk bookstore beneath the loggias of the

Doge Palace were setting up their displays. I caught up with several American delegates at St. Mark's landing and boarded the water-bus to San Giorgio's Isle. A professor from a Midwestern university sat next to me. The captain of the waterbus gunned the engine and tooted his horn at a gondalier, as he prepared to cross the choppy waters of the basin. With the engine roaring in the background, the professor glanced at my Sony tape recorder and Minolta camera. "I see you've brought all your spy equipment with you," he said, addressing me from the corner of his mouth, much like the agents one would expect to see in the movies. I acted as if I did not hear him and the man remained silent for the duration of the ride.

The morning conference session was boring, so I caught the first waterbus back to St. Mark's. As the craft moored up to the column of the winged lion of St. Mark, a pushing match ensued before the exit ramp. At first I thought that the engine exhaust bothered some of the passengers and then saw what the real reason was: a voluptuous girl in her early twenties, built along the lines of Sophia Loren, was having problems keeping her wet bosom inside her flimsy blouse. She had been splashed during the ride and two "chivalrous" Italians attempted to shield her from the gawking crowds by generously pressing their bodies against her. Everyone filed out like cattle behind the girl, and I bumped into the coy American who befriended me at the Cipriani banquet.

"Aren't you going to your hotel?" I asked, noting that he was heading in the opposite direction toward the clock tower.

"No, I've got to meet someone in a hotel . . . if you know what I mean."

I winked, "Yeah, I do." I really didn't know what he meant, but I was beginning to have an idea. It appeared that U.S. government intelligence agents were operating both overtly and covertly in Venice during the meeting, and the cooperating members of the American delegation had mistaken me as part of the operation.

At 10:15 P.M. Diane and I were alone in the Europa Hotel cocktail lounge finishing our drinks after what I thought was one of the most significant receptions I had ever attended abroad. I not only had talked in depth with KGB Colonel Nikolai Beloussov, master-mind of the Christine Keeler-British War Minister John Profumo sex scandal in England, but I learned a great deal from Russians who should have been guarded more closely by their KGB watch-dogs. I noticed a man in a wrinkled gray suit staring at us from the corner of the lounge. His glare bothered Diane because he was making it obvious.

"Let's go," I said to Diane, uncertain whether the man was a girl watcher or whether he would follow us. We walked into the lobby of the hotel and out the entrance into the empty courtyard. It was pitch black outside and drizzling. I held Diane by the arm and waited, watching the hotel entrance. Sure enough, the door opened, and the man in the wrinkled suit came out. "Let's get the hell out of here," I said. We hurried along a dreary passageway that smelled of cat urine and made an L-shaped turn at the Hotel Budapest sign. I had an eerie feeling escorting my wife through a black abyss, where all I could hear were our shoes against the wet walkway and canal water splashing against the buildings. The chilling footsteps of a mysterious stranger were close behind. We picked up our pace and crossed a bridge leading to the columned archway of St. Mark's square. I heard voices around the corner, and to our relief, seated at an outdoor cafe on the perimeter of the square was part of the American delegation. Our tail disappeared behind the columns. I didn't know who he was, but there was no question that he was assigned to tail us. It was spooky, because the man could have been a foreign agent who knew that I had been assisting the CIA, and he may have found out that I learned that the Russian moon rocket was on the launch pad in Tyuratam and would be launched before Apollo 11. As it turned out, the Russian super-booster blew up on the launch pad several months later, but in Venice I had no idea as to what extremes the Russians would go to protect the secret of the launch vehicle and timetable.

Venice, Saturday, May 10, 1969: At 9:30 A.M. on San Giorgio's Isle, Diane and I joined Georgiy Zhivotovskiy—the head of the Russian delegation, who was wining and dining us throughout the week —in the mini-auditorium to see the Russian film spectacular on the Soyuz 4 and 5 manned spacecraft missions. I recorded the sound track of the commentary and photographed the Russian space hardware. On my right was an American engineer frantically trying to record the pertinent film data on his note pad. By now it was clear that part of the American delegation was involved in a coordinated intelligence collection operation, and I had a fairly good idea who was involved. There was the clannish group of seven men from prominent American firms who seemed unusually nervous throughout the conference, as if they were doing something illegal. They seemed to be stepping over each other's feet, like members of a vaudeville team, carrying on whisper-like conversations and mustering only stares at the Russians. Their state of mind was best depicted when a member of the team approached Diane and asked: "How do you have the nerve to wear your Air Force Association pin?" To my knowledge, not one member of this frustrated group ever made substantive contact with the Russians, though each tried on numerous occasions. Then there was the engineer

63

who would not walk with me along the Grand Canal because he had to meet someone in a hotel; and the professor on the waterbus who asked if I had all my spy equipment with me.

Paris (Le Bourget Field), Thursday, May 29, 1969: The Russians were displaying their space hardware in what was called the C3 Building. As I was conversing with two Russians, a stocky Oriental with pad and pencil stood at my side, attempting to write down the Russians' answers to my questions. The Russian exhibitors later gave me a personal tour of their display, and during most of this period, the Oriental was within arm's reach. His contorted face indicated that he was having problems hearing what was being said, and his behavior emulated that of the American team in Venice; I would learn later that he was not the pestiferous foreign news correspondent he pretended to be.

Paris (Le Bourget Field), Friday, May 30, 1969: At the French Mirage fighter aircraft display, three men wearing sunglasses, though it was heavily overcast, were busy photographing and measuring the jet's dimensions. One man was holding a transparent plastic grid of one-inch squares over the inlet—the front of the engine—while another photographed it. A third man took notes. All three looked American, had cuffs on their trousers, and were inside the roped-off area unnoticed by their French hosts. Across the way near the Russian aircraft display, a Russian exhibitor, most likely a KGB agent, was filming Americans who were examining and photographing the Russian hardware. The air show was swarming with espionage agents and it appeared that many of the agents justified their presence on the basis that they could return with films and photos of other agents, who had similarly convinced their superiors that their presence at the air show was needed for the same reasons.

June 4, 1969: Having had our fill of Europe on this trip and getting that "let's go home" feeling, Diane and I boarded International Air Bahamas flight 102 in Luxembourg and flew to Nassau, Bahamas. In the back of my mind were the numerous episodes in Venice and Paris which indicated that the United States government intelligence apparatus was involved in extensive operations abroad using engineers and scientists from private institutions. From outward appearances it seemed that the espionage games played at international events would come to a grinding halt if the agents from one of the countries suddenly decided to stay home. Based on what I had seen in the secret facility, I wondered whether the Venice and Paris intelligence operations could stand on their own merits; specifically, what was the intelligence value of the information acquired by our government in relation to the money expended?

Our connecting Eastern Airlines jet in the Bahamas took us over the stormy waters of the "Devil's Triangle" to the Palm Beaches. Here, I resumed wearing my other hats—intelligence analyst and propulsion engineer for Pratt & Whitney and self-appointed investigator of the Building 828 domestic and foreign operations. I kept telling myself that what FTD did was none of my business, but for some unexplainable reason, I couldn't buy that argument; I had to learn more about it.

6

At Pratt & Whitney I met Justin F. Gleichauf, the mustached chief of the CIA Miami field office, and handed over about twenty pounds of brochures and photos, including a seventy-three-page intelligence report summarizing what I had learned from my Eastern bloc contacts. Gleichauf, who was approaching a quarter of a century of service with the CIA and was first introduced to me in 1965 by William T. Dwyer, a former FBI agent and chief of plant protection for the Florida Research and Development Center, was head of the CIA office that turned in the first reports in 1962 that the Russians were introducing offensive ballistic missiles in Cuba.

Gleichauf was overwhelmed with my intelligence take on the Venice trip—it was my best job to date—and he was speechless over our encounters with the Russians, particularly Georgiy Zhivotovskiy, who had invited us to dinner and late evening cocktails throughout the conference. Gleichauf was astounded that Zhivotovskiy wanted me to meet him in Argentina later in the year so that we could discuss in private his tentative invitation for me to visit the Soviet Union as a guest of the Academy of Sciences.

"Zhivotovskiy has to be authentic," Gleichauf mused, "because there aren't many Russians who have the authority to extend an off the cuff invitation to visit the Soviet Union. Are you going to Argentina?" he asked anxiously.

I knew that he wanted me to go, but the CIA didn't want to get involved financially in the event something went wrong. I had a close relationship with Gleichauf and I felt that I could talk with him on an informal basis and get to the heart of a discussion without wasting time on formalities, but it was an unusual relationship. Diane hit the nail on the head when she once quipped: "Should anything go wrong, the secretary will disavow any knowledge of your actions."

"I'll have to get time off—that might be a problem—but you can plan on me being there." I was similarly curious about Zhivotovskiy; the senior level KGB intelligence officer was assessing me as a potential spy for the Russians—they would love to penetrate Pratt & Whitney—but the Russian was proceeding cautiously before coming forth with his pitch.

"Good!" Gleichauf said, taking out his yellow legal-size pad to commence the usual debriefing. Gleichauf in my opinion represented the epitome of the professional intelligence officer. His Miami outfit, sometimes referred to as "contact services," would collect useful intelligence from cooperative sources who had been in touch with members of the Eastern bloc. In Gleichauf's case, this included Communist Cuba. He was always polite and left me with the impression that the CIA—at least the Miami field office— would not strong-arm a source if he or she wanted to be left alone.

July 3, 1969: I completed arrangements to visit the agents in Building 828. Gleichauf indicated that he had no objection if I gave FTD a copy of the technical intelligence I had given him, though he asked me to inform my FTD contacts that the CIA would officially write up my material for U.S. intelligence files. Both my superiors, H. Norm Cotter and Lowell Ruby, thought it would benefit the company if I gave FTD the Venice and Paris data. Accordingly, Cotter authorized the company's photo laboratory to make prints from my Kodak slides of the air show and the Russian movie in Venice.

July 8, 1969: I took a late-evening jet to Dayton and checked into the Falcon Motel, conveniently located in Fairborn, Ohio, on Route 444 near Wright-Patterson Air Force Base. As I was unpacking my pajamas, I heard a loud thump on my door. I opened it and standing before me was an FTD agent attired in Bermuda shorts. His crew-cut assistant—the all-American boy—leaned against a railing waiting for me to invite them in. The former became known to me as *Super Smart* and the latter as *the Snake*—names coined by the Eagle. Super Smart complimented me on the annual secret report I authored, and then presented a problem.

67

"We're not happy with East Hartford's performance. We'd like to abrogate our relationship with East Hartford in favor of an airbreathing [jet engine] agreement with Pratt & Whitney in Florida."

I recognized immediately what the problem was. FTD had a working agreement with Pratt & Whitney's East Hartford headquarters, similar to the agreement they had with Pratt & Whitney's Florida Research and Development Center. The Eagle was coordinating the East Hartford program with FTD while I was coordinating the Florida program with FTD; the East Hartford agreement concerned jet engines, and the Florida agreement concerned rocket engines. It appeared that FTD wanted to consolidate both the jet and rocket engines intelligence evaluation programs with Pratt & Whitney and have the Florida branch—namely me—be responsible for the overall program. The real reason for this, however, appeared to be that the Eagle's assessments of Russian jet engine technology differed significantly from FTD's official assessments which were being distributed throughout the Defense Department. And since the Eagle was sending copies of his assessments to other branches of our government, there was no question that at some future date a high-level Defense Department official would ask why FTD was not incorporating the Eagle's work in its studies. Generally, FTD gave the Russians credit for advances in technology that the Eagle thought was unwarranted. At times, the Eagle was blunt in his opinions of the FTD effort, and he was critical of the intelligence data that FTD sent him to evaluate. Being careful to enunciate the more conservative Florida policy—"Don't upset the Air Force"—I told Super Smart: "I'll bring up your proposal with Ruby and Cotter."

Super Smart frowned and picked his nose. Looking at the floor, he replied, "If you don't want to accept the responsibility for the Pratt & Whitney airbreathing foreign technology program, then I have to assume that East Hartford [headquarters] represents the official company position."

"Currently, that is the understanding," I answered. "We handle the rockets and East Hartford does the airbreathers."

"If that's your official position," he said, looking at the Snake, "then you leave us with no alternative but to discontinue sending Pratt any foreign airbreathing data." I was shocked at the ultimatum: an FTD agent, a member of the Air Force, was actually threatening to discontinue sending a leading jet engine contractor information about foreign jet engine development unless the contractor changed its internal policies and acquiesced to his demands.

"Let's do this," I said, hoping to salvage a delicate working relationship. "You know we're working on the FX [jet] engine; we therefore have the need to know. Send data that might help us in that effort. If we see something important, I'll let you know, but all official reporting on airbreathers would still have to be done by East Hartford."

"That's the problem!" he retorted. "We don't want to work with East Hartford! We want to work with Florida, and if we send you data, we want you to give us an annual report. We were very happy with your rocket report; we want one like that in airbreathers."

"We [Pratt & Whitney] prepared the rocket report at no cost to you. We can use data on advanced Russian jet engines, but we don't have the manpower in Florida to commit another man on the foreign technology effort to prepare another report. All we want is access to reports already published by the intelligence community on Russian jet engines. It would be in the national interest, you know!" I was beginning to get hot under the collar, but I tried not to show it. It was idiotic that I had to take the Florida position—"Don't upset the Air Force."

"Pete, that's not the point," Super Smart yelled. "We need an annual report from you to help us prepare our assessments for the DIA [Defense Intelligence Agency]."

"If we don't prepare an airbreathing report for you, we get no airbreathing data?"

"That's about the size of it."

"I really can't believe that you'd cut us off like that. You represent the Air Force, and we're developing an engine for the Air Force, so there's no interservice rivalry. What the hell's the problem?"

"It's interesting that your primary competitor doesn't feel this way!" Super Smart replied pompously. He was careful not to mention Fat Wally and General Electric. The Foreign Technology Division was playing the competitors against each other. If Pratt & Whitney did not accept his "offer" to cooperate with FTD, he intended to give the Russian data exclusively to General Electric, playing the role of a kingmaker. What he did not know was that Fat Wally of General Electric and the Eagle of Pratt & Whitney had been in touch with each other and the question of the competence and efficiency of the Foreign Technology Division organization was discussed privately. Among other things, they concluded that FTD lacked the expertise to evaluate properly Russian weapons systems, and it was mutually understood that FTD indeed pitted corporations against each other to achieve its objectives. I had heard rumors to this effect, mainly from the Eagle, but gave them little credence because Stan Zelazek of the company's marketing department intimated that there was a personality problem

69

between Super Smart and the Eagle. Now, in a second floor room of the Falcon Motel, I had reason to believe that the rumors were true, and under the circumstances, there was little a corporation dependent on Air Force contracts could do about it. I was torn between being blunt and candid, like my colleague in East Hartford, and being diplomatic per instructions from Ruby and Cotter.

The Snake joined in on an unwarranted attack against the Eagle, and after a while, both FTD agents sounded like a broken record, with one exception: the Snake wanted me to give him a list of company engineers proficient in airbreathing propulsion technology; experts from the Florida division who could work with FTD. We broke up the meeting after midnight and agreed to get together in Building 828 in the morning.

7

Wright-Patterson Air Force Base, Wednesday, July 9, 1969: I was
met in Building 828 by James Bartley, a stocky middle-aged civilian
intelligence analyst who wore sunglasses indoors because of an
eye problem. The former marine had found a home in FTD, and in
addition to his weekly scoutmaster duties in Fairborn, Ohio, and
night courses he was taking in Russian history, Bartley was a member of Captain Harold Gale's technology group. He reserved a conference room and invited analysts in the complex to consult with
me. Compared to the CIA and the Defense Intelligence Agency,
from the sampling of men I was introduced to in Building 828, it
was my impression that the average age of FTD's analysts was
dismayingly on the young side, in the twenties and early thirties.
Experience and knowledge normally contribute to an efficient
intelligence organization and good leaders; obviously I had yet to
meet the real movers behind the Building 828 operation.

The analysts were elated over my Venice and Paris write-ups
and the album of photographs, and they appreciated receiving the
notes directly, because according to Bartley, this saved FTD the
trouble of requesting the data through official government channels; another analyst admitted that communications between

71

FTD and CIA were below par, and this was aggravated by the fact that the CIA was not required by law to give FTD anything if it chose not to.

In the afternoon, as I was briefing analysts from the systems group, a short man entered the room carrying a pad and pencil—it was the Oriental from Paris.

"Hello again," I said, addressing the Oriental. "I thought you were a news correspondent with UPI at the air show." The disturbed yellow man, embarrassed because I had recognized him, plopped his pad on the table as if to say: "Shut up and get on with your presentation."

Another agent was called into the meeting because I had brought photos of the Russian film shown in Venice. The exuberant agent knew that I had taped the sound track of the film—someone from Venice had reported this—and he asked if FTD could borrow the tape. I promised to forward the recording when the CIA was through with it. There followed a raging controversy as to whether the Russian film shown in Venice was the same as the Russian film shown at the air show at Le Bourget. It seemed that there were better ways to spend hard-earned tax dollars; I don't know what they would have done if the Russians had shown film premiers in all the world's capitals.

I outlined the importance of the recent Russian experiments concerning the refueling of spacecraft in orbit, and during the late afternoon I met privately with the Fox, a crafty FTD intelligence officer who took his work seriously. He had read my coverage of the Venice conference and he wanted to talk about it. The Fox said that he was affiliated with the Operations Directorate, the cloak and dagger part of the Air Force intelligence which operates from both Building 828 and another complex on the base.

"What did you think of the Americans attending the meeting?" he asked.

"Some Americans were involved in a collection operation." I named names, including the slapstick routines of the engineers who were outright nervous and awkward.

The Fox, a compulsive chain smoker, took a puff from his cigarette and finally spoke: "I'm glad you told me this."

"For your general information," I added, "the KGB kept tabs on most Americans who attended the conference. If anyone had to be debriefed on a regular basis, you should assume that your debriefing headquarters were located by the KGB within hours after contact was made."

I looked into his perceptive eyes, hoping to find a sign of acknowledgment. He glanced at my Venice report again. "Would you be interested in working with us?" he asked. "I know you're working for the CIA, but damn it, Pete, your work is good and we could use you!"

"Thanks for the compliment. First of all, I'm not working for CIA, or any other intelligence organization. I've volunteered my notes to the community, but I've never accepted any financial assistance, nor have I been offered any."

"You mean the CIA has been getting your notes for nothing?" he asked incredulously.

"That's right. I'm sure that they've been made available to FTD."

"I haven't seen any of them! I wish we had known about you earlier. The first time I heard about you was in Venice!"

"Venice!"

He laughed and flicked his cigarette ashes on the floor. "We kept getting reports that we had to talk with James. I asked: 'James who?' They said: 'Pete James.' I said: 'I know a Pete James from Pratt & Whitney Aircraft, but he's in Florida.' They said: 'No, this Pete James is not in Florida. He's here in Venice!' They said you could answer our questions because you and your wife were getting along great with the Ruskies. Some guys claimed you were working for us and we weren't leveling with them. I denied it, but they didn't believe me. Things got so screwed up . . . hell, it was a fiasco! One guy said that he was being followed. Imagine that." The Fox chuckled. "Some of these guys think they're a regular James Bond or something."

I was alarmed that he didn't believe the reports from his own agents. "I wasn't joking about the surveillance in Venice. Zhivotovskiy was responsible for the Russian operation and his people kept tabs on the Americans. If one of your men said he was being tailed, take him seriously—he probably was."

The Fox examined the report again. "Fantastic!" The Venice fiasco, as he described it, had left FTD with little worthwhile information. "Pete, you came up with more than the rest of the team, and you didn't cost us a cent!" he exclaimed, slapping the report with the back of his hand.

"How much does it cost you to organize a collection effort?" I asked.

"What collection effort?" he asked facetiously. The Fox read the summary of my first dinner meeting with Zhivotovskiy. "It was a fiasco!" he said, shaking his head.

"Sounds like your people came back with nothing."

"Worse than that," he replied, lighting another cigarette. He tossed the match on the table, missing the ash tray.

"For the price of some airline tickets, you didn't lose too much."

"I wish it were only that. You'd be surprised." He threw the report on the desk. "You want to work for us?"

"I'm not interested at this time. Anything we work out would have to be approved by Ruby and Cotter."

"You going to Argentina?"

"I'll make it one way or another; the last trip cost us $3,500, so we'll be saving some this summer to swing Argentina."

"Will you let us see what you come up with?" I nodded. "Thanks. You don't know how much it's appreciated. Don't let Big Brother know about our discussion."

"Who's Big Brother?"

"The CIA. They debrief travelers. We could get in trouble if they thought we were trying an end run on them." When it came to foreign operations involving American citizens, FTD feared the CIA, almost as if it didn't want me to open a Pandora's box.

Three intelligence analysts joined us and asked about the Russian propellant transfer experiment in space discussed in my Paris write-up. As I outlined the implications of the Russian venture, an analyst interrupted: "Does the CIA know about this?"

The man to his left frowned and said, "The CIA has all of his reports!" There appeared to be no love lost between the two intelligence organizations.

The day's discussions left an impact on me because perhaps for the first time, I realized that U.S. overseas intelligence operations were not as well organized as I thought they were. I had created an image in my mind of a flawless intelligence establishment operating like a well-greased machine, manned by experienced and professional agents. I found the opposite; there was something wrong with an intelligence unit that couldn't do better than a U.S. citizen who operated outside the government system.

8

The Air Force Secret Facility, Thursday, July 10, 1969: I visited the secret facility to research material for my next annual report. I felt more at ease during this visit because I knew my way around and I could work with the information systems specialists on a personal level. Having studied Russian rocket technology for a year, I knew the names of significant Russian facilities and personalities who were heavily involved in their defense program. The facility had eight staff assistants working on my requests, and no one complained, which astonished me, because I was running them ragged. One girl with an armful of secret cards exclaimed: "I want you to know, Mr. James, that we've never pulled this many cards for anyone before . . . not even one-tenth as many!"

"I believe you," I replied. "I can only promise you that this data will be put to good use. I have six months. I hope to do something that has never been done before."

"Okay, I just wanted to make sure that you knew what you were getting yourself into."

The outline of my next annual report materialized before me; in addition to what the Air Force expected, I had my own ideas, including a separate report listing thousands of Russian personalities and significant details about their activities and how their work related to overall Soviet space and military programs. I wanted to do this on behalf of the thousands of nameless spies who had risked their lives to acquire the information. The amount of intelligence filed within the facility was incomprehensible, and it was no secret that the majority of the collected intelligence would go unseen by analysts' eyes. Why were men asked to risk their lives to gather intelligence that is not used? Who was responsible for determining our technical intelligence requirements? This was another aspect of our operations that needed to be looked into.

After two fruitful days at the secret facility, I boarded a jet to Palm Beach and thought about the U.S. intelligence situation. It looked altogether different since I had gotten my feet wet and met with this nation's intelligence specialists on both the military and civilian sides of the house. One thing was certain and the late director of the CIA, Allen Dulles, made this point on several occasions: the craft of intelligence requires good collection operations as well as good analysts to review the intelligence collected. I was not only dismayed over the ineptness of FTD's collection operations abroad, but after almost one and a half years of association with FTD, I was distressed over the quality of its assessments. Several points disturbed me:

(1) The competition between the CIA and the DIA, and thus, FTD, was not always in our national interest. Whereas competition ideally helps improve a product, the competition between the two intelligence organizations was vicious and caustic; instead of cooperating with each other, members of the military intelligence services withheld intelligence from the CIA, so that the DIA could scoop the CIA and thus come out looking like a knight in shining armor. The reverse was also true: during the Cuban missile crisis, the CIA withheld data from the DIA so that the CIA could scoop the military and generally discredit the DIA before the President. The idea behind competing intelligence organizations is to offer our policymakers more than one interpretation of the same intelligence data. With FTD withholding data from the CIA and the CIA not legally obligated to share its data with DIA and FTD, each organization was attempting to analyze intelligence information using different pieces of different puzzles; not one intelligence organization in the United States had access to all the available pieces to the same puzzle, even though the CIA was chartered by law to be the center for all intelligence information; that is why it is called the Central Intelligence Agency.

(2) The Air Force secret facility contained thousands and thousands of raw intelligence reports collected throughout the world

by attachés, paid informers, agents, engineers, and scientists. Much of the information was acquired at great financial investment by the government, but it was filed away untouched by analysts; it did not make sense to spend a fortune collecting information that would not be analyzed.

(3) There was something drastically wrong with the FTD-private industry relationship. FTD had numerous aerospace corporations under contract to perform analysis work for it. Each company would conduct a detailed study like mine and submit it to FTD. This information would be evaluated by FTD's analysts and incorporated into the drafts of FTD and DIA intelligence reports. The drafts would then go through a lengthy approval cycle. By the time the finished intelligence assessment was published and disseminated to the users of the intelligence, the material was old. In fact, the cycle would usually take between *one and two years*.

(4) The users of technical intelligence reports—the aerospace industry and scientific and research laboratories—were not receiving the reports. Because of job security and other reasons, the reports were being pigeonholed by FTD. I was appalled at Super Smart's performance in the Falcon Motel. He was telling a representative of the company that built the jet engines that power the Douglas A-4 Skyhawk, the General Dynamics/Grumman F-111 variable-geometry tactical fighter aircraft, the Boeing B-52 bomber, the Boeing KC-135/C-135 tanker transports, the North American F-100, the McDonnell Douglas F-101, the F-105 Thunderchief interceptor, the YF-12A interceptor and SR-71 reconnaissance aircraft, that Pratt & Whitney Aircraft could not receive jet engine intelligence reports compiled by the Foreign Technology Division and the Defense Intelligence Agency unless the company promised to prepare a special yearly report for FTD. If Pratt & Whitney did not agree, the intelligence reports would be sent to General Electric, Allison, and other corporations competing in the jet engine field. It was alarming that agents in Building 828 had the power to distribute selectively intelligence data to companies of their own choosing, giving the selected companies an edge over their competitors. Besides being unfair, the FTD role of kingmaker blatantly infringed on the free enterprise system; it merited investigation.

(5) While I had not encountered this personally, the Eagle told me that the cards he had selected at the secret facility were screened by Building 828 agents who claimed to be enforcing the "need-to-know" security restrictions. He said that the cards forwarded to him were carefully selected so that he would arrive at certain predetermined conclusions. In effect, he was charging the Air Force with controlling supposedly independent intelligence assessments of

Russian weapons systems by monitoring the information sent to evaluators they had under contract. And this included screening open literature publications as well as the classified data. Since FTD contractors were not necessarily being sent the same information, their assessments could not be checked against each other. Thus, when FTD put together its story for DIA behind closed doors, its "finished" assessments agreed with its predetermined assessments, and the conclusions by FTD's evaluators in private industry supported FTD's finished product as well; it looked legitimate to outsiders, and the irregularities couldn't be cross-checked because the evaluators were prohibited by FTD from comparing notes with each other, allegedly because the government might accuse them of conspiring, price-fixing, or violating anti-trust laws. This was another area that I wanted to look into.

(6) After talking with FTD intelligence analysts, I learned that they were far removed from the real world, having lost touch with the current state-of-the-art and technology in the aerospace industry. Some of their assessments lauded Russian technical achievements and mentioned a Russian lead of so many years over the United States, when in fact the United States was ahead of the Russians in the areas cited; their erroneous assessments clouded the areas where the Russians really were ahead.

(7) Another problem I encountered was that some groups in Building 828 were convinced that the Russians were embarked on a particular program, and consequently were close-minded about considering intelligence information that indicated otherwise. Besides the major gaps in intelligence analysis, FTD groups were much too compartmentalized; one group did not know what another group was working on and there was little cross-flow of information.

I gave Lowell Ruby and Norm Cotter a verbal briefing of my three day visit to the Air Force base and the secret facility, and I supplemented it with a memorandum to document what had transpired. The cover sheet of this memorandum read: "Private: All Persons Having Access To This Document Must Sign Below; No Other Copies Of This Document Are Authorized." I wanted to inform Pratt & Whitney management in no uncertain terms of the clandestine nature of the company's foreign technology program with FTD, the direction we were heading, the possible pitfalls, and the fact that FTD wanted more names—the list again. Additionally, since I was the company's foreign technology expert, I wanted proof that my superiors were fully informed of FTD's intentions, because no government agency outside the Air Force Systems Command was monitoring its operations, and some FTD agents were abusing the secret trust of their sensitive positions. I wanted to cover all possibilities, especially if the company's foreign technology program blew up in my face.

My memorandum was circulated, read, signed, and returned three days later. The signators included: (1) Lowell Ruby, my technical supervisor and project engineer in the systems analysis department, (2) Norm Cotter, Ruby's boss and chief of the systems analysis department, (3) Richard Mulready, chief of the advanced propulsion department, (4) Richard Coar, engineering manager of the Center, and (5) William H. Brown, assistant chief engineer.

I also prepared a supplement to the aforementioned memorandum and hand delivered it to Lowell Ruby and Norm Cotter. This document, which I typed at home, contained a detailed account of my conversations with the Fox. Excerpts are shown below:

I had a four hour exchange with [the Fox] and briefed him on what I learned at the Venice conference. At the end of our discussion [the Fox] stated that there was no question that we submitted more valuable information than his entire team. He is also looking forward to receiving the CIA's summary of our report. . . . FTD found the movie photographs extremely valuable. . . . Needless to say, our Venice movie photographs were timely. . . . [the Fox] wants to establish daily communications with P&WA and inquired whether there were any government facilities in the area. He made it clear that we were free to contact him and have dossiers prepared at their expense on any Soviet personalities. . . . He also said to contact him if we need anything we can't get through normal channels. . . . [the Fox] privately asked me (1) to participate in the FTD collection operation and (2) if he could contact the CIA and P&WA for approval. I politely declined his offer, but stated that I would provide them with some suggestions at a later date.

We should remain very much independent of their collection operations for a number of reasons. I personally feel that the FTD collection operation leaves much to be desired, and for that reason is dangerous. I seriously don't think that members of his team are aware of what is really going on, or how competent the Soviet operation is. [The Fox and Super Smart] remarked that the FTD operation in Venice was so mixed up that it must have fooled the Soviets. That is not true. The Soviets had five KGB agents that I know of who were operating very effectively. Three of them were primarily concerned with counterespionage. Zhivotovskiy was coordinating their overall effort. . . . Another top-notch operator at the conference was Nikolai Beloussov, who was officially listed as Soviet Air Attaché at the Roma Embassy. Beloussov is directing the Soviet espionage effort from that embassy. His activities have recently been under surveillance by the Agency. He was expelled from England at the request of the British Secret Service because they determined that it was Beloussov who masterminded the Christine Keeler-Profumo sex scandal that embarrassed the British government and forced numerous officials who opposed the Communists to resign. . . . Beloussov's right-hand man was Istomin, another KGB agent from the embassy who was listed as an engineer.

The FTD collection operation is no match for the trained KGB agents that the Soviets send to these conferences . . . it is obvious that (1) their risks are not commensurate with their returns and (2) the FTD collection operation should be overhauled. In summary . . . I recommend that we continue to remain independent of their operations and pursue a middle of the road course, with FTD on one side and the CIA on the other.

In short, by July 1969 I thought it was my responsibility as the program manager of the company's foreign technology effort to sound the alarm, so that Pratt & Whitney would not be drawn into any foreign operations with FTD that it would later regret.

9

August 7, 1969: I was working on my second annual report on foreign rocket technology when Lowell Ruby handed me a letter mailed to Pratt & Whitney by Major Dennis L. Askelson, a contracting officer with the Department of the Army in Fort Eustis, Virginia. Askelson stated that it is Defense Department policy to provide all government contractors pertinent foreign technology information during the performance of their work on government contracts. He asked Pratt & Whitney to make Army-related foreign technology requests through the Army. This was my first exposure to a foreign technology effort by the Army, so I telephoned the Eagle in East Hartford and asked if he knew anything about the Army effort. He indicated that the Army was concerned mainly with materials development, surface-to-surface tactical missile programs, and helicopters.

The Askelson letter begged the issue because the Eagle and I were having problems getting an official listing of the titles of U.S. government intelligence reports. Our requests of this nature to FTD were categorically rejected. FTD had a number of corporations under contract, but it controlled the dissemination of intelligence reports to private industry and, above all, it kept the list of available documents secret. Therefore, even though it was Defense Department policy to make these reports available to government contractors upon request, in practice this was not the case. We couldn't request what we didn't know existed. I doubted whether Congress or high-level Defense Department officials knew about this situation, and, belonging to a conservative "don't rock the boat" company, my hands were tied. To make matters worse, Lowell Ruby told me that General Manager W. L. Gorton would personally escort out the door any Pratt & Whitney engineer who did anything to upset the Air Force. "Call the Russian embassy!" the Eagle suggested facetiously. "They'll probably give us the titles [of the intelligence reports] over the phone."

To combat the FTD monopoly on defense-related intelligence, I decided to spearhead a one-man effort to collect, analyze, and disseminate intelligence information to the highest government officials I could reach. I hoped that if I could exceed the performance of the Building 828 team in some areas, it would draw the attention of the right officials and result in a reevaluation of FTD's mission function. My second annual report on foreign rocket technology could be my sounding board for the "intelligence analysis" part of the plan, and my planned Argentine trip could cover the "intelligence collection" aspect of the plan. I requested a week's leave of absence to attend the Argentina International Astronautical Federation meeting and was told by Lowell Ruby that my request would be considered.

The Eagle forwarded the tentative program schedule for the October meeting and noted that several high-level Soviet personalities would be attending. I prepared a list of questions that I thought could be answered from conversations with the Soviets and forwarded it to Gleichauf, so that the CIA could be kept abreast of my plans. Shortly after mailing the data to Gleichauf, I received a cryptic telephone call from an intelligence specialist having close working relations with the CIA. He said that my Venice-Paris report contained something that was very significant and the CIA was trying to get more information on the subject. He extended the personal thanks of CIA analysts whom I did not know and added that they hoped I would attend the Argentina meeting to follow up on the Venice-Paris data.

Gleichauf telephoned two days later and asked whether my Argentine request had been approved; on the basis of the CIA communications alone, there appeared to be a lot of behind-the-scenes activity on the conference. He said that the CIA did not wish to interfere with the operations of Pratt & Whitney and the matter was strictly between the company and myself, but he hoped everything would turn out all right, and he volunteered to talk with General Manager W. L. Gorton if the company had any reservations about the merits of my reports to the CIA. About an hour after the Gleichauf call, Lowell Ruby notified me that Engineering Manager Richard Coar had rejected my request.

"There's nothing I can do," he replied apologetically.

"I'm only bringing it up again," I said, "because the customer [i.e., the CIA] is willing to talk personally with Gorton."

"He is?" Ruby asked incredulously. While Gleichauf had no intention of pressuring anyone from Pratt & Whitney, I knew how the company's internal politics operated: someone from the government wished to speak with the general manager to reverse an arbitrary decision that cut off the flow of foreign intelligence to the CIA. Gleichauf once described me as his best source, so he probably had a personal stake in it too. Ruby reeled back and thought it over. Jumping to his feet, the gray-haired project engineer rushed into Cotter's office. Minutes later, both men came out. "Pete," Cotter said, "he won't have to talk with Gorton. You get one week, same rules as before." (I.e., I paid for the travel expenses.) While in this instance the company's fear of offending the U.S. government worked in my favor, I couldn't help but think that it was a hell of a way to run an organization!

September 26, 1969: With a few days remaining before my departure, Stan Mosier, an aggressive company engineer engaged in the design of advanced jet engine components for the Air Force, asked me to contact FTD immediately to obtain its latest intelligence reports on advanced lubricants. Because Super Smart and the Snake had indicated that they might send some foreign airbreathing data to us in Florida on a conditional basis, I dispatched a letter describing the problem, identifying the Air Force Aero Propulsion Laboratory at Wright-Patterson Air Force Base as the official contracting agency, and listed the pertinent documents I already had on file. I requested FTD's assistance and expressed interest in receiving both classified and unclassified reports. Super Smart telephoned me several days later and said that the data would be waiting for me when I returned from my "southern vacation."

October 3, 1969: At 1:30 A.M. I was seated next to a Spanish-speaking couple in the tourist section of a LAN Chile Boeing 707 jetliner. The plane knifed through a storm over the Caribbean and flew along the western coast of South America, where the crimson sky silhouetted the rugged Andes mountains. Due to a last minute change in our plans, Diane would join me one day later. On this trip I learned a great deal from my Soviet contacts, and Georgiy Zhivotovskiy, the senior-level KGB intelligence officer, was true to his word: he invited us to visit the Soviet Union in 1970 as a guest of the Academy of Sciences, but there was a special condition—I was secretly to pick up my visa in a Russian embassy on the European continent before departing for Moscow. The intelligence I learned from the Soviets during this and other conferences is summarized in my first book, *Soviet Conquest From Space*.* There was one episode in Mar del Plata, Argentina, that relates to the *Air Force Mafia* story.

Mar del Plata, Argentina, Thursday, October 9: 1969: Nervously puffing a Havana cigar, Georgiy Zhivotovskiy, the senior-level KGB intelligence officer, excused himself while his associates, Igor Prissevok (Russian intelligence officer and translator) and Gennadi Dimentiev (Russian space manager), made themselves at home around the coffee table. We continued our technical exchange on the mezzanine floor of the Hotel Provincial in spite of the fact that the formal sessions were in progress in the main hall. As Dimentiev was sketching a spacecraft in my note pad, an American engineer affiliated with a West Coast aerospace firm moved closer to us, as if he were a pawn on a chess board; I had seen him at the registration desk, then next to a pillar, and he finally settled down on a sofa about fifteen feet from us. I lowered my voice, hoping to maintain the privacy of our discussion, but after a few minutes, the engineer got up, walked over to our table and spread his newspaper over the unused portion. With nose buried in the paper, he monitored our discussion, much like the agents one would see in the movies. Earlier in the week he had asked me to introduce him to the Russians, but with the space conference almost over, and having had little success with the Russians, the fidgety engineer was beset with another problem: justifying his expenses to his "employer" for the week. I glanced at the engineer, hoping to make him feel uneasy, and I succeeded. I was burning alive inside; the leech would prepare a report based on the fragments of the conversation he had heard, he would insert a few subjective remarks of his own to smooth out the gaps in the conversation he did not hear, and he would pass off the information to his superiors as his own work, based exclusively on his personal conversations with the Russians—more erroneous data and junk to clog up our intelligence files. Having visited the Air Force secret facility and talked with its agents and analysts, I knew that there was no way they could tell how the leech had acquired his data or whether the data was factual, fabricated, or both. In fact, since FTD would not use a lie detector on its employees—something that the CIA routinely did—to help un-

*New Rochelle, N.Y.: Arlington House, 1974 ($8.95).

cover unethical practices by its personnel, I wondered whether it even cared. The FTD chiefs behind the Argentine operation would similarly keep mum, because something was better than nothing, and they too had to justify their expenditures, if only to make their operation cost-effective in comparison to the CIA's.

After parting with Prissevok and Dimentiev, leaving the aerospace engineer at the table "reading," I watched him from across the mezzanine. Within seconds, he got up, left the newspaper on the coffee table, and joined Gloria, an Argentine hostess at the registration desk.

Including the Venice and Paris trips, our 1969 travels would cost us about $5,000. But in my opinion it was worth every cent, because I was learning a great deal about the Russian space and defense establishment and I was assisting our country in what I believed to be a worthwhile effort. Besides, I planned to write a book on what I had learned when my usefulness to the CIA ended. As the engineer flirted with Gloria, I remembered what Gleichauf once told me, and I understood fully what he meant: "One reason why your work is so highly regarded [by the CIA], Peter, is that it is all voluntary. . . . You don't have to fabricate a story because no one holds your purse strings. Your only reward is knowing that you are helping your government."

From an intelligence standpoint I knew that I controlled the Mar del Plata conference from the moment I touched down in Argentina, when I met Zhivotovskiy at the Buenos Aires Metropolitan Airport enroute to Mar del Plata. The thought entered my mind to forward a copy of my Argentine report to Senator John Stennis, who was overseeing U.S. intelligence operations for the Senate, with the idea of telling him it was a gift from a concerned taxpayer. If he could compare it, prepared at no cost to the American taxpayer, with everything the FTD spooks had been able to put together on the conference, I was sure he would find that the taxpayer was being hoodwinked into subsidizing costly boondoggles around the world in the name of national security. But the time to approach Congress had not yet arrived.

From outward appearances my plan—to have someone high in government look into FTD's collection operations—had possibilities; FTD and CIA intelligence reports are identified by code numbers, so reports on the Argentine meeting could always be recalled for review by a Senate committee behind closed doors.

Monday, October 13, 1969: I reported to work with the foreign and domestic intelligence I had acquired in Argentina. Betty McCracken, the head of a security subcontrol station for my department, signed over several secret reports that were forwarded by

Super Smart while I was in Argentina. It was FTD's response to my September 26 request on behalf of Stan Mosier for advanced foreign lubricant data. To assist the Air Force Aero Propulsion Laboratory in the development of advanced airbreathing technology, I hoped that FTD would forward its most recent intelligence assessments on the Soviet effort. Instead, Super Smart had sent worthless 1964 and 1965 reports; data that would have set Mosier's program back five years or so, if used. I telephoned Super Smart. "The data you sent us is old. Don't you have anything better?"

"Sorry, Pete. That's the best I have."

"How about your colleagues? Don't they have anything?"

"There are recent reports on the subject but they're the property of another group that's had a long-standing feud with us."

"In [Building] 828?"

"Yeah."

"Since we're under contract by the Air Force, I'd appreciate it if you asked the other group anyway."

"No way!" he barked. "It's unfortunate that we have personality conflicts in our organization, but we do, and there is nothing that can be done about it!"

After exhausting all other possibilities I tried the unavoidable: "Can you please give me the name of the man who has the reports? I'd like to call him myself."

"No!" he thundered back, almost breaking my eardrum.

"I assume you have a good reason," I replied, knowing that he didn't want his industry contacts to communicate with other groups in Building 828.

"Yes . . . we're not allowed to give out any names." He was hiding behind a façade of good security practice.

After hanging up, I realized that FTD's promise to provide Pratt & Whitney with airbreathing data "in the national interest" was a hoax; it was interested only in its own empire, and everyone else be damned. It appeared that each group in Building 828 was free to work out its own deals with private industry. It had a good thing going and the reports were its trump card. A complaint to Air Force headquarters was warranted, but Norm Cotter and Lowell Ruby had adopted the general manager's policy that nothing should be done to upset the Air Force, allegedly because it might cost the company the FX jet engine contract which would soon be awarded.

10

November 3, 1969: I received an envelope postmarked November 1, 1969, and addressed to me at our home. It was from Super Smart. Excerpts are shown below:

> Last summer in a conversation the possibility of a spring vacation in Southern Europe was mentioned. To get funding for the trip, it's always nice to be giving a paper at a conference in the tour area. I just happened to hear about a conference in Rome that might be of interest to you. Just for my own entertainment, I wrote up an abstract that might be accepted by the meeting sponsors. Feel free to rewrite into your own words. The abstracts should arrive at the address below by 30 November 1969. . . . Be sure to make your corporate affiliation clear in the abstract submission letter. I'll be able to help with the actual paper later if you so desire.

In essence, Super Smart was proposing that I present a report at a conference in Europe. In return, FTD would reimburse me for my expenses, and probably more. Acceptance of the offer would make me a bona fide agent of the U.S. government, bind me to a briefing before the conference, a debriefing after the conference, and possibly something during the conference. More importantly, I would have to sign a secrecy oath which would seal my lips forever. He also wanted me to contact the conference organizers and list Pratt & Whitney Aircraft as my affiliation—the cover story—yet he had written the abstract of the report in an attachment to the letter and volunteered to write the report if I consented.

The Eagle once told me that the military intelligence services use scientists and engineers from well-known aerospace firms and scientific research establishments as pawns both to collect intelligence and to mislead the Soviets by presenting reports that contained erroneous data. He said that the latter was a serious practice because the purpose of a scientific conference is to exchange ideas, and these conferences were attended by dedicated scientists throughout the world who often wrote books, articles, and reports which referenced material presented at the meetings. Many U.S. firms were not aware of this facet of FTD's operations and, in some cases, the personnel involved were high-level managers in U.S. industry under private contract with FTD. While the false information may have confused the Soviets on occasion, the Eagle thought it was "third rate" and the Soviets were on to it. The private working agreements also created a lasting and binding relationship between executives of the aerospace industry and Air Force intelligence officers, and thus the Department of Defense; this has led to conflicts of interest and has set the stage for the procurement of billions of dollars of unneeded aerospace systems, since the aerospace managers on FTD missions could report about a Russian capability that in fact did not exist; the military intelligence services would notify the Defense Department of this capability; the Defense Department would order the development of aerospace systems to counter the alleged Soviet work; and the aerospace firms would be awarded contracts to develop these systems, managed by the military. It was a neat cycle.

Having both collected and analyzed intelligence, having visited the Air Force secret facility, and having observed the FTD spooks abroad, I saw FTD as the silent partner in this process. As a rule, Russian scientists attending international meetings would approach the author of a presentation afterwards so that they could discuss it in more depth. If I were part of the FTD team, part or all of my paper would have been ghost-written by agents in Building 828. Thus, after discussing it with the Soviets, FTD agents would debrief me, and from this debriefing, they would prepare a raw intelligence report, similar to the ones sent to Pratt & Whitney on the 5 by 8 inch cards. Ideally, the raw report would contain an objective unevaluated summary of what I had learned from the Russians. However, by controlling the subject matter of the papers presented at international conferences and the content of debriefing reports, FTD was in effect controlling the data base of raw intelligence that would be stored in U.S. intelligence files and eventually analyzed by independent evaluators. Thus, analysts who were not familiar with the background of FTD's overseas operations would suddenly be swarmed with a deluge of seemingly legitimate unevaluated reports on an alleged Soviet activity. Not knowing that agents in Building 828 were manipulating them, the independent evaluator would support FTD's already predetermined conclusions. Armed with controlled intelligence information for dissemination to Congress and its civilian chiefs, FTD—a silent partner in the military-industrial complex—could secretly dictate the design, development, and procurement of billions of dollars of military hardware without any outward sign of an irregularity. The taxpayer was in effect being lambasted on both ends; he was supporting FTD's secret operations at home and abroad, and he was supporting the military programs justified by FTD's intelligence assessments. It was a vicious circle, and unless the silent partner was exposed, I could see more money going down the rat hole and FTD's empire getting larger and beyond control.

I supported a viable military-industrial complex vis-a-vis our national security, but it was quite clear that the covert agreements with FTD had no visible means of control by Congress or the public, they infringed on the free enterprise system, and they were obviously not in our national interest. Needless to say, I did not accept Super Smart's offer. Instead, I resolved to delve further into FTD's operations; I had only scratched the surface.

11

Gleichauf visited Pratt & Whitney during the second week in November. Leo Faucher, the new chief of plant protection who replaced W. T. Dwyer, no longer questioned me about the material I was transmitting to the CIA. Gleichauf locked my 110-page Argentine report in his briefcase and said the CIA was extremely grateful for my efforts.

After Gleichauf left Pratt & Whitney I received a call from an Air Force intelligence officer who cryptically asked me to give FTD a copy of my Mar del Plata report. His agents responsible for "south of the border" operations reported that I was having extensive contact with the higher echelon Russian scientists throughout the week. "It's imperative we talk with you," he said. I told Ruby and Cotter of the call and they concurred that FTD should indeed be given the write-up.

November 11, 1969: Lowell Ruby and I boarded a Delta jet for Dayton, Ohio. My gray attaché case was crammed with the Mar del Plata report, other sensitive Russian-related documents and a copy of Paul Bethel's book, *The Losers,* an account of the Communist advance in Latin America. If the plane had been hijacked to Cuba, it would have been interesting.

Wright-Patterson Air Force Base, Wednesday, November 12, 1969: Ruby and I attended a "threat analysis" foreign technology briefing presented by personnel from both the Air Force Aero Propulsion Laboratory and the Air Force Aeronautical Systems Division, with FTD intelligence analysts listening from the sidelines. The briefing chairman gave his analysis of FOXBAT, Russia's advanced all-weather interceptor aircraft. During the question and answer session, I asked the briefing chairman when the intelligence community thought the Russians would deploy FOXBAT outside the USSR in satellite countries or other friendly nations. He laughed at my question as if I should have known better than to ask. "From past experience," he replied confidently, "you can bet they won't let FOXBAT out until another ten years—probably around 1980." As it turned out, the Russians deployed FOXBAT in the Middle East about a year later. I had asked the question because there is a world of difference in analyzing intelligence about a weapon system as described on FTD's five- by eight-inch cards and the weapon system itself. The Israeli Six-Day War in 1967 was a boon for Western intelligence because it showed the importance of capturing modern weapons systems; the West needed to capture a FOXBAT intact, because FTD's assessments on the system weren't worth the paper they were written on. The chances of this happening were remote, however, unless the Russians deployed the aircraft in a combat zone outside the USSR.

After the briefing I visited Building 828 and met with the Fox. In a conference room screened off from other FTD personnel, I gave him technical excerpts of the Mar del Plata report, but I withheld political and biographical data because in my opinion FTD did not have a need-to-know and this would have unnecessarily exposed both Americans and Russians to retribution from their superiors.

"Pete," the Fox said, "will you be here tomorrow?"

"I'll be at the [secret] facility. Why?"

"We'd like to talk with you again. I want the chief to see this. Is that all right?"

"Use your judgment." He appeared to be preparing another pitch to enlist me in FTD's clandestine operations. I decided to play it by ear and let him make the first move.

With FTD taking the position that Pratt & Whitney could not receive recent foreign jet engine intelligence data unless the company provided it with an annual report, and with the material it was willing to send appearing as if it had been prepared by the KGB's directorate of misinformation, I wanted to see what the Directorate of Foreign Technology of the Aeronautical Systems Division could offer. I was not acquainted with the organization of

91

the Air Force, but I did know that the Foreign Technology Division and the Aeronautical Systems Division were separate units of the Air Force Systems Command, and the Aeronautical Systems Division had its own intelligence outfit, allegedly independent of FTD. During the FOXBAT briefing earlier in the day, a man from the Aeronautical Systems Division's spy shop—the Directorate of Foreign Technology, not to be confused with FTD—asked me to drop by his office for a chat.

I drove to Area B of Wright-Patterson Air Force Base later that afternoon and met with Francis Simon and Lt. Larry Ehle in the basement of Building 14, an L-shaped complex of the Aeronautical Systems Division. The men were to the point. They outlined the activities of their unit that they thought would be of interest to Pratt & Whitney. This included "threat analysis," the evaluation of Russian fighter aircraft and bomber weapons systems. Both men claimed that if Pratt & Whitney signed a foreign technology contract with the Aeronautical Systems Division it could supply the company with more Defense Intelligence Agency reports than FTD was giving us. Simon claimed that his unit had access to all pertinent jet engine foreign technology information, whereas FTD was restricted to study special areas of technology and systems of interest. As I listened to their pitch, a clear and ominous pattern was developing; it seemed that each branch of the United States government was somehow involved in intelligence, and each branch had a "better deal" to offer than the other, yet to participate in the better deal an "understanding" was required. The men proposed a loosely-worded, no-cost contract with Pratt & Whitney, similar to the company's arrangement with FTD, except the company had never signed a contract with FTD. They wanted, however, to include both Pratt & Whitney Aircraft in Florida and its headquarters in East Hartford, Connecticut, in the contractual agreement.

In what I thought was the most revealing disclosure of the day, Simon said that McDonnell Douglas Corporation had an arrangement with them and was using it to good advantage. According to Simon, his unit was sending McDonnell Douglas the latest intelligence information on the Russian FOXBAT. He proudly showed me a photograph of the proposed McDonnell Douglas F-15 air superiority fighter and pointed out the similarities between the F-15 and the Russian FOXBAT. What intrigued me was that the Aeronautical Systems Division had contracted Fairchild Hiller, North American Rockwell, and McDonnell Douglas in a competition to develop this nation's next generation air superiority fighter, called the "FX" in the earlier days and redesignated the F-15, and though the winner of the competition was to be announced in December, about a month away, the Directorate of Foreign Technology of the Aeronautical Systems Division was slipping McDonnell Douglas intelligence information on advanced Russian aircraft. Even if Fairchild Hiller and North American Rockwell had working agreements with the Directorate of Foreign Technology, the rules of the game permitted one company to be favored over another, and thus be given the best and most recent intelligence information. This clearly was not in our national interest, and under the circumstances it appeared that only a congressional investigation could rectify the situation. The chances of this happening, however, were nil because Congress did not know of the practice and the aerospace contractors on the short end of the stick would not buck the Air Force.

Simon's presentation was impressive. He suggested that Pratt & Whitney send a manager to the air base to discuss his proposal on an official basis. While I thought the proposal was outrageous from a national position, it was still in Pratt & Whitney's interest to consider it since no other jet engine company, according to Simon, was under contract with his unit.

12

November 13, 1969: I visited the Air Force secret facility and selected more cards for possible use in my second annual report on foreign technology. While reviewing a Defense Intelligence Agency report, Super Smart, whom I thought was in Dayton, knocked on the door and entered the room. "Pete," he began, "your Mar del Plata report has opened more wounds in the [intelligence] community; one faction supports your findings, another is vehemently against you."

"Could you elaborate?" I asked.

"Forget it. When you're on top, some people will take a shot at you."

"We're all working for the same team, aren't we?"

"Sure, but to put it bluntly, some of our people are jealous of your success, which brings up why I'm here. We'd like you to work for us [FTD]."

"I'm interested in your proposition because I can't afford to keep paying for these trips. What do you propose?"

"Don't worry about the money. Money is no problem. We could use you." The intelligence officer pointed his finger at me to make his point.

"One reason why I've been successful is that I've been able to operate independently of the community. The Russians haven't pegged me as a government spy, because I'm not a government spy. If I agree to work for you, I would like it understood that I want no contact with anyone from FTD outside the United States. I'm not interested in being debriefed on a daily basis."

"Pete, I'm alarmed to hear this, coming from you. By being in daily contact with us you would have the support of the organization. We could help you! Our people in the States could give you feedback as things progressed. We could tell you what questions to ask them [the Russians]." So that was it. I suddenly realized why the cost of an overseas collection operation escalated beyond that of paying for a number of airline tickets, hotels, and meals. That was only a fraction of the total cost. The real cost of the operation was communications and support personnel. During an overseas operation, Building 828 is connected by a secured communications network to our embassies abroad. Depending on where an operation is planned, the nearest American embassy is used. Supported by military intelligence officers and attachés who maintain contact with the collectors of the intelligence information, agents in Building 828 had absolute control over the subject discussed between FTD operatives abroad and Russian scientists; FTD was not only ghost-writing papers presented at international meetings, but it was making sure that Russian scientists were asked certain questions. By maintaining daily contact with their operatives abroad, Building 828 controllers could elicit intelligence favorable to FTD. They could eradicate what they considered to be unfavorable intelligence by simply ordering their pawns to pursue another line of questioning in their discussions with Soviet scientists. FTD was stuck with what I had given the CIA, and it therefore had no control over it; this may have been what Super Smart meant when he said that my Mar del Plata report "opened more wounds in the community."

He continued: "If you don't want contact with our people, we could have one of our scientists give you our questions."

I was appalled at his suggestion. I didn't need a lower echelon officer to tutor me on the types of questions that I should be asking the Russians. He should have known better than to suggest such a thing, especially since he had read both my Venice and Argentina reports. Getting tied up with FTD's overseas leeches was the last thing on my mind. There had to be no other explanation: Super Smart was more interested in getting me under contract with FTD, so that the CIA or his other rivals in the intelligence community could not use my services, than he was in obtaining worthwhile information from the Russians. This also explained why the CIA was losing the services of some of its scientific sources: FTD was hijacking them. If I signed up with FTD, it meant that it could control the intelligence that I was reporting, since FTD, not Gleichauf, would file the report. It was empire building all over again, and I was to be another FTD pawn. In Kim Philby's memoirs, *My Silent War*, the Soviet master spy said that he did not hesitate to join the Soviet intelligence service because "one does not look twice at an offer of enrollment in an elite force." In theory, that advice would probably apply to any American who was approached by a member of the U.S. intelligence services. Now, in the Air Force secret facility, Uncle Sam, under the guise of the Foreign Technology Division, was again asking me to join its overseas intelligence operations. I was not only hesitant, but I questioned the eliteness of this intelligence organization.

"Aren't there other groups that could also benefit from my reporting?" I asked.

"Sure, and they're all jealous because we have you." Super Smart was alluding to the Pratt & Whitney-FTD letter agreement of 1968. We were heading for an impasse: if I worked for FTD, I worked under its ground rules. I didn't want to put a damper on our relationship, so I tried diplomatically to drop the subject: "Let's wait and see how Ruby and Cotter react to me getting involved like this."

"I suggest you tell only Cotter about this," he said.

I nodded and changed the subject: "Earlier in the year, Ruby forwarded eight copies of my first annual report to FTD. He attached the names of Air Force officers in the Pentagon that we thought would benefit from the report. Do you remember?"

"Yes, I do," he replied, shuffling his feet.

"Did you ever distribute the reports?"

"No . . . we didn't."

"Why not? The Pentagon certainly has a need to know."

"It's a long story," he said with a drawl, as if wanting to change the subject.

"You indicated that it was one of the best you've received. Why are you holding on to it?" Super Smart ignored the question and sifted through the cards on the desk. The Eagle once told me that FTD had extracted the meat out of the annual report and passed off a censored version of the work as its own. Using a secret classification, FTD gave neither Pratt & Whitney nor me any credit. The Eagle felt that FTD would never give my work visibility because it would invite other members of the intelligence community to solicit my assistance. As Super Smart groped for words I realized that

I had again sold the Eagle's judgment short. "I see. They're pigeonholed in a filing cabinet," I said sarcastically.

"No . . . They're in a cabinet, but anyone who wants to use them can."

"Our agreement is with FTD. I guess what you do with the reports is your business."

He smiled. "Pete, when you work for us"—he was back on the overseas collection operations again—"you work for *Uncle Sam.* It's altogether different."

"In what way?"

"You have Uncle Sam's full support. Your name goes on file in Washington. If you get in trouble, and that sometimes happens, your government is behind you: the State Department, the diplomatic corps . . ."

"I thought I already had that promise as a private citizen. That's what the passport is about, isn't it?"

"If you're under contract with us, they'll work twice as hard!"

"Like they did for Lieutenant Bucher and his [Pueblo] crew?" If you get caught, government or no government, you're through!"

"If you're caught without any official connections, you're really through. In this business the rules are different. Pete, we expect you to protect yourself—always." Super Smart's eyes grew larger, as if to accentuate his point. "But when you're beyond that stage, when you're in trouble, that's where Uncle Sam comes in. *If you don't work for us, protect yourself!*"

His last remark had a disturbing cryptic meaning. "It's senseless to bicker over semantics. The worst thing that could happen to me is to be absorbed into this bureaucratic mess. I'm interested, but only if I operate independently of your shop."

"Pete, you've got a problem. You tell the truth too much!" Super Smart put his arm around my shoulder. "Send me the name of a conference you want to attend, and let me work from there." I wasn't sure whether he was serious or whether this was a ploy to get me on board. One thing was certain about the intelligence officers at FTD, and I was not alone in my evaluation of them: they often lied to achieve an objective.

November 14, 1969: I was assured by Air Force agents that the Mar del Plata report would be handled in the strictest of confidence and be put to good use. They asked me to think over their proposition to spy for them and promised to keep in touch. I spent the remainder of the morning at the secret facility, watched the Apollo 12 astronauts launched to the moon, and boarded a jet for Florida in the evening. While I had every reason to feel good—the intelligence community lauded my work and Pratt & Whitney management was very pleased with the positive uproar created by the annual foreign technology report and my participation at international conferences—I was greatly disturbed because the superficial back-scratching was not getting to the heart of the problem: FTD was running nonproductive, costly intelligence operations and producing grotesque intelligence assessments that in the words of some highly respected private observers were "worthless" and "fraudulent." This was a grave problem that I wanted to look into in more depth because FTD's assessments influenced the design specifications of weapons systems that would be the cornerstone of our national defense in the coming decades.

The upsetting aspect of this dilemma was that the Foreign Technology Division would not acknowledge that a problem existed; in fact, it was interested in building an even larger empire and plans were under way to expand the Building 828 complex, but thank God, the funds for the project were being held up. The Florida Research and Development Center would not do anything, even though Ruby, Cotter, and other managers knew of the situation; they were afraid of offending the Air Force. And Justin F. Gleichauf indicated that the CIA's hands were tied because the Agency had no jurisdiction over the military intelligence services. Whereas it was my objective to prepare a comprehensive intelligence report that might embarrass FTD intelligence officers covering the Mar del Plata meeting, I only succeeded in helping them justify their expenditures; my Mar del Plata coverage would be added to their returns from the conference. FTD could get away with it because sources of information were not disclosed. If I had refused to turn over the Mar del Plata report to FTD altogether, I would have been treading on thin ice with Pratt & Whitney.

This still left me with a final option: my second annual report on foreign technology. If I could do a better job than FTD in evaluating foreign technology, and get the report distributed outside Building 828, the right people might start asking questions. I was torn between what Pratt & Whitney wanted, what the Air Force wanted, and what I thought was right and in the national interest. I could feel myself being drawn on a course that would lead people in Pratt & Whitney and the Air Force to doubt my loyalty. I also began asking myself if I were truly acting in the national interest and whether I might do more damage than good by not playing along with FTD.

With the air base visit out of the way, I started serious work on the second annual foreign technology report. In my association with FTD, the problem that some intelligence analysts raised was that their work was grossly over-edited by their technical superiors so that the "finished" intelligence product was unrecognizable from what was submitted. Their main complaint was that new assessments had to be compatible with previous assessments, even if the previous assessment was known to be wrong. This procedure could be described in two words: job security. When a good report was published, it was usually pigeonholed by analysts who wanted to make a name for themselves; it was a cutthroat operation in Building 828 and this is what happened to my first annual report; the Eagle was also convinced that my first report was not disseminated to the Pentagon because some sections differed from FTD's official position.

I found that FTD intelligence reports seldom told the reader how valid or accurate an assessment is, nor did they indicate whether the assessment is based on hard intelligence or speculation. This problem was called to my attention by the Eagle when he learned that FTD analysts were passing off passages of KGB-approved Russian textbooks as finished intelligence. He forwarded several technical translations of Russian textbooks and asked me to compare the "finished" FTD intelligence assessment with the Russian textbooks. The FTD assessment led the reader to believe that the conclusions were based on an extensive evaluation of all available intelligence information and the paragraph in question in the FTD report was classified "Secret—No Foreign Dissemination" to perpetuate the fraud. Examination of the translated Russian textbook, however, showed that the FTD intelligence assessment was nothing more than a direct quote from the translation with a few changes such as "The Soviets say" or "They say" added to the lead sentences in the textbook. The pencil changes in the textbooks appeared to have been prepared for a typist so that the material could be woven into the body of a "finished" intelligence report. I showed H. Norm Cotter the textbooks before shipping the evidence of FTD plagiarized intelligence analysis back to the Eagle in East Hartford for filing.

From a planner's point of view, I concluded that it would serve no useful purpose if my next annual report were tailored after the FTD reports. Above all, I felt that the annual report had to be independent of the military and civilian intelligence establishments, and its main objective would be to provide high-level aerospace managers and planners with an informative summary of Soviet space and defense programs. This was more than the letter agreement between Pratt & Whitney and FTD spelled out, but that did not matter. I felt obligated to write an assessment with no strings attached, no axes to grind, and with the idea of letting the chips fall where they may. Whereas other companies' annual reports to

FTD were generally thirty to forty pages in length, to do the job right, I was thinking in terms of a Cecil B. De Mille production—400 to 500 pages. Once I got this report distributed, it was my plan to use it as a launching pad to go after the agents in Building 828 and have their whole operation investigated.

The following day Norm Cotter told me that Captain Harold Gale of FTD telephoned him to notify Pratt & Whitney that FTD was exceptionally pleased with my performance. Cotter was impressed because Gale called for this purpose alone. With Cotter before my desk, I summarized the discussions I held in the basement of the L-shaped building with Simon's spooks from the Aeronautical Systems Division. As Cotter was similarly disappointed with FTD, he gave me the go-ahead to pursue negotiations with the Aeronautical Systems Division. I felt like an aerospace Judas: FTD—the *elite* force—was praising my work, and I had embarked on a course that would ultimately challenge its competence and blow open its unethical operations.

13

November 25, 1969: I received a handwritten note from the Eagle, who was aware of my disillusionment with FTD. He had been asked to review and endorse the draft of an FTD intelligence assessment on a Russian weapon system. After "many painful hours," he wrote, of trying to produce a polite and printable critique to FTD, the Eagle found that it couldn't be done without jeopardizing his position with Pratt & Whitney. His earlier description of the FTD report, which he modified into a printable response to FTD, included terms such as fraudulent, fantasy, fabrication, bureaucratic empire building, questionable integrity, technical trash, no, not so, foolhardy extrapolation, and unjustified speculation. The Eagle said that the FTD report recommended a vastly expanded program for testing old Russian hardware and was very carefully contrived to give FTD complete autonomy in all areas of related foreign activity. He felt that he had an obligation to defend his friends in other branches of the government, and he did so with a more diplomatic, but succinct letter to FTD. It was his opinion that the FTD report was an indefensible intelligence report, and it contained unwarranted and imaginative speculations that could not be supported by the available evidence. He reminded the recipient of his letter that the emphasis in technical reporting should be on objectivity, not subjectivity. In conclusion, he criticized the FTD proposal for recommending the extensive testing of old Russian hardware, and he doubted that anything worthwhile could be learned from the investment. He suggested to me that the FTD report was written to justify setting up an enormous Air Force bureaucratic empire with unlimited funding and very little supervision from Congress. He thought the money could be better used if it were simply invested by private industry in corporate research and development programs.

The Eagle's diplomatic response to FTD still took courage on his part; I suspected it wouldn't take long before someone in Building 828 put the screws to him. Whether Pratt & Whitney headquarters in East Hartford would buckle under pressure by the "Air Force" was one thing, but I knew where the Pratt & Whitney division in Florida stood on such issues.

November 26, 1969: At the request of *the Swimmer*, an impulsive, flamboyant Pratt & Whitney project engineer who had a hand in the company's decision to assist FTD in 1968, I forwarded to FTD a Pratt & Whitney Aircraft proprietary document entitled *Engine Performance Analysis Methods*, which described in detail some of the company's in-house secrets and jet engine analysis techniques. This particular document was requested by Super Smart, who was using the agreement to his advantage. Though Pratt & Whitney was not benefiting from its arrangement with FTD, Super Smart, using the prestige of the Air Force, was successful in slowly milking the company of sensitive and proprietary documents—reports that were normally locked in company files, away from competitors. Inasmuch as FTD intelligence officers were chummy with the company's competitors, I advised the Swimmer against sending the data.

"I'll assume full responsibility for any repercussions," the Swimmer said, combing his hair. "Pete, you worry too much. Send it."

December 23, 1969: McDonnell Douglas Corporation was selected by the U.S. Air Force Aeronautical Systems Division as prime airframe contractor of the F-15 air superiority fighter. The first contract called for the design and manufacture of twenty aircraft for development testing and was worth over one billion dollars. Pratt & Whitney was still vying against General Electric to build the engines for the F-15, and the engine contract award was expected in several months. The similarities between the McDonnell F-15 fighter and the Russian FOXBAT, and statements made to me by Francis Simon of the Aeronautical Systems Division Directorate of Foreign Technology, a month before the contract was awarded, indicated that McDonnell used much of the foreign intelligence given it by the Air Force, and it was questionable whether McDonnell's competitors—Fairchild Hiller and North American Rockwell —had been given the same information.

If I had the authority, I would have called for an immediate congressional investigation into the relationship between the foreign intelligence secretly given McDonnell by the Aeronautical Systems Division, the one billion dollar contract awarded McDonnell by the Aeronautical Systems Division, and whether a cigar-smoking general in the Air Force had railroaded the F-15 air superiority fighter program into McDonnell's lap because he simply wanted a "hot-rod" FOXBAT and McDonnell was willing to go this route.

February 3, 1970: At FTD's urgent request, and with Lowell Ruby's approval, I forwarded to FTD a classified copy of a popular company report entitled *Components Design Handbook, Air Force Reusable Rocket Engine Program . . . Demonstrator Engine Component Description.* The Foreign Technology Division had reams and reams of telemetry intercept data from Russian launches that it could not break down into understandable language because it did not have specialists who understood advanced rocket test information. In contrast, U.S. aerospace contractors such as Pratt & Whitney, Rocketdyne, and Aerojet had teams of specialists who were analyzing this type of data on daily rocket engine test-stand firings. Rather than permit U.S. aerospace experts to see the telemetry, FTD "closeted" the information, ostensibly for "national security reasons." Had FTD allowed the experts in private industry to look at the data, part of the FTD operation would have been alleviated from spinning its wheels; it might at least have been assigned to other make-work projects like listening to the sound tracks of Russian propaganda movies to determine if the films had been shown in other cities. Thus, when FTD's budget for the next fiscal year would be reviewed by the Air Force Systems Command, FTD Commander George Weinbrenner could still show that analysis was a major part of FTD's overall mission. As it turned out, the Air Force was spending a fortune using sophisticated worldwide telemetry stations to gather intelligence that analysts in Building 828 neither understood, nor cared to analyze.

Though I transmitted the *Components Design Handbook* to FTD as it had requested, I could not transfer the years of experience accumulated by Pratt & Whitney engineers familiar with an advanced rocket engine test-stand data. And this is what FTD really needed if it was going to produce reliable intelligence assessments. But this didn't seem to bother the FTD; one disgruntled FTD analyst who had his fill of make-work projects later told me that everything in FTD was geared to increase both its budget and empire, as if this super-secret organization had other long-range objectives not necessarily related to foreign technology.

The following week I received a copy of a letter written by the Eagle to an Air Force officer who had a low regard of the FTD operation. The Eagle said that he was convinced that efforts devoted to reviewing unclassified 5 by 8 inch cards were frivolous and the resulting yield had been disappointing. (I.e., the KGB did an excellent job of monitoring Russian scientific and technical reports released to the West, and FTD was wasting the taxpayer's money with its massive open literature exploitation program.) I agreed with the Eagle: on my bookshelves were about one million dollars of Russian technical publications translated by FTD, yet Pratt & Whitney engineers who reviewed the material found less than 1 percent of it to be of any value, and in those cases, the Russian literature was useful in establishing trends only; the publications were too old to be of any technical value. Even more disturbing was the fact that FTD would bill the government as much as $50,000 to translate a single Russian textbook! I couldn't believe that this was a legitimate expense and I wondered whether over the years it had built up a secret fund for umbra operations that even Air Force headquarters didn't know about.

Both the Eagle and I were disturbed over the cost-effectiveness of the bureaucratic paper mills in Building 828 and the Air Force secret facility. What was even more alarming, however, was that the military intelligence services expended about 90 percent of their budget on collecting intelligence and about 10 percent of their budget on analyzing the intelligence collected. These figures indicated that if one wanted to look for waste in the espionage establishment, the spooks had to be investigated. In FTD's case, this meant the Operations Directorate. It was ironical that Congress and the public had been stampeded into investigating the CIA over the years, but right under their noses—headquartered in Building 828 of Wright-Patterson Air Force Base—was one of the world's largest spy networks, which in many ways was redundant to the CIA yet practically unknown.

Being funded through the Air Force Systems Command, FTD spooks had carte blanche authority to travel just about anywhere in the world at the drop of a hat. In the name of national security, FTD spooks were gallivanting around the country saying goodbye to friends and asking questions that could be handled easily over the telephone. Others were taking "business" vacations—at the taxpayer's expense—or "staking out" plush European hotels for weeks because a Russian might check in.

Though it was my objective to increase the flow of useful foreign intelligence to Pratt & Whitney, I felt obligated to protect what I considered to be the national interest of the United States. It was my belief that even though I was an employee of Pratt & Whitney, my loyalty was to the United States first and the company second. Ideally, the company was supposed to act in the national interest when working with the government, but this was not necessarily the case. I was convinced more than ever that FTD had to be investigated, but I still didn't have enough evidence to present an open and shut case. Besides, there was something about the secrecy of its overall mission that sent a chill down my spine. There was one subject I was afraid to discuss, even with the Eagle, for it was unthinkable, and I had no evidence that the officers in Building 828 were heading in this direction. But it haunted me.

14

February 9, 1970: The Eagle privately contacted officials from the Directorate of Foreign Technology of the Aeronautical Systems Division and made tentative arrangements for executives from United Aircraft Corporation, the parent corporation of the Pratt & Whitney division, to discuss a possible foreign technology contract. The FTD arrangement was not productive, we were not receiving the type of intelligence that we had hoped to get, and it was worth seeing what Simon's spooks in the basement of the L-shaped building could offer. The plan was for Pratt & Whitney to be represented by officials from both the Florida and Connecticut divisions.

The following week all hell broke loose. The Eagle was in trouble. Super Smart reportedly sent an ultimatum in the form of a memorandum dated February 11, 1970, to Fred Polhemus, Pratt & Whitney's field representative for Wright-Patterson Air Force Base, in which it was stated that unless the Eagle was replaced as the corporation liaison representative with FTD, the Foreign Technology Division would assume that Pratt & Whitney desired no further association with it. This was explosive because the Air Force was scheduled to announce the winner of the F-15 engine award—the Aeronautical Systems Division had selected McDonnell to build the F-15 airframe the previous December—and the company, at least the Florida division, could not afford a run-in with any branch of the Air Force; at least not now!

To justify his attack against the Eagle, Super Smart tore into a report that the Eagle had written for FTD. This Pratt & Whitney management-approved report contained conclusions that were contrary to FTD's assessments of Russian weapons systems, and it concluded that the Russians were not as advanced in certain technical areas as the military intelligence services wanted everyone to believe. Excerpts of the memorandum, which Super Smart later intimated to me had been read by Colonel George Weinbrenner, commander of the Foreign Technology Division, are shown below:

> Memo: *Evaluation of Pratt & Whitney Report, PWA-3869,* 11 Feb. 70. This one is worse than any report ever received by us, no-cost or otherwise. I prefer to attribute the contents to the author, rather than the corporation, since I have met many fine people in Florida. We terminated relations with the originators of the previous worst report, which this surpasses, but prefer not to do so here, if possible. If [the Eagle] is not replaced as the corporation representative, we will have little recourse except to consider that Pratt & Whitney does not desire further association with us. Interestingly, this is occurring as the excellent relations with their competitors improve.

The memorandum, which was interpreted by Pratt & Whitney headquarters as an attempt to intimidate both the Eagle and Pratt & Whitney, implied that if the corporation did not replace the Eagle, then FTD would provide intelligence information to the corporation's competitors, again playing the role of kingmaker. If Super Smart had known that Fat Wally of General Electric and the Eagle were corresponding privately, I seriously doubt that he would have written: "Interestingly, this is occurring as the excellent relations with their competitors improve." From what I could gather from the Eagle, FTD was also having problems with General Electric; Fat Wally was similarly disappointed with the quality of work coming out of Building 828, and he too was attempting to do something about it. It appeared that FTD was trying to get everyone in line before it had an epidemic on its hands.

The ruthless attack on the Eagle during a critical period in Air Force-Pratt & Whitney relations was not taken lightly by my superiors. H. Norm Cotter had me make a copy of Super Smart's memorandum, and after showing it to Lowell Ruby, who shook his head in disbelief, Cotter set about notifying other Pratt & Whitney managers that a volcano was about to erupt. I notified Gleichauf that a problem was brewing between FTD and private industry so that the CIA wouldn't get caught in the crossfire. With the Eagle on the ropes, I again evaluated my position and the wisdom of sitting on the sidelines.

Later that afternoon, while I was in the washroom, the Swimmer—the flamboyant Pratt & Whitney project engineer who ordered me to send company secrets to FTD—showed me a paper with four names on it.

"Recognize any of these names?" he asked.

"Yeah. Two are FTD." The Snake was on the list. "Where'd you run across them?"

"A meeting out West." The Swimmer glanced over my shoulder at the empty urinals. "Come on up to my office for a second, will ya? We need some privacy."

He closed the door to his office and looked out the window over the pond, combing his hair. "Pete, they asked me to spy for them at an upcoming deal in Europe. They pick up the tab. What do you think?"

"The decision is yours, but make doubly certain you know what you're getting into. It should be approved by Norm [Cotter] and Leo [Faucher, the security chief]."

"I don't even know who the hell these guys are. They could be FTD, CIA . . . hell, they could be Russians for all I know!"

"For what it's worth, I've been approached, too. I couldn't get them to agree to do it my way, so I never signed up."

"What's your way?"

"No contact with them!"

He laughed. "Thanks, Pete."

I returned to my desk and reflected on what was happening. When Lieutenants Pfeifle and Penswick requested a list of Pratt & Whitney engineers who attended specialist conferences in January 1969, I cautioned Ruby and Cotter about FTD's ulterior motives. Three months later, Captain Harold Gale succeeded in obtaining a list. After my Venice and Argentine trips, FTD espionage agents had repeatedly asked me to join their operations abroad, using my job with Pratt & Whitney as a cover. Approaches were made verbally and in writing, bypassing the company. Now the Swimmer had been approached. This time contact was made at a conference held in the United States. With FTD having a list of company engineers in its possession, I wondered who else had been secretly approached. In essence, it took FTD about two years to include the Florida facility in its espionage operations from the date the company agreed to evaluate technical translations for them.

With the Swimmer's disclosure, things were coming quickly

into focus. Lowell Ruby, who was getting further bogged down in company programs, transferred his foreign technology files to me. In going through them, I ran across a November 1967 memorandum written by the Swimmer in which he recommended that the Florida division pursue a relationship with FTD. Since I had attended meetings in Athens, Madrid, Belgrade, Venice, Paris, and Mar del Plata, the Swimmer had called me into his office to pick my brains because he assumed that I was being funded by either the CIA or FTD. Finding out that this was not the case, he probably regretted telling me anything.

But there was another interesting aspect of FTD's motives which I now suspected. When Super Smart and the Snake met me in the Falcon Motel on July 8, 1969, it appeared that the decision had already been made in Building 828 to involve the Pratt & Whitney Florida division in clandestine operations abroad. But they had a problem: the Eagle was in their way. The Eagle not only insisted that FTD agents keep their hands on the table with palms up whenever he dealt with them, but he was designated as FTD's East Hartford contact man, and he would not allow FTD to deal with anyone in East Hartford behind his back. I was FTD's Florida contact man, but I was not about to tell my superiors and other company managers, who were twenty years my senior, how to behave—especially when they welcomed contact with FTD's agents. I could only warn them and put my objections down on paper in the form of memoranda, for whatever they were worth. With Super Smart intimidating the Eagle and East Hartford and suggesting that he had met many fine people in Florida, and with the Swimmer having been approached by the Snake and other FTD agents to spy for them, it was now clear that FTD had launched a concerted offensive—spearheaded by Super Smart's February 11, 1970, attack on the Eagle—to split Pratt & Whitney into two camps—Florida versus East Hartford —and it hoped to expand its espionage operations abroad by signing up recruits from the Florida division.

The following morning the Eagle was asked before his superiors to explain the reason for FTD's attack on him. That afternoon, in a ruling which blew the roof off the Florida division, Colonel George R. Weinbrenner, commander of the Foreign Technology Division, was officially notified by Pratt & Whitney headquarters that the company had no intention of replacing the Eagle, and furthermore, the company stood behind his assessments. It was the headquarters' position that the Eagle diligently prepared an objective assessment of the Russian capability and it was improper for FTD to ask the company to replace him because his views differed. By the reaction of the managers in Florida, I wondered whether the Florida and East Hartford divisions belonged to the same company; my superiors were willing to let the Eagle go down the tubes to preserve the company's image with the Air Force.

With East Hartford having swiftly countered FTD's assault, I began to shore up Pratt & Whitney's defenses in Florida. We needed an alliance with Simon's spooks in the basement of Building 14 of the Aeronautical Systems Division. My logic was this: FTD agents were relying on the 1968 letter agreement with Pratt & Whitney to justify having personal contact with company engineers, and thus recruit spies. Since Simon claimed that his outfit could give the company more reports than FTD, an agreement with Simon meant that the company could abrogate its 1968 agreement with FTD, and FTD would have to wheel and deal elsewhere. I called the Eagle and he concurred that FTD had to be dumped. We agreed to meet in Dayton to launch the counter-offensive.

15

February 18, 1970: I flew to Dayton, Ohio, and met the Eagle and his friend, Eugene Kiefer, an executive of United Aircraft Corporation, the parent corporation of the Pratt & Whitney division. The three of us stayed at the Imperial House North Motel to get our signals straight before the meeting with Simon's spooks.

Wright-Patterson Air Force Base, February 19, 1970: In the basement of Building 14 we were introduced to Major R. A. Rowley; his technical deputy, James Foreman, a cigar-smoking civilian who buried his face in a technical report, showing us only his crew cut and black horn-rimmed glasses; Francis Simon, who invited us; and Lt. Larry Ehle. These men were representing the Directorate of Foreign Technology of the Aeronautical Systems Division, though from the secrecy of their basement layout one might have concluded that they were running a bookie joint.

Using a blackboard for their presentation, the men drew organization charts showing how their outfit tied in with the Defense Intelligence Agency (DIA), Central Intelligence Agency (CIA), and the Foreign Technology Division (FTD). Their charts showed that the bulk of the espionage work was handled by DIA, Air Force, and CIA—this was nothing new—but FTD held a preeminent position in one particular area: the determination of scientific and technical intelligence requirements. I was sick! FTD, which was not a member of the United States Intelligence Board, headed by the Director of Central Intelligence Richard Helms, who was chief of the CIA at the time, was not even up to date with the state-of-the-art in the United States. And it determined technical intelligence requirements? This explained why our spies were collecting volumes and volumes of intelligence that was never analyzed. It was shocking: agents throughout the world were risking their lives on behalf of Uncle Sam because they believed that the intelligence they were being asked to acquire had a direct bearing on the national security of the United States, when in reality, the information had a bearing on the survival of FTD hacks who needed make-work intelligence to justify their own existence.

According to the blackboard presentation—and I got Simon's people to give me a quick and dirty sketch afterwards for my own files—spies in the field receive instructions mainly from CIA and DIA intelligence officers, but these men relied on FTD to determine the type of scientific and technical information to be collected in the field. *The other point in the presentation was that the military intelligence services were doing the lion's share of the defense intelligence analysis work, having just about eliminated the CIA from this area.* Though the Directorate of Foreign Technology was independent of FTD, Simon's outfit had to coordinate its intelligence and requirements in the field through FTD because both organizations were part of the Air Force Systems Command. In other words, FTD was really in the driver's seat. The main message was clear: the Foreign Technology Division has a stranglehold on this nation's efforts to exploit foreign technology and has its fingers in almost everything, whether it concerns the analysis of intelligence, the collection of intelligence, or the determination of the type of technical intelligence to be collected. With other intelligence experts privately challenging the competence of the FTD operation, I wondered whether our country would be in for a rude awakening during the next international crisis, and whether our best spies in the Soviet Union would be arrested beforehand because they had compromised their cover by collecting worthless intelligence on orders from Building 828.

After a lengthy two-hour discussion, James Foreman agreed to forward to Pratt & Whitney a contract which the company could either sign or use as the starting point for further negotiations. I found the proposed contract acceptable, but after listening to their briefing, I seriously doubted that Pratt & Whitney could avoid FTD's tentacles. I left the air base without visiting Building 828.

February 23, 1970: In a memorandum to H. Norm Cotter I recommended that Pratt & Whitney contact the deputy chief of staff of intelligence in the Pentagon to seek a general briefing on the Air Force foreign technology directorates and their intended function vis-à-vis government contractors. It seemed that the U.S. government was involved in intelligence operations on such a grand scale—even Army intelligence was now sending feelers to the Eagle's contacts in East Hartford—that each military branch had the authority to contact private industry to conduct intelligence analysis work for it.

Meanwhile, in East Hartford, the Eagle summarized his assessments of the military intelligence groups' activities for his superiors. He noted that the current cost-effective fad in the military intelligence services is to impress the civilian managers in the Defense Department and other Washington policy-makers with the outstanding success of their organization in intelligence analysis by alluding to the number of private contractors supporting no-cost contracts with the military services; since the working agreements are no-cost, similar to the Pratt & Whitney-FTD agreement, it appears to outsiders that the military, and thus the government, is getting a great bargain. Additionally, outsiders naturally assume that the military group having the greatest number of agreements is the most competent; the relative incompetence of the military activity is not considered in assessing its cost-effectiveness. Having seen the internal facilities of various directorates of foreign technology, the Eagle concluded that their main functions, in spite of all their talk to the contrary are (1) paper shuffling, (2) massive processing of printed data, and (3) spooky collection activities, with emphasis on the action instead of the information.

With our eyes on FTD, however, both the Eagle and I recommended that the company continue private negotiations with Simon's spooks and consider the proposed contract that James Foreman promised to forward. Unknown to us at the time we made these recommendations, the secret controllers in Building 828 had been kept fully apprised of Pratt & Whitney's back door dealings with Simon's spooks; this was confirmed when the Eagle and his friend Eugene Kiefer from United Aircraft subsequently paid their respects to FTD Commander George Weinbrenner in a "Gunfight at OK Corral" meeting at Wright-Patterson Air Force Base. While Super Smart's letter intimidating the Eagle and East Hartford headquarters and FTD's ambitions to recruit Pratt & Whitney spies were on the agenda, the company lost its ace-in-the-hole—the potential agreement with Simon's spooks—

113

when Commander Weinbrenner pulled out his trump card: in his office was none other than James Foreman, the cigar-smoking technical director of the Directorate of Foreign Technology!

It was my guess that since FTD had been unsuccessful in reaching a jet engine understanding with the Pratt & Whitney Florida division, it had asked its neighbors in the Directorate of Foreign Technology—Simon's spooks—to make the approach with the idea that FTD would play the role of the silent partner. This made sense because a condition of James Foreman's contract was that the Florida division had to be included in any agreement reached. Concurring with my assessment, the Eagle conjectured, "Our brush with this crowd convinced me that they were trying quite hard to set something up, and the meeting Gene and I had in the bird commander spook's office, along with several flunkies, served as further evidence of the devious conduct, evasiveness, yet penetrating ambitions of this whole crowd." Needless to say, when the James Foreman contract was received at the East Hartford headquarters, the "neat deal" was rejected. I dug in and waited for the assault on the southern front.

It was a sunny day and I was working on my second annual report when two men entered the second floor of the Florida Research and Development Center. They were ignored by the busy engineering staff. One man carried a black attaché case; the other was the Snake. Both entered the Swimmer's office. The door was closed. I was to learn later that spies recruited by FTD are signed to a secret contract that is brought to the recruit's place of business. Carrying a black attaché case, FTD contract couriers are usually accompanied by another agent to witness the signing, but not always. To my knowledge, the flamboyant Swimmer, in search of a James Bond adventure abroad, was the first manager in the Florida division to sign a contract to spy for FTD; the warnings in my memoranda as early as July 15, 1969, were ignored.

February 27, 1970: The United States Air Force selected Pratt & Whitney over General Electric to develop the engines for the F-15 air superiority fighter aircraft. The contract was worth almost half a billion dollars, and this was only the beginning. If the government decided to mass produce the fighters, the resulting multi-billion dollar production contract and improvements would keep the company busy for about two decades. With the worrisome albatross removed from General Manager W. L. Gorton's neck, I was hoping that the Florida division would pursue a more independent course from FTD. I would find that I was dead wrong.

The value of the Foreign Technology Division and Defense Intelligence Agency intelligence data was again questioned when I was

114

called into H. Norm Cotter's office. Even though Pratt & Whitney was awarded the F-15 engine contract, there was concern within the Air Force about the projected cost of the Pratt & Whitney engine, and this was amplified by the Senate investigations on aerospace spending, spearheaded by Senator William Proxmire (D-Wis.). In a discussion between Grant Hansen, assistant secretary of the Air Force, and a Pratt & Whitney East Hartford executive, Hansen reportedly asked, "Why can the Russians build simple low-cost engines, while we can't? What are they doing that is different? Why is the F-15 engine so damn complicated?" The questions reverberated throughout the Pratt & Whitney executive offices in East Hartford—they feared Proxmire and respected Hansen—and filtered down to Florida, where the engines were being developed.

The data I had on file on the Russian FOXBAT engine were nil, thanks to FTD's ineptness and the competence of the Russian security system. The lesson I learned in this special one-week assignment was that our intelligence data base on Russian aircraft systems was inadequate and the Defense Intelligence Agency and FTD's assessments of other Russian fighters were not only dangerously wrong, but their reports were written as if the assessments were known facts rather than erroneous speculations, as it turned out. The military intelligence services were grossly negligent in this area because their assessments were being used by aerospace corporations to design aircraft systems to counter the Russian threat—systems that would be flown by American pilots.

When I investigated this practice in more depth, one FTD analyst candidly admitted to me that FTD assessments of Russian technology were required on a regular basis, even if no new information was acquired since the last assessment. To comply with these requirements, FTD intelligence reports would be padded with almost anything analysts could lay their hands on, either to salvage their jobs or further the careers of their superiors. Another reason for the blatantly erroneous FTD assessments was that their analysts were misplaced in their job assignments. As an example, on March 18, 1970, I forwarded several volumes of jet engine reports and college-level lecture notes to Building 828 to assist a particular analyst who was evaluating Russian jet engine systems. This data was requested by the analyst after he visited the Center to learn the fundamentals of jet propulsion systems. A number of project engineers bluntly told me that the analyst was "over his head" in his job assignment and it was frightening that FTD's intelligence assessments of Russian technology in this man's "specialty" would be used as the basis for defining the design specifications of future U.S. weapons systems.

In another damaging indictment of Air Force intelligence, the Eagle sent me paperwork and a copy of a private memorandum he had written to R. T. Baseler, vice president of the Pratt & Whitney Aircraft division in East Hartford; copies of the memo were also sent to seven other high level company executives. The paperwork showed that William S. Gerros, a contracting officer with the Air Force Aeronautical Systems division, informed Pratt & Whitney in an official Department of the Air Force letter dated March 11, 1970, that the General Electric Company Aircraft Engine Group in Cincinnati, Ohio, had been awarded a $4,998,000 contract by the Air Force. It was the Air Force's judgment that General Electric's proposal to a forthcoming government-funded jet engine test program of foreign hardware was technically superior to Pratt & Whitney's. In the memorandum to Pratt & Whitney executives, the Eagle noted that the General Electric program accepted by the Air Force at a cost of almost five million dollars was identical to Pratt & Whitney's proposed program *with the exception that Pratt & Whitney offered to do the same job for roughly one and a half million dollars less.* Though "technical excellence" was the reason given by the Air Force for selecting General Electric over Pratt & Whitney, the Eagle pointed out that a General Electric engineer with close Air Force Foreign Technology Division connections (1) wrote the government's request for a proposal, which was sent to private aerospace firms for a reply, (2) wrote General Electric's response to the government's request, (3) reviewed all proposals received by the government as an "unofficial consultant," and (4) played politics with the government very well.

Under the circumstances, the secret dealings between Air Force intelligence agents and the military-industrial complex warranted investigation, as did the award of the contract to General Electric (identified by Air Force Aero Propulsion Laboratory Request for Proposal number F-33657-70-R-0320). There were enough incriminating memoranda of unethical intelligence activities floating about the company's East Hartford and Florida divisions to light a good-size fire and send smoke signals all the way to Washington—but no one was making a move to get the story out, as if the company had its own skeletons in the closet and morality was something that only the poor suckers outside the company's gates, the taxpayers who were footing the bill, were concerned about. It brought to mind something that Jack McDermott, a devout Catholic and conscientious company program manager, said during lunch in the cafeteria. We were talking about the high costs of jet engines and the company's financial investment before and after a contract is awarded. McDermott asked his colleagues: "Where do you draw the line? Which comes first: the company's interests, or the national interests? If the government is willing to fund a project you don't think is worthwhile, do you accept the money and do what you are told, or do you tell them they're wasting their money?"

With the final typing of my second annual foreign technology report plodding along, I addressed myself to a problem that had been nagging me for half a year—getting the report distributed outside the U.S. intelligence community. The opportunity came unexpectedly one afternoon when John Enders of the Executive Office of the President visited our Florida facility. In a meeting with engineering manager R. J. Coar, H. Norm Cotter, and me, Enders said that President Nixon had a group privately investigating the effectiveness of our intelligence services. In what I thought was a revealing colloquy, Enders asked engineering manager Coar what he thought of the company's program with FTD. Coar laughed, picked up a copy of *Aviation Week & Space Technology*—the authoritative weekly publication read by most aerospace engineers—and said, "I get my weekly foreign intelligence right here!" Coar threw the magazine on his desk and grinned at Cotter; too bad FTD Commander George Weinbrenner wasn't in the office —he may have learned something that neither Pratt & Whitney nor his subordinates were willing to tell him.

Enders was interested in my analysis of the Russian space program, and before he left, he asked me to send the Executive Office a copy of my annual report when it was printed. I called Capt. Hal Gale later and asked that Pratt & Whitney be permitted to distribute the report outside the intelligence establishment. "It's against our policy to authorize distribution of the report," Gale said bluntly. "It would be best in the long run if the final report were sent to us only." A confrontation was in the making. Under no circumstances did I want FTD to summarize my report; I wanted my printed conclusions to reach other government officials, not FTD's interpretation of my conclusions. I unloaded the bomb.

"Hal, John Enders from the Executive Office visited us the other day. He would like to receive a copy." There was silence on the other end of the line.

"I'll check with my superiors but I doubt anything would change from what I've already told you." The captain was playing it by the book. I felt as if I were sitting on a time bomb and a break in relations with FTD was inevitable, yet on the surface everything seemed okay. The most important task I had was to get the report printed and distributed to the right people before someone from the "Air Force" telephoned General Manager Gorton and requested that the company not distribute the report "because of security reasons."

With the Enders visit fresh in my mind, I drafted a three-page memorandum summarizing my views on the "foreign technology problem" and submitted it to Norm Cotter, asking permission to forward it to Enders. He rejected the request. Condensed excerpts from the memorandum are shown below:

(1) One of the best services that the intelligence community can provide the aerospace industry is to provide timely and useful intelligence data and assessments. In general, this is not being done because of the time, upwards of two years, required for the intelligence community to (a) evaluate the individual assessments submitted by industry, (b) integrate industry's assessments with its own, (c) write a concise "finished intelligence" report, and (d) approve, publish, and distribute the final product. Another factor that contributes to the problem is unnecessary compartmentalization on the industry level, due to numerous separate agreements with various branches of the intelligence community. This practice has not only led to redundancy of effort, but has restricted legitimate interested parties from presenting an alternative viewpoint and using the available information in its raw form. Accordingly, I propose that an Aerospace Industry Intelligence Council be created to ensure that the intelligence community is more reponsive to the requirements of the aerospace industry. It is further proposed that during council meetings *all* branches of the U.S. intelligence community (a) be represented, (b) participate in the floor discussions, and (c) submit identical "intelligence assessments data-packages" to council members for the aerospace industry. This would expedite the transfer of timely and useful intelligence data to the aerospace industry and eliminate costly redundant compartmentalized projects. (2) Approximately 11,000 translated pages of Soviet reports and textbooks were reviewed by over one hundred Pratt & Whitney aerospace engineering specialists. Less than 1 percent of the technical translations were found to be of any value and in those cases, the documents were more useful for establishing trends rather than their technical content. It is suggested that the merits of this costly technical translation program and/or the method of screening foreign technical documents for exploitation be reevaluated.

The aerospace industry intelligence council I proposed was designed to eliminate the role of the kingmaker within the military intelligence community by forcing all of the services to treat each corporation equally. The plan would permit aerospace experts to talk about foreign technology directly with their peers, without waiting two years or so to find out what their peers were thinking, as orchestrated by the military intelligence services. The formation of the council was also a frank admission that the U.S. intelligence community was inept in the analysis field and that it was time that American aerospace experts evaluated the work of their Russian counterparts, something that was already being done with great success within the Soviet Union under the direction of the KGB.

There were memoranda circulated in Pratt & Whitney concerning the incompetence of FTD personnel and their operations, and both Lowell Ruby and H. Norm Cotter had made known their own views about the waste of company time and money on the FTD venture, but they admonished me for attempting to get these views released outside the company, allegedly because the resulting furor would affect the company's relations with the government.

April 17, 1970: I was sent memoranda covering correspondence between the Eagle and Fat Wally of General Electric, and between Fat Wally and FTD Commander George Weinbrenner. The memoranda showed that in 1969 Fat Wally had similarly proposed a joint industry-intelligence council to FTD Commander George Weinbrenner. The commander tabled it and responded with wiggly circumventing prose as if he were a politician campaigning on election eve. Fat Wally's proposal, if accepted, would have diminished FTD's control over intelligence assessments. The importance of the memoranda between Fat Wally and the Eagle— foreign technology experts from two major jet engine contractors —was that they could not rely on FTD to provide their companies with reliable and useful foreign intelligence, and attempts to approach FTD with the problem were rebuffed.

The absurdity of the FTD translation program reached its pinnacle the following day when I received a handwritten tongue-in-cheek note from a Pratt & Whitney engineer who had been asked by FTD to evaluate a particular translation. His note to me read:

> . . . One polite reply [to FTD] might be: FTD-MT-24-202-69 [FTD report number] discusses the problems associated with two phase flow turbomachinery. P&WA has diligently reviewed this report and considered the facts presented in terms of past and possible future products of the corporation. P&WA does not con-

119

ceive to create a steam powered aircraft engine, nor does P&WA have any confidence that coal will become a common fuel for aircraft propulsion powerplants. As such there are no useful data in the report. In fact, it is worthless and most damn fools would not have wasted the U.S. government's money having this idiotic nonsense translated.

April 22, 1970: Both James Bartley and his superior, Capt. Hal Gale of FTD, called to inform me that FTD had no objections if Pratt & Whitney distributed my foreign technology report to the Executive Office or other government facilities, providing that the Air Force Rocket Propulsion Laboratory in Edwards, California, approved our distribution list. "You're fortunate," Gale said. "It's highly unusual for us to consider such a request, let alone grant it!" Gale may have objected to my plans, but FTD had no legal jurisdiction over the distribution of the secret report because it was prepared by the company under an Air Force Rocket Propulsion Laboratory contract to justify the use of classified information.

I had a personal stake in the report: I had incorporated most of my CIA notes—acquired through personal expenditures in excess of $10,000—in it, and there were some aspects of the Russian ICBM arms build-up and advanced space systems that deserved dissemination within the Executive Office and the U.S. government in light of the Strategic Arms Limitations Talks (SALT) that were being held with the Soviet government.

Having written my second annual report, I was now free to learn more about FTD's intelligence collections operations before I alienated the division completely. I learned that a conference was being held in Pisa, Italy, during the summer of 1970. The timing was ripe for another trial balloon.

16

I wrote to the Fox in Fairborn, Ohio, using a post office box number
he had given me, and told him there was a one-week conference
being held in Pisa, Italy, that interested me. I wanted to cover
the Pisa conference because my analysis indicated that some of
the Russians scheduled to participate in the meeting were involved in the Russian space shuttle program. I needed to talk with
the Russians, but I couldn't afford to travel to Pisa in the summer
and to Germany in the autumn to participate in the annual space
conference that I normally attended at my own expense. I therefore wished to explore the possibility of sharing my notes with the
Air Force if it covered my expenses to Pisa, but one condition I
would not compromise on was "no contact with FTD agents
abroad."

Within days the Fox called. The FTD spooks from the Operations
Directorate were interested in the Pisa proposal. "Where would
you like to be contacted?" he asked. "Home or at work?"

"At work," I answered. I wanted the meeting to be monitored
by company security officers—a hands-on-the-table approach—
because intelligence organizations, East or West, use whatever
means suitable to keep their intelligence agents in line; this task

121

was made easier by secret binding agreements between the intelligence organization and the agent. After talking with the Fox, I briefed Norm Cotter on the situation, and called the CIA field office in Miami. Gleichauf said he would be happy to ride shotgun on the meeting.

A week passed. Then one morning Justin F. Gleichauf and a man from Air Force intelligence drove through the guarded gates of the Pratt & Whitney rocket and jet engine facility. Gleichauf introduced me to Fred Meisetz, a blue-suited middle-aged heavyset man whose hair was combed back, exposing a receding hairline. With his briefcase and neat appearance, Fred looked like a super sales-man, one of the many vendors who visited the company daily. Leo Faucher, supervisor of plant protection, escorted us into an office, and asked his assistant, Ernie Woleslagle, to monitor the meeting. Woleslagle closed the door to the small office, as H. Norm Cotter joined us and took a seat to my left. Cotter appeared to be sizing up the FTD agent, while Gleichauf, who looked about as formal as I had ever seen him, may have been worried that I would stop assisting the CIA because FTD was willing to finance this and most likely other trips. Fred Meisetz brought up the Pisa confer-ence, and I indicated that Zhivotovskiy and Beloussov (KGB agents) might also be covering the meeting.

"Zhivotovskiy?" Fred asked.

"Yes, do you know him?"

"By picture only." Fred looked experienced, but disturbed, as if wishing he could talk to me in private. Besides myself, he felt the weight of six eyes on him, watching his every move. "You know Beloussov?" he asked.

"We met in Venice. He's worth talking to."

"Do you know who Beloussov is?"

"Yes. He masterminded the Christine Keeler-John Profumo sex scandal." Woleslagle leaned forward, as the conversation began to interest him more. Fred nodded. I briefed him on the Zhivotov-skiy invitation and the arrangements we had made in Mar del Plata. "Since you're willing to subsidize my expenses to Pisa, would you be willing to cover me on a trip to the Soviet Union?" Fred looked at the floor, carefully thinking out his words, as if about to make an address before the United Nations.

"Yes, but you have to have a written invitation from the Academy."

"I don't have a written invitation. Only a verbal agreement with Zhivotovskiy."

"What do you know about Zhivotovskiy?" he asked.

"He's one of their top intelligence officers," I said, handing

122

Fred a green notebook containing my Venice and Argentine reports. I turned to a special section covering Zhivotovskiy's dossier.

"Have you shown this to anyone?"

"We have filed all of Peter's reports," Gleichauf answered quickly, representing the CIA's interests.

"I've never heard of a verbal invitation from the Academy," Fred said looking at Gleichauf. "Have you?"

"No, neither have I."

"We can't fund you to Russia unless you have a written invitation."

"You mean to prove I was invited?"

"No. Unless you get invited officially, they won't show you anything. Their bureaucracy is ten times worse than ours."

"Zhivotovskiy promised to show me quite a few things, including institutes in Moscow and Novosibirsk."

"Without an invitation, you could spend three weeks with Zhivotovskiy drinking coffee in a restaurant."

"He's always kept his word before." I really wanted to say that I learned more having dinner with the Russians in restaurants than his best people did doing anything else.

"Who did Zhivotovskiy say you could see?"

"Grodzovskiy, Maykapar . . . "

"Maykapar?" he interrupted. "Seeing Maykapar would be worth the trip alone."

"That's what I'm saying. You're welcome to see any notes I take, but pick up the tab."

Gleichauf cut in: "You have our permission to help out Peter with the expenses, and debrief him after the trip, but we will prepare the report through our shop."

I outlined my conditions: no contact with agents or attachés in Europe.

Fred thought it over: "To Pisa, yes; Russia, no. I've never run across anything like this before. It's too dangerous. You never know what might happen. We've never had problems with official invites. If the Academy invites you, they give you the royal treatment."

"I'm aware of the possible risks," I said. "But we learn more my way. I prefer to talk with their people in private informal surroundings."

"Do this." Fred said. "Go to Pisa and get one of their scientists to invite you officially. Then we'll start the paperwork on the Russian trip."

"I don't need another invitation," I replied. "I already . . ."

"Now wait a minute!" Cotter interrupted. "We've always

cooperated with the government, but we won't send anyone on an intelligence assignment. If Pete attends a conference, it's because of corporate business." Cotter scanned the Pisa conference paperwork on his lap. "I see nothing at this conference that would benefit the company." Cotter was right: the reports scheduled for presentation in Pisa were of no interest to me either; I was interested in talking with the Russians, but I couldn't give anyone a guarantee that I would learn anything of value in Pisa, just as I had no guarantee about the Argentine meeting, though it turned out to be a grand slam for the CIA by the time it was over.

Feeling the pressure of this awkward situation, Fred replied: "Yes, it is also our position that Pratt & Whitney must benefit."

"I'm planning to attend the Konstanz [Germany] meeting later in the year," I said. "Their conference format is more in line with Pratt & Whitney programs. See if your superiors would be willing to switch Konstanz for Pisa."

"I'll put in your request," he said.

Gleichauf broke in: "Peter, before I forget. Two men from the Foreign Technology Division would like to talk with you about Argentina. Will you see them?"

I addressed Cotter: "Would you object if I saw them at work?"

"If it relates to your foreign technology assignment, no."

"I'll see them," I said to Gleichauf.

"They want two or three days, Peter." FTD apparently had a number of follow-up questions on my Mar del Plata write-up.

Fred put the papers back in his briefcase. "I'll turn in your request on the Russian trip," he said, "but I don't think they'll fund it without an invitation."

"Well, that's a decision for your organization. If I can't depend on my own government to support the proposal, I'll go the route myself." Fred suddenly looked up, as if what I had said evoked a Pavlovian response.

"What I'm saying is for your own protection!"

"I'm aware of that."

Three days later Gleichauf telephoned. Fred officially notified the CIA that FTD turned thumbs down on my proposal. I was not surprised: it either learned that I was probing into its clandestine operations or it feared that support of my independent activities— no contact abroad—would give FTD operators already under contract ideas of their own. Under the circumstances, I saw little reason to waste my time with the two FTD analysts who wanted to see me. FTD was spending a fortune on inept collection operations, and I no longer felt obligated to bail it out with free information; the

CIA had already debriefed me on Mar del Plata and it didn't make sense to support a redundant activity.

"Mr. Gleichauf," I said, "please notify FTD that I do not wish to discuss Mar del Plata anymore, and if they have any further questions, I'd like them to be channeled through your shop."

"I'll relay the message, Peter. You can be assured that you will have no unwanted visitors!" Private American citizens can rely on the CIA to keep the military intelligence services at arms length if they wish; the military has agreed to notify the CIA of its overtures to citizens to perform spy missions. Using the CIA as such a buffer, I could see myself involved in a tug of war, trying to maintain my independent status on one hand and trying not to upset the Air Force and the company on the other. I was losing the battle.

I fed the alligator in the Center's pond for several afternoons before the expected call from FTD came. "Mr. James! I have been told you refused to see two of our men," the authoritative gravel voice on the other end said. It was Mr. Nicholas Post, one of the top officials at FTD headquarters and the man who first contacted Pratt & Whitney in 1968 and initiated the foreign technology agreement.

"Yes sir. That is correct."

"Could I have your reason?"

"I have two reasons. First, your organization showed no interest in a related proposal I made to one of your officers during his recent visit to our Center and . . . "

"What proposal was that?"

"It's private. The Operations Directorate [i.e., the FTD spooks] can fill you in."

"What is your other reason?"

"All material relating to my October 1969 trip has been reported through appropriate and authorized channels."

"What authorized channels?"

"Those channels that legally authorize contact between the U.S. government and a private citizen on this matter."

"I'm alarmed at your position!" he cried. "You have information that relates to our national security: you can help my people in the performance of their work! You're an American! How can you refuse to help?"

"The information has already been transmitted to a qualified body. Besides, I *volunteered* most of this to your organization. I was not obligated to give you anything. I'm sure you're aware of that."

"We have questions on the data you gave us!" he yelled.

"Direct your questions to the authorized personnel [CIA] whose job it is to handle inquiries like yours."

"Mr. James, Pratt & Whitney Aircraft signed an agreement to assist us in evaluating foreign technology. Your uncooperative attitude cannot possibly do our relations with your company any good!"

He was trying a power play. "I'm sorry sir, but the letter agreement my company has with FTD is to evaluate the material that you [FTD] send us. It does not give you the right to probe into my personal affairs, or more specifically, conferences that I attend. Your organization does not have jurisdiction over these matters. I strongly suggest that you handle this through official channels and according to the rules!"

"Is that your final position?"

"That is my final position." We hung up.

I immediately notified H. Norm Cotter about Post's call, and because Post had made a veiled threat that Pratt & Whitney would suffer if I didn't play ball with FTD, I volunteered to withdraw from the foreign technology program.

"Norm, if you find I'm a liability, don't hesitate to . . ."

Cotter laughed. "Don't worry about it."

"They might play games because of this."

"Pete, I'm not worried what some rinky-dink captain might do. What bothers me is that this rinky-dink captain with a chip on his shoulder might be promoted to a colonel, and then, some day in the future, he could hurt the company; they [FTD] could do us more harm than good. Your personal affairs are none of their damn business. Don't worry about it."

Cotter was fed up with FTD, but he was still willing to live with it. I was not. By now, however, I really didn't have a choice; I was on its list.

17

In a memorandum distributed in the East Hartford and Florida divisions, the Eagle sealed the fate of future agreements with the military intelligence services and fanned the flames of the underground war against FTD by elaborating on his earlier remarks. He said that no-cost contracts by the military intelligence services are part of their current popular pastime, designed to show congressmen, the Executive Office, and the Defense Department that the military is doing an outstanding job for the U.S. government in foreign intelligence assessments since they have an impressive list of prominent corporations working for them at no cost; the military intelligence services can build their empire larger and faster if their viewgraphs shown in Washington contain a growing number of special arrangements with private industry, regardless of the quality of the work performed. With prominent companies "supporting" its effort, the military has found it easier to sell its clandestine intelligence programs to its Pentagon chiefs.

In a scathing indictment of the FTD operations, the Eagle continued his campaign and wrote to the Pratt & Whitney office in Washington and reminded Fred Polhemus, the paunchy company field representative recently transferred from Dayton, that FTD's attacks against East Hartford were entirely predictable because the company's headquarters would not endorse FTD's plagiarized reports or its unwarranted and expensive translation program. The Eagle noted that it was not private industry's duty to conduct sub-sophomoric tutoring sessions for technically deficient FTD officers, absorb endless abuse from insecure FTD analysts, or endorse pre-determined, defective, or plagiarized intelligence assessments. Requests by FTD, the Eagle said, should be checked out in advance because its requests have usually been refused as improper by both the State Department and Federal Bureau of Investigation. (I.e., FTD's requests for company proprietary or classified information sometimes violated either the Espionage Act, because FTD cir-cumvented normal security procedures, or the State Department's export controls regulations, because FTD's overseas operations circumvented the State Department's Office of Munitions Con-trol.) In summary, the Eagle did not believe that Pratt & Whitney's name should be used by FTD in a presentation in Washington in which it is implied that the company endorses a "national scan-dal;" he advised Polhemus to inform decision-makers in Wash-ington that Pratt & Whitney did not give blanket endorsement of the FTD "cost-effective story."

The FTD campaign to discredit the Eagle escalated. He soon found himself under surveillance, and during one trip to the Air Force secret facility, while he was busy reviewing raw intel-legence reports, someone conducted a thorough search of his mo-tel room. No valuables were taken, but his briefcase and notes had been rifled, and when nothing incriminating was found, his working notes had been clumsily replaced. It was his guess that FTD spooks had conducted the illegal search with the hope of finding classified notes in his possession. Armed with this type of evidence, the "Air Force" could again demand that the Eagle be replaced as the company's liaison representative with FTD, or better yet, that the Eagle be dismissed. The Eagle suspected that the director of the Air Force secret facility was collaborating with the burglar(s) because of the director's more than casual interest in the Eagle's motel reservations, flight timetable, and itinerary. In a subsequent visit to the facility, the Eagle threw a curve ball at the spooks by giving the director erroneous information and changing motels; the director almost had a coronary when the Eagle unex-pectedly announced his early departure from the facility.

Meanwhile, FTD continued in its efforts to penetrate the Florida Center. In addition to the Swimmer, Dr. Marv Glickstein, a heat transfer specialist at the Florida Research and Development Center, was contacted to participate in an FTD cloak and dagger operation in Southern France. The Glickstein connection had an interesting background. When the subject of "the list" first came up in January 1969, Lieutenants David Pfeifle and Barry Penswick were involved. Glickstein was involved in the April 1969 discussions with Capt. Hal Gale at the Center on advanced Soviet brazing materials. On this trip Captain Gale returned to Wright-Patterson Air Force Base with a list of company engineers who attended a technical discussion he presided over; Dr. Glickstein was on the list.

When FTD finally made its pitch, Dr. Glickstein was contacted on the second floor of the Center by none other than Lt. Barry Penswick and another colleague from FTD. The deal never went through; it was my understanding that corporate headquarters in East Hartford got wind of it and turned thumbs down, allegedly because of unacceptable financial arrangements that could embarrass the company if anything backfired. The Eagle may have had a silent role in the decision.

The Glickstein affair raised other questions which tended to undermine FTD's credibility in the intelligence field. It is not my intention to take anything away from Dr. Glickstein, whom I have always known to be an exceptionally polite, bright, and honest person, but if anyone were to be sent on an intelligence mission abroad to deal with top-notch Russian agents, Dr. Glickstein would be the least-likely candidate. On the other hand, he could do no worse than the leeches FTD already had on their payroll. But FTD was playing another game. It was riding on his credentials—one of the few doctoral engineers on the Center's payroll—and this tended to add credibility to the FTD cost-effective story, since it had key individuals from prominent aerospace companies on its payroll.

On July 13, 1970, my foreign technology report was ready for publication. I submitted the proof copy of the title page to Lowell Ruby. He was surprised to see my name on the title page as the author, since I had declined to identify myself as the author of the previous report. "You're signing your name this time?" he asked.

"Yes, I've invested too much in it not to."

One hundred copies of Volume I and twenty copies of Volume II* were printed on July 15, 1970. Including illustrations, the bright red covered report numbered over 800 single-spaced typed pages and was entitled, *Annual Report on Foreign Rocket Technology (1969-*

*Volume I of the report was written primarily for U.S. government aerospace managers and planners and members of the U.S. aerospace industry; Volume II was prepared exclusively for the U.S. intelligence community, and it contained dossiers covering the technical activities of thousands of key Russian personalities (scientists and espionage agents).

1970) and assigned the Pratt & Whitney report number, PWA FR-3760. The report, a sequel to the first report, was classified "Secret— No Foreign Dissemination."

I distributed fifteen copies of both volumes to FTD, eighteen copies of Volume I to the Pratt & Whitney Aircraft management in Florida, and six copies of Volume I to the management in East Hartford. The Eagle was sent both volumes, and H. Norm Cotter and Lowell Ruby reviewed and approved the contents of both volumes as well. One of the personalities on the distribution list in the East Hartford facility was "Bay of Pigs" Richard M. Bissell, Allen Dulles' former deputy at the CIA. Bissell, a victim of the Kennedy purge after the Bay of Pigs fiasco, was also involved in the headquarters foreign technology program.

Friday, July 17, 1970: At 4:30 P.M. I telephoned Captain Gale at FTD and he confirmed that the foreign technology report had arrived and was being processed by its security department. He suggested that I spend several days with its analysts. H. Norm Cotter and Lowell Ruby, who was elated with the report—in fact, when Ruby got his copy, he rushed it downstairs for the just-promoted assistant general manager R. J. Coar to read—asked me to fly up to Wright-Patterson right away to answer questions the report would generate.

18

Monday, July 20, 1970: I boarded a Delta jet for Dayton with the feeling that this would be my last visit to the base: the report was finished and I had no intention of writing another. I checked into the Falcon Motel in Fairborn, Ohio. As before, there was a loud thump on the door—Super Smart and the Fox. They briefed me on the background of Nicholas Post's telephone call after I refused to see two FTD analysts in Florida.

"We apologize," the Fox said, "if you thought the call was an attempt by the Air Force to intimidate you."

"There was no other interpretation," I replied. "Forget it."

According to their story, my Mar del Plata report raised hell with the systems group in FTD because it conflicted with their most recent intelligence assessments. The problem was compounded by an internal power struggle between the technology and systems groups. When Gleichauf notified FTD that I would not see the two men, the systems group, which had requested the debriefing, cried foul and claimed I had been advised by the technology group not to see the men.

"Why would they think that?" I asked.

"You might as well tell him," the Fox said. "He's already admitted the decision was his own."

"Well," Super Smart began, "the two men who were going to debrief you"—he grinned—"they weren't really interested in debriefing you. They had another mission. They . . . they were being sent down to discredit you."

"To discredit me? How?"

"Believe us, it can be done. A few days with you, and then a report covering the debriefing to the commander, and your report [to the CIA] would be worthless."

"Pete," the Fox said, "for your sake I'm glad you turned down their request. Some people around here were already questioning their tactics. We fought it, but were overruled. When you turned them down, we got fingered and got called on the carpet. They complained to the commander [Weinbrenner]. That's why the [Nicholas Post] telephone call. They wanted to hear it from the horse's mouth. Whatever you said, it cleared us. As it turned out, you made their [the systems group] job more difficult. Pete, get some sleep. We'll see you in the morning." While their explanation seemed plausible, I still interpreted the Nicholas Post telephone call as a veiled threat.

Their explanation about the underhanded tactics of the systems group was worth looking into. I suspected that this was the case, but I had only circumstantial evidence. What they said was profound: any raw intelligence report from the field could be discredited by FTD, *providing that their agents are allowed to debrief the source of the report.* Since the CIA had filed my report, it was officially a part of the U.S. intelligence files. Thus, FTD's only recourse was to discredit me by submitting another report for the files. *The rules of the intelligence establishment, however, prohibit any government agency from filing a debriefing report without having personal contact with the person to be debriefed.* Once contact is made, FTD could report what a source had said during the FTD-conducted debriefing, and because words can be subject to interpretation and the source seldom gets to see the final debriefing report, the work sails through the intelligence files unchallenged. The shocking aspect of this mode of operation is that if FTD had set up the machinery arbitrarily to discredit a CIA raw intelligence report, it didn't require much of an imagination to figure out what they were secretly doing with their own raw intelligence before filing it with the community.

Wright-Patterson Air Force Base, Tuesday, July 21, 1970: I drove past the Air Force Museum to the base, signed in at the control center, and parked near Building 828. The receptionist called James Bartley for me as an armed Negro security officer behind a partition reviewed the paperwork on his desk and glanced occasionally at the closed circuit television screens before him. "Pete," Bartley said, grasping my hand firmly. "I've been going through your report. How'd you ever find the time to write so much?"

"I had a year. How's it going?"

"The place is buzzing. We're tickled to death with it. How long are you here for?"

"The week."

"Good. Everyone wants to talk with you. I'll start scheduling the appointments. I guess you know you've stirred up a hornet's nest."

"Oh, you mean the telephone call?"

"No, I mean the report!"

"What's happening?"

"You've put the systems group on the defensive."

"Exactly who in the hell are they?"

"They handle the launch vehicle and space systems assessments. We're separate from them. They assess current systems. We assess the technology."

"So what's the problem?"

"In one area they spent millions to reach the same conclusion you did."

"What else?"

"You documented something they said was not so about a year ago. Now the commander [Weinbrenner] is asking questions."

"Sounds like this could be an interesting week."

James Bartley led me into a conference room. We were joined by Captain Gale, other members of the technology group, and a senior-level pipe-smoking civilian. Everyone rose, and Captain Gale introduced me to Fred Van Dame, chief of the Technology Branch of FTD. Van Dame said he read the report and liked the way it was organized. He was impressed because in some areas I arrived at their conclusions by relying entirely on personal contact with Eastern bloc scientists. This was an important point because an FTD analyst I had talked with earlier said that Melvin Laird, the secretary of defense at the time, was raising hell with the intelligence community because it was squandering defense funds to acquire trivial information that could be obtained at nominal cost if good judgment were exercised.

"How many specialists worked on the report?" Van Dame asked. In the past I maintained the façade that the entire Center contributed to the foreign technology report, when in fact it was my work. I decided to level with him.

"We were faced with budgetary problems; I was the only one who could work on it. My technical supervisor Lowell Ruby approved it."

He removed the pipe from his mouth and tapped it against his shoe. "How many man-years went into the study?"

"Less than one man-year. I worked on other programs as well." I did not want to lessen Pratt & Whitney's contribution to the report, but I did not wish to leave Van Dame with the impression that it required a team of experts to do the job.

"I want to personally compliment you on an excellent and monumental report . . . your section on the organization of Soviet research and development is good. You've done something that we seldom do. You brought many related programs together and showed how they relate to each other. I intend to distribute it to all of our groups. There's something there for everyone!"

"That was one of my objectives."

"Your command of the political aspects of the problem impresses me. Are you a political science major?"

"No, but I studied Soviet political-military strategy to write it."

"I'm still concerned over the allocation of resources to do the job. What were your primary sources?"

"Open literature publications, HUMINT [human intelligence] from the facility, and personal contact."

He leaned forward. "Which source would you consider the most valuable?"

"Personal contact."

"What do you think of HUMINT?" the branch chief asked.

"I've read many HUMINT reports where the meaning of what transpired in a conversation I was party to was completely distorted. To read the HUMINT report you would draw a different conclusion than if you listened to the spoken version. Sometimes the Russian may have been joking—Zhivotovskiy often did this. Unless the analyst knows the man personally, he cannot tell. In other reports I've read, the material is presented completely out of context." I was referring to the leeches, but did not elaborate.

"That's interesting. Will you write another one next year?"

"Probably not. The general assessments are good for five years or so."

As the branch chief was leaving the room, James Bartley whispered, "Pete, I'm glad you met him. He was elated when your report came in. It gave us all a big boost."

Bartley bought me coffee in the Building 828 snack bar, and as we were walking back to his office, he said, "Hold it, Pete. I want you to meet someone." Two officers, each carrying a cup of coffee, were approaching. When they were within hearing distance Bartley shouted: "McAllister, I want you to meet Pete James. Pete, this is McAllister." The officer's name registered: he was one of two FTD analysts who wanted to debrief me in Florida about Mar del Plata. Whereas I had expected to see an experienced forty or fifty-year-old intelligence officer, McAllister, a frail college-age boy, gave one the impression that if he were involved in intelligence, then anyone could be. The boy was shocked: the Floridian he wanted to see so badly—the one who was causing the furor—was standing before him.

"It's a pleasure to meet you Mr. McAllister," I said, intentionally not recogizing his rank. He bobbed his head up and down. "I'll be here for three more days. I hope we meet again." He kept bobbing his head and hurriedly joined his colleague a few paces ahead.

"I suppose you know who that was," Bartley said with a grin. Bartley wanted me to meet the officer, apparently to set up a confrontation.

"Tell McAllister I'll gladly talk with him or any group in the facility." That was what Bartley wanted to hear; he immediately telephoned his superiors and relayed the message.

After hanging up, he said, "Pete, more people are hearing about the report. They want to talk with you."

"Good." I had yet to meet the movers behind the Building 828 operation. "What's the latest reaction?"

"Fantastic. You can't imagine what you've stirred up. The systems group has the commander convinced that launch vehicle assessments can only be made if he approves a telemetry intercept program. You know how much that costs? Well, never mind. After they made an assessment from the intercept data, your report came in, and in one area you came up with the same results at a fraction of their cost."

"That's good, isn't it?"

"Sure, but things are boiling here because of it. There's another group we've disagreed with for years. Your report shows they're wrong, and you've done a good job in supporting your conclusions. You can't imagine what's going on!"

Bartley and I were discussing the organization of the Soviet military-industrial complex when a captain from the FTD materials group—I vaguely recognized him from somewhere—and a civilian entered the room. After Bartley introduced us, we exchanged views on Soviet laser research. The civilian, Roy Frontani, was particularly interested in the section of the report in which I analyzed the significance of Soviet laser experiments in relation to research in East Germany, and how this effort related to Soviet ambitions to build a major space-based laser weapon system. The captain's face kept haunting me. It finally came: though we had never spoken to each other, he was Robert M. Dunco, a graduate of my class at Case Institute of Technology in Cleveland, Ohio, in 1962. It was interesting: two Case graduates, one employed by the government and one by private industry, were sitting face to face in Building 828, using their technical skills to assess the Soviet capability in the areas of materials and weapons technology so that the United States could develop more efficient weapons of mass destruction.

Roy Frontani complimented me on the materials section of the report—he welcomed my independent analysis—because he had arrived at the same conclusion, but was having difficulty in getting the intelligence community to look into the Russian work in more depth.

Later in the afternoon I was introduced to the gravel-voiced Nicholas Post, the technology adviser of the Technology Branch at FTD and the man who first contacted Pratt & Whitney in 1968 with the foreign technology proposal.

"Mr. James, what is your opinion of Have Stork [the Air Force secret facility]?" I thought he was going to discuss the telephone incident, but apparently not.

"In my opinion, the facility is very organized, but there are a lot of reports filed and ignored because the government doesn't have an organized approach in evaluating the raw data."

"What's wrong with our approach?"

"Under the current system the government depends on a few individuals who might luckily uncover something of significance. If they run across something that's significant in another field, they ignore it because it's not related to their own work."

"So that's why you wrote Volume II," he said. "Tell me about it."

"If I came across something that even looked interesting, whether it concerned space stations, the political climate within a Russian university, or the prospects of a scientist being promoted or transferred, I red-flagged it for more detailed analysis. When I was done with Volume I, I had over 10,000 items not used directly in the report, but I knew they would be of interest to intelligence analysts working in other areas. I categorized the items by Russian personalities, ending up with over 3,000 names. So Volume II is a who's who in Russia, spiced with useful intelligence; I also prepared it as a personal reference for international conferences."

Post was impressed with my attitude of not dumping information because I could not use it in Volume I. "I'll make sure Volume II gets put to good use," he said assuringly. We shook hands and he walked past an officer standing in the wing of the conference room, waiting to talk with me.

"I'm glad you had kind words about the [secret] facility," Bartley said.

"Why?"

"Because that was his baby. He dreamed it up."

The officer, Capt. "Chip" Toby (phonetic spelling) of the missile systems group, took a seat opposite me. I studied his grim expression as he leafed through Volume I of the red report. The minutes of silence dragged on, interrupted occasionally by the turn of a page and the movement of an ash tray. I broke the ice: "Have you read the report?"

"Yes, we've seen it," he replied with eyes glued to the report.

"Well . . . where do we disagree?"

"I don't concur with your space systems assessment." In a ten minute classified exchange I learned that the captain and his colleagues were officially on record supporting a different assessment, and with my report now being distributed in FTD, they had to defend their position. I was waiting for the captain to use the standard argument that since he was a member of the intelligence establishment, he naturally had access to better data. He finally did: ". . . You must admit," he said, looking up for the first time, "that you arrived at your conclusions using only the information you had available at the time. Isn't that so?"

"All studies are conducted on this basis. The intelligence community may have access to more sources of information than I, but that doesn't detract from the reliability of my data. Besides, in the area we disagree, the community has consistently blown its assessment for the past five years."

"I have complete confidence in our methods," he replied.

"What do you know about the Academy of Sciences or the work done in the Moscow Aviation Institute or Georgiy Petrov's Institute of Space Research?" I asked. The captain returned with a blank stare. "How about Valentine P. Glushko's design bureau?"

"I'm not up to speed on these facilities," he sheepishly admitted.

"How about Academician G. L. Grodzovskiy, Oleg Belotserkovskiy, Jouli Khodarev, Boris Petrov . . . Georgiy Ulanov?" I was now naming the cream of the crop in the Soviet Union; high-level academicians I had met personally, and in some cases, men who had invited me to their hotel room for a drink of Stolichnaya vodka or Georgian cognac. The captain shook his head. The pattern was becoming increasingly clear; he admitted that the FTD systems group relied almost entirely on telemetry intercept and other costly electronic surveillance programs. "Why don't you use HUMINT?" I asked astounded.

James Bartley interrupted: "Pete, our organization is set up so that the systems and technology groups are separated. We [the technology group] rely on technical translations and HUMINT; the systems group uses telemetry and other sources."

"I don't understand why all available sources are not considered when an assessment is made. You people have everything under one roof." It was appalling: FTD's finished intelligence assessments were being passed off as the best estimates available, based on all available intelligence data, when in fact their assessments were made on the analysis of a limited amount of their own data base. And it came as no surprise that FTD did not have the so-called "black briefcase" which contained "new" information that would make me change my assessment. The "national scandal," as the Eagle called it, included an unknown number of "authorities" in the intelligence establishment who were using the covert nature of their work to explain inconsistencies or outright erroneous assessments: the alibis that the Eagle and I frequently heard—"We've just received information that is currently being processed which supports our position . . . In our confidential files we have information that . . . Our expert who is not here right now believes . . ."—were nothing short of devious excuses for perpetuating a hoax on persons who legitimately wanted to get at the truth.

I felt morally obligated to get my report distributed to as many officials outside the espionage establishment as possible because the issues could then be debated, and it would force some analysts to come out of the woodwork and defend their assessments.

19

Wright-Patterson Air Force Base, July 22, 1970: James Bartley was reviewing Volume II of my report when an Air Force intelligence agent popped his head through the door. "Pete, you just gave HUMINT [human intelligence] a big boost!" He waved and went on his way. That was the very last thing I wanted! HUMINT to FTD meant a massive military-controlled bureaucratic maze of kingmakers who used American engineers and scientists as pawns. I didn't want Volume II of my report to be used to increase the budget of the Operations Directorate—the spooks—for HUMINT operations; the HUMINT used in the report was based mostly on my personal contacts with the Russians; only a fraction of the government HUMINT was used. In a sense, I made the job easy for them, for in Volume II, all classified sources of information were identified by code numbers only; my contributions were intentionally woven into the maze of FTD code numbers to protect me as a CIA source when I traveled abroad. To an intelligence administration official, however, the report would appear to support the thesis that government-sponsored HUMINT was paying off. There was nothing further from the truth, and the double standard bothered me: on one hand, I was told by FTD clandestine operators that my coverage of the Venice and Argentine conferences in 1969 was better than their team effort—my personal evaluation of raw intelligence reports corroborated this—and on the other hand, FTD included my reports, prepared at no cost to them, in their pool of HUMINT reports to justify their budget. As a concerned intelligence analyst and taxpayer, I resented this practice.

After lunch, I reminded James Bartley that if McAllister et al. wished to debrief me about Mar del Plata, I was available. In what he said was a major policy decision by the Operations Directorate, McAllister was ordered to stay away from me. How ironic: several months earlier FTD was willing to fly two men across the country to debrief me; now they wouldn't give the same men the authority to walk a hundred yards to see me.

Wright-Patterson Air Force Base, July 23, 1970: In a surprise move, the spooks from the Operations Directorate called James Bartley in Building 828 and asked if I would be willing to have lunch with them at the Officer's Club. I agreed. At noon Bartley got into my rental car in front of Building 828 and directed me to an innocuous-looking building—it resembled a warehouse—where Fred Meisetz, the agent who visited me in Florida to discuss the Pisa proposal, was waiting. Huffing and puffing, Fred climbed into the back seat and we drove to the Officers Club. We were joined by Michael Hughes, a well-built administrator whom I was told was responsible for planning Air Force clandestine operations in Europe; he was in charge of the spooks. Hughes asked about my dealings with the Russians in Venice and Mar del Plata, and as our dialogue progressed, Fred spiced up the conversation with salty jabs at the Russians I named. Hughes then got to the point:

"Pete . . . I'd like to explore something with you. I'd like your thoughts."

"Go ahead." The serious countenances of Fred Meisetz and James Bartley telegraphed that they may have known what Michael Hughes had on his mind.

"The French and other West European countries are progressing significantly in a number of areas. As you know, they've committed a fantastic amount of their resources on R&D [research and development]. How can the United States find out the results of their work without treading the same ground they've covered?" I scratched my nose and waited for him to finish the pitch. "If our researchers could visit the European laboratories and research centers . . . Let me explore this with you . . . If the Air Force were willing to cover your expenses, would you be willing to visit some European aerospace firms and report to us what you may have learned?" My God, I thought. When Pratt & Whitney was first sent

140

classified intelligence reports in 1968, what caught my attention was that FTD was collecting intelligence on our allies. Hughes wasn't just "exploring" this with me. They already had the program in operation, and it was being supported by FTD's secret worldwide network of embassy attachés and agents. It was a clandestine grab for power. They had infiltrated American industry, they manipulated the military-industrial complex through secret intermediaries, and they were now trying to move into the European market.

"Your proposal would have to be approved by Pratt & Whitney and . . . "

"It's our policy that such a trip would have to benefit the company first!" Hughes interjected. Seeing that I was skeptical, and not wanting to convey the impression that this was a clandestine proposal, Hughes elaborated: "The company benefits first, the individual second, and the Air Force last. We would use our facilities to assimilate the data. We would disseminate the results of this effort to Pratt & Whitney and other [U.S.] research centers."

"I'm not interested," I replied. "Besides, I've done quite well operating independently." Hughes reached for a glass of water, perturbed over my cocky stance. "I'll tell the people in Florida of your proposal."

"It's best not to mention our meeting," he replied.

This was both a clandestine power play to set up another covert bureaucratic empire with no controls and an FTD end run to spy on our European allies—France, West Germany, Great Britain, et al.—using agents from American firms and universities. Besides setting the stage for a major international incident with unknown consequences, the Hughes plan depended on the "cooperation" of American firms, it meant that aerospace executives from private industry could secretly recommend government-funded programs with FTD playing the role of the silent partner, and it again elevated FTD into a preeminent position of secretly contributing to a higher defense budget while simultaneously manipulating the internal policies of American corporations and the foreign policy of the United States government.

The alleged real beneficiaries of such a program—American aerospace corporations, research centers, and universities—were already pursuing agreements and information exchanges with their European counterparts to be competitive with each other; aerospace corporations had their own sales and marketing departments for this express purpose, and they didn't need the spooks in Building 828 and the Operations Directorate to "coordinate" the work.

Hughes paid for the lunch. As we were parting in front of the Officers Club, he said, "You've got the wrong idea about the conferences. *It's easy to forget things after they happen!*"

"I take notes."

"You don't have any support your way!" he shouted with restraint, alluding to FTD's worldwide communications hook-up with Building 828.

"That also makes me more flexible. I'm my own man." He fought to control his temper and succeeded. Michael Hughes had explored my thoughts at lunch; I would neither endorse the Hughes plan nor accept his thesis that I needed FTD's spooks abroad to quarterback me. His icy glare conveyed what his colleagues already knew: I was "bad news." To make matters worse, the chief spook knew that I no longer gave a damn what they thought.

I dropped the two men off at their hideaway, shaken over the implications of the Hughes plan, and returned to Building 828 with James Bartley. I said goodbye to my contacts and on Friday, July 24, 1970, I visited the secret facility to thank them for their past assistance, and for the real reason: to see them for the last time—I wanted out.

20

July 31, 1970: I summarized the highlights of the FTD trip for the Florida management in a five-page memorandum. The main thrust of the memo was to show that FTD's programs were not cost-effective and that the Operations Directorate—Michael Hughes, et al.—wanted to work closer with the company.

With H. Norm Cotter's written approval, I hand-carried seven copies of Volume I and two copies of Volume II of the foreign technology report to Faucher's security department for transmittal to the CIA. I had yet to get the report distributed widely because of a bureaucratic approval cycle that required signatures from both the expected recipients of the report and Captain Robert Probst, an officer of the Air Force Rocket Propulsion Laboratory in Edwards, California.

August 12, 1970: Ruby called me into his office: "Pete, we have a problem! The red foreign technology report was on his desk. He leafed through it. "Coar [assistant general manager] read the report again and wants it rewritten."

"Rewritten?" I asked incredulously. "It's already been distributed to FTD."

"I know. Those have to be called back."

"Called back?" I parroted. "What's the problem?"

"Some sections are too controversial. You've got to get the politics out of it."

"But I conducted a systems analysis. It's all integrated, and politics is just as important as science and technology."

"We can't have Washington thinking that the corporation is telling them how to run their business. The report has to be rewritten or Coar won't allow it out of the plant. The boss has made the decision."

"The CIA has the report."

"I know. They'll have to return it."

"You know they'd make a copy before returning it. Don't you think they should be allowed to keep it?"

"I guess you're right. But no other copies leave the plant until Coar approves the rewrite. Write a memo summarizing the changes, and let me see it." I returned to my desk, greatly disappointed over the ruling. The thought of sanitizing the already-approved report was absurd. Now, Pratt & Whitney management in Florida was doing exactly what some FTD officials were doing —tampering with an intelligence assessment for political expediency.

The next day the Eagle telephoned and recommended that I send Senator John Stennis my file on the "FTD story" since the military intelligence services were being investigated by both Defense Secretary Laird and Congress. "The time's ripe for a knockout punch!" he said. I agreed, but I didn't feel like losing my job over it.

August 14, 1970: W. L. Gorton, Pratt & Whitney Aircraft division vice president and general manager of the Florida facility, received a letter from FTD headquarters commenting on my foreign technology report. Col. Benjamin F. Smotherman, on behalf of FTD Commander George R. Weinbrenner, extended his gratitude and appreciation to Pratt & Whitney Aircraft for the foreign technology effort and the "outstanding study" on Russian rocket technology. As was the case in 1969, the Air Force found that the 1970 report was both comprehensive and timely, and it exhibited "high competence" on the part of the personnel involved. Smotherman named Lowell Ruby, Captain Probst of the Air Force Rocket Propulsion Laboratory, and me in the letter and said we were to be commended for our "outstanding performance" in the study. The fact that Captain Probst had nothing to do with the study was beside the point, and it indicated that FTD's pat-on-the-back system included the liberal use of congratulatory letters to pump up everyone's ego. It worked on General Manager Gorton the previous

144

year—Gorton even sent a copy of FTD's 1969 platitudes regarding my first report to Pratt & Whitney President Bernard Schmickrath in East Hartford to show how highly the "Air Force" regarded the Florida Center.

August 19, 1970: I submitted to Lowell Ruby a memorandum summarizing the changes in the report to comply with management's directives. On page four of the memorandum I wrote:

> The above changes in my opinion free the report of politically sensitive conclusions. This includes the Strategic Threat section, which discusses the Soviet political-scientific-military-industrial complex. If P&WA feels that discussion of this complex is politically sensitive, it would be best to omit the entire section (pages 385-429).

Ruby made the decision as soon as he read the memorandum: the Strategic Threat section—which discussed the clandestine Soviet ICBM arms build-up, and implicitly questioned the defense policies of former Defense Secretaries Robert McNamara and Clark Clifford and served as a warning to our SALT negotiators—would be deleted.

Suddenly I began receiving frantic calls from the company's Government Mail Control Center. In the confusion of making the revisions, no one bothered to stop the Pratt & Whitney field representative from notifying leading U.S. space and defense officials about the existence of the report. Requests to obtain the report came from private aerospace corporations, the Defense Department, the National Aeronautics and Space Administration, and the Executive Office of the President. I asked the girls in Government Mail Control to sit on the report until the revisions could be made.

August 28, 1970: I sent a management-approved nine-page memorandum to the technical publications department summarizing the political changes. I reviewed the revisions, page by page, with technical writer Tom Bridges. In what seemed like the longest day of my life, I watched Bridges execute the instructions of the memorandum and delete the life and blood of the analysis with each stroke of his pencil:

> Prologue: Delete the photos of Lenin, Stalin, Khrushchev, Brezhnev, and Kosygin." (Pratt & Whitney wanted to de-emphasize the role that Soviet political leaders played in science and technology because it might upset the Nixon-Agnew team.)
>
> Page 1. Delete—"It is hoped that this study will encourage the U.S. intelligence community to (1) pursue in depth those areas that

145

are of immediate interest to the U.S. aerospace industry (i.e., Soviet space shuttle developments, etc.) and (2) provide the industry with useful and timely technical feedback for use in the planning and development of U.S. hardware." (It was the concensus of Pratt & Whitney managers that the foreign intelligence FTD was sending the company was both untimely and worthless, yet the company would not go on record and acknowledge that there was a problem.)

Page 10: Delete—"The Soviets will continue to deploy and conduct extensive R&D [research and development] on advanced ABM's because they believe that it is both strategically and politically advantageous to do so." (Again, since the U.S. was in the midst of an ABM (antiballistic missile) controversy, Pratt & Whitney wanted no part of a discussion on ABM's.)

Etc., etc., etc., for 429 pages in Volume I.

Of all the deletions in the report, the removal of the strategic threat section because of political sensitivity to the interests of the corporation was the most serious. It integrated the analysis of hundreds of preceding pages and summarized in blunt language the scope of the Soviet arms build-up.

I was disillusioned with both my superiors and our espionage establishment. At home I reviewed the notes I had transmitted to the CIA since 1965 and I assessed the situation: my 1969 annual report had been written for the intelligence community, but it was pigeonholed by a handful of men in Building 828; my collection efforts at various international conferences at no cost to the CIA were used by FTD to justify its own overseas intelligence operations; my 1970 report was written for military and civilian aerospace managers and planners, but it was whitewashed to accommodate the whims of a few managers at Pratt & Whitney. The rewrite of the once-approved report was the last straw.

I learned from experience that the intelligence community and private corporations paid more attention to complaints from outside their organizations than from within. I had to stop procrastinating and start work on a book! The question I asked myself was: how could a man who authored reports under the "secret" label, but authored nothing in public, write a believable book that could survive the inevitable—an attack by the military intelligence services and misguided government officials to discredit both the book and the author? Two books had to be written: the first would be a firsthand report on the Russian strategic threat—an expanded unsanitized version of my 1970 secret report, updated by more meetings with the Russians; the second would blow the roof off of Building 828. The Russian book had to be written first, so I could establish my credentials. With both books out, the right people might ask the right questions and FTD would be investigated by a responsible government body. The more I thought about it, the more I became obsessed with this challenging and possibly dangerous project. It was insane, but I felt driven, as if I had an unwritten moral obligation, a debt I owed to a society which had deferred me from the military draft—first because I went to college, and second because I joined a government defense contractor— and to men who were dying in Vietnam because our politicians in Washington couldn't make up their minds and were not being truthful to the American people.

Since I would soon depart for Europe to attend conferences in Italy and Germany and visit my friends with the Messerschmitt-Bolkow-Blohm firm, I knew that upon my return to the States, FTD agents would again ask the CIA for permission to debrief me, and the aggravating cycle would repeat itself. Rather than make it appear that I desired no further association with FTD—Gleichauf of the CIA knew that this was my position—I devised a plan that would allow me to disengage from FTD without alienating my superiors. It was no secret in Building 828 that I had refused to cooperate with their agents on the Mar del Plata matter. And knowing that I had been blackballed by the Operations Directorate—for all practical purposes the Operations Directorate was an annex of Building 828, and the spooks in Building 828 worked hand in hand with the spooks in the Operations Directorate—I telephoned James Bartley and proposed to spy and analyze intelligence for FTD. For the aforementioned reasons, I knew that they would have to reject my offer before my departure. Thus, when I returned to the States, if FTD had any ethics remaining, it would leave me alone and allow the CIA to debrief me. Reliable James Bartley—I regretted using a man I respected—called, and true to form, the spooks in the Operations Directorate wanted no part of my "offer." Among other things, this meant that in theory, Nicholas Post would have no reason to place another telephone call and announce that he was "alarmed." All in all, I hoped that these machinations would give me the independence I needed to keep FTD agents at arm's length.

September 1, 1970: Norm Cotter called me into his office. "If Brown [chief engineer] is hauled up to Washington," he said, "and asked how the [foreign technology] report got distributed outside the company, we want to be able to produce a letter saying the Air

147

Force asked us to do it. Is that understood?" I nodded. "We don't want Washington thinking we're competing against the government [in the intelligence field]."

Now it was coming out in the open. My annual report gave one the impression that Pratt & Whitney had a team of espionage agents operating in Florida. If read in its entirety, the report not only questioned the competence of officials in Washington, but it layed out in black and white the scope of FTD's overseas intelligence operations; one had only to read between the lines in Volume II. Fearing that the wrong United States senator might run across the document, H. N. Cotter wanted to be able to prove that the company was following "Air Force" orders, especially if FTD was later charged with meddling with private industry or both FTD and the company were charged with meddling with foreign policy. Volume II identified all raw intelligence report numbers used in the preparation of the annual report, and some of these numbers could be traced to FTD foreign operations. In lieu of the Hughes plan, the report was political dynamite. As Pratt & Whitney management would later learn, its policy of covering itself by getting everything down on paper, would leave for government investigators a trail wide enough to drive a Mack truck through.

After Cotter made his point perfectly clear, I called Lieutenant David Pfeifle—he was very complimentary of the foreign technology report during my last visit to Building 828—and explained the problem to him. Pfeifle understood the urgency of my request: if the systems group in Building 828 heard about it, one call to General Manager W. L. Gorton, explaining why the letter could not be sent, and it was all over. Three hours passed before Pfeifle called. "Pete, it's taken care of. A letter recommending that the report be distributed is going out today to RPL [Air Force Rocket Propulsion Laboratory]. You'll get a copy."

I thanked Pfeifle and rushed to Cotter's office, confirming that the letter was being sent.

September 8, 1970: With only three days before my departure, I sent Captain Probst of the Air Force Rocket Propulsion Laboratory in Edwards, California, a letter requesting approval to distribute the censored version of the foreign technology report (PWA FR-3760-A, dated September 1, 1970) to the personnel I listed in an attachment. Ruby promised to handle the distribution of the report during my absence.

Diane resigned from Pratt & Whitney after almost eight years of service and she was off to Madrid a week ahead of me to start a well deserved vacation; I would pick her up enroute to the Rome conference.

21

In September and the first part of October 1970, Diane and I attended international meetings in Rome and in Konstanz, Germany, and visited engineers from the Bolkow Space Division near Munich. Relative to past conferences we had attended, our activities in Rome and Konstanz were noticeably monitored by individuals who could be best described as employees of reputable American aerospace firms and innocuous government facilities. I was to learn subsequently from a CIA source that these FTD operatives had prepared dossiers on us, and the information they collected included a breakdown of whom we met, what we discussed, when, and where. This was my reward for wishing to remain independent of FTD's overseas operations.

Rome, September 14, 1970: Diane and I lounged at poolside on the lush fifteen acre estate of the Cavalieri Hilton Hotel on Monte Mario, as members of the international jet-set splashed playfully before us. A shadow crept over our table and a familiar voice said, "Good afternoon." Dressed as a civilian was an Air Force official I respected. "Is the company [Pratt & Whitney] paying your expenses?" I shook my head. "How about your friends in the Midwest [FTD]?"

"No."

"Oh, I forgot, you're working for Washington [CIA]."

"No, I'm not."

"You did, didn't you?"

"Never."

"I was told you did." This indicated how private my conversations in Building 828 really were. The official watched a shapely bikini-clad girl floating on her back, and then nodded toward my Minolta. "You've always been busy with your camera."

"I need the pictures for my personal files. The data *you know who* [FTD] prepares are erroneous."

"I know," he mused. "They've got to update their records. Even their pictures [of Russian scientists] don't match the names [beneath the photos]. Are you going to make yours available?" he asked, eyeing the girl again.

"I doubt it." Giving FTD a correct match of names and photos was a drop in the bucket compared to what really had to be done.

"If you let me have your negatives, I can make extra prints at no cost to you."

"No thanks." I was through bailing out FTD and allowing them to use my work to support their "cost-effective" story. The Air Force official bid us well and left quietly.

Rome, September 15, 1970: I was in the foyer of the Consiglio Nazionale Delle Richerche, waiting for the technical sessions to commence, when Vladimir Istomin, the blond-haired attaché of the Russian embassy in Rome—he assisted Zhivotovskiy and Beloussov during the 1969 Venice conference—entered the room. Using the translating skills of Boris Goudz, another member of the embassy staff, I asked Istomin to cable Moscow and inform Zhivotovskiy that I could not accept his invitation to visit the Soviet Union due to my workload at Pratt & Whitney. As Istomin recorded the text of the cable in his black notebook, Dr. Ivan Soukhanov, a supervisor from the U.S. Library of Congress, listened intently to our exchange. Professor V. G. Mikeladze, chief of a major aerodynamics laboratory in Moscow, joined our discussion. Suddenly, Dr. Soukhanov approached our group and volunteered to be my interpreter. Remembering that a branch of the Library of Congress was tied up with FTD—this little gem was something Lowell Ruby had brought back from the FTD-sponsored El Segundo meeting of 1968 —I suspected that the Library of Congress supervisor may have had another reason for volunteering his translating services. It was no secret in FTD that I would deal only with the CIA in the future. Feeling sympathetic toward the elderly Soukhanov, I did, however, allow him to ask Mikeladze to deliver a personal message from me to a Russian scientist named V. V. Sychev, whom I expected to meet in Germany later in the month; Soukhanov was so elated that he suggested that he act as my interpreter throughout the week. I declined the offer.

Rome, September 16, 1970: As arranged with the Russian embassy staff, I was notified that Miss Keldysh had just arrived from Moscow and she was attending the sessions on the upper floor of the Consiglio Nazionale Delle Richerche. I wanted to see her before the conference delegates heard she was in Rome, for I was sure her name would trigger a reaction from any intelligence specialist studying advanced reusable rocket-powered aerospace planes. I opened the door to the dark lecture room, and seated in the back row among fifty overheated scientists watching the slide presentation was a brown-haired lady in her forties who looked more like the head of a garden club than a renowned engineer. Istomin introduced me to Miss Keldysh as two American aerospace engineers on the other side of the room strained their necks to get a glimpse of the mystery lady.

After the presentation I left the room with Miss Keldysh and her Russian escorts. In the foyer the two aerospace engineers, who by now must have had wrenched necks, eavesdropped while pretending to converse with each other. I thanked Miss Keldysh for her time and asked her to give my regards to her husband. After Miss Keldysh left the building with her escorts, the two engineers caught up with Diane and me.

"Who is she?" one of the men asked. This was a peculiar encounter: I didn't know them, they didn't know me, but we knew each other.

"That was Miss V. V. Keldysh, sister of Mstislav Keldysh, president of the Academy of Sciences of the Soviet Union and wife of Professor Georgiy Maykapar, one of the best aerodynamicists in the world." I intentionally poured it on, with windowdressing and all.

"Did you learn anything?" the other asked. I shrugged. "What did you learn?" he asked again. My blood pressure rose; another damn leech trying to justify his expenses. I ignored him.

"Diane, let's find a restaurant!"

"Will she be here tomorrow?"

"See you later," I said, hustling Diane toward the Viale delle Scienze. I admonished Diane to stay away from the duo because from the looks of things, if they failed to make substantive contact with the Russians, they might panic and claim I hindered them on their mission.

"That can be serious, can't it?" she asked, talking above the screeching tires of a Fiat, whose driver must have thought he was in the Monza Autodrome.

"Only to the men responsible for this boondoggle. It'll be a reflection of their competence in the long run. They'd file a complaint through official channels to cover themselves, and it might reach [general manager] Gorton, though I doubt it; that would be admitting that the clowns used aerospace engineers as pawns, and it would open a Pandora's box; they couldn't survive a Senate investigation."

Rome, September 17, 1970: After giving his presentation, suave Vladimir Sosounov, head of a department within the Ministry of Aviation in the USSR, stepped down from the rostrum and joined us, taking the seat to my left. Besides looking as if he had just stepped out of a shower, the Russian aeronautical engineer had outdressed other members of his delegation, and if his diplomatic answers to the piercing questions on Soviet-Israeli relations were an indication of things to come, it appeared that the Central Committee of the Communist Party was grooming Sosounov for a higher level position. Placing his notes on the floor, the Russian said: "Peter James, I have present for you . . . a Matryoshka!" He placed the Matryoshka, a colorful red and yellow wooden doll about four inches long and shaped like a bowling pin, into my palm, and still holding the upper half, he twisted it until it came apart; a similar doll, about half as large, rested in the exposed cavity. The handsome Sosounov asked us to join him for a drink at the conference snack bar, so we could discuss his friend Zhivotovskiy and the invitation to visit Russia in more depth. "When you come to Moscow next year," Sosounov said, "you must attend the Bolshoi Ballet."

Suddenly, an American aerospace engineer I barely knew walked up to me and said, "Hi, Pete!" as if we were bosom buddies. Before I could answer, the engineer turned to Sosounov and said, "I'm Arnold and I work for the Marquardt Corporation. I'd like to talk to you about scramjets." The engineer coldly looked at me and said, "Excuse us!" He held Sosounov by the elbow, walked the Russian over to a sofa, and unloaded a barrage of questions. Sosounov held up his hand, looked in my direction, and asked me to join them. Under normal circumstances, I would have declined to give the engineer a chance to talk with a Russian. In five years I had never interrupted a conversation between an American and a Russian, but I wasn't about to let the coarse engineer get away with a cheap stunt like exploiting a friendship that didn't exist. To the discontent of the engineer, I accepted Sosounov's invitation.

"Have you heard of Orlov and Mazing?" he asked Sosounov.

Incredible! It was like reading a rejected script of past conferences. Orlov and Mazing, two Russian authors whose works have been translated by FTD, jointly wrote a textbook on advanced jet engines; their work has been plagiarized, taken out of context, and referenced in many FTD reports to show how much the United States "lags" the Soviets in scramjet technology. Sosounov took a deep breath and nodded, as if the question telegraphed knowledge privy to the KGB. In what I thought was a masterful performance, the experienced Sosounov took the offensive and elicited from the engineer information about his company's experimental test programs. I wondered whether the engineer realized that he was playing Russian roulette with his company's secrets, or more importantly, whether the company knew it.

Konstanz, Germany, Wednesday, October 7, 1970: The Russian Mikeladze had personally delivered my Rome message to V. V. Sychev in Moscow, and as prearranged, I met Sychev privately in his Konstanz hotel room to explore Soviet continued interest in a science and technology agreement, a subject Zhivotovskiy and I had discussed in Argentina. Sychev recommended that I talk with Gennadi Dimentiev, a high-level Russian space manager attending the conference. Since Soukhanov, the Library of Congress supervisor who translated the message for me in Rome, knew that I planned to meet Sychev in Konstanz, and I knew that FTD would be covering the Konstanz meeting, I assumed that the Building 828 spooks and their pawns would place me under surveillance and attempt to leech on my exchanges with the Russians. At precisely 11:55 A.M. I met Gennadi Dimentiev and his translator Yuri Riazantsev on the back terrace of the conference hotel. After a lengthy discussion, and as Dimentiev was proposing that I notify the U.S. Department of State of Soviet interest in a technology exchange with the United States, a mysterious conference delegate made a beeline for our isolated table. Dimentiev immediately picked up the copy of *Aviation Week & Space Technology*—I had brought the publication to show the Russians the type of technology I hoped they would declassify and make available to the West —and placed it face down just as the "curiosity seeker" made a pass of our table. At the time, I assumed that it could have been a meaningless incident, but after I learned in the States about FTD's *James file,* I realized that there was more to it than what appeared on the surface.

I had done quite well in Konstanz with my Russian contacts, meeting them practically around the clock. The leech from Mar del Plata—he was now becoming a regular conference attendee—approached Diane and me as we dined in the hotel and said: "I heard you were with the cosmonauts last night!" I nodded and buttered my bread, wishing he would leave. "Maybe I'll see you tonight," he said.

"I prefer to talk with them in private," I responded. An hour later, after another meeting with Sychev, I returned to our hotel and saw Diane in the telephone booth; she was confirming our Swissair reservations. Suddenly, the Mar del Plata leech crept up to her booth, listened for a few seconds, and not being able to hear her soft-spoken words, he literally opened the door and yelled, "Who are you calling? The States? Miss your mother?" The leech saw me and quickly left. This incident, which later became known as "the telephone booth act," appeared to have been the leech's attempt to destroy the rapport I had developed with the Soviets, because most people knew that Diane often delivered my messages whenever I was busy. If I had to place money on it, I would have guessed that the Mar del Plata leech had launched his "espionage career" by first being debriefed by the CIA. After attending a few meetings, FTD moved in and promised to cover his expenses in exchange for owning his soul. He apparently bought the deal for the prestige value, because he was the type of person who enjoyed impressing his fellow workers with the "world traveler" routine. Why Diane was being subjected to the surveillance and harassment was another question. But the telephone booth act and other overt acts of surveillance signalled to me that in 1970, FTD's spooks were operating with more authority and leeway in the performance of their intelligence missions abroad than they had at previous conferences. Their presence in Konstanz was obvious, and they were there in full force.

Lindau, Germany, October 7, 1970: As I was lining up an appointment with members of the Eastern bloc the following day, an ex-Air Force officer, whom Diane and I barely knew—we subsequently began calling him *the Red Baron*—asked us to join him for dinner. I politely declined, feeling that my time could be better spent with the Eastern bloc researching material for my book. The Red Baron persisted, and I again declined. His aggressiveness and adamant proposition that we have dinner with him was noteworthy because he wouldn't look me in the eye. Little did I know at this time that I may have averted a major confrontation with FTD's operatives, for I was to learn later through a personal horrifying experience that "dinner invitations" were used by "Uncle Sam" to intimidate American citizens in the name of national security.

A passenger ferry on Lake Constance, October 7, 1970: Academician Georgiy Ulanov was conversing with me as a sweet little old lady, a representative of the United States Air Force at Wright-Patterson Air Force Base, stood but thirty feet away, holding a Japanese-made Canon camera. She raised the camera, zoomed in on Ulanov with a telephoto lens one would expect to see at the Hialeah Race Track, and snapped the Russian's picture. Seeing that Ulanov was visibly disturbed, she approached us and addressed me: "Peter, how are you! I have your picture!" Ulanov quickly excused himself, disgusted over the attempt to cover up what would later become a dossier photograph in U.S. intelligence files.

Konstanz, Germany, October 8, 1970: Dr. Ivan Soukhanov, the Library of Congress supervisor who translated for me in Rome, said he had to talk with me right away. The discouraged Soukhanov explained that the Russians suspected he was a CIA agent —"They think all Russian Americans are CIA agents," he said—and consequently he was having problems learning anything of significance. "Some day," Soukhanov reflected, "I would just like to take a trip to Europe with my family without having to worry about answering questions. I'm getting too old for this."

"Would someone [in the States] be unhappy if you couldn't get answers to their questions?" I asked.

"Yes," he replied, taking out a wrinkled scrap of paper from his inside pocket. "Can you help me?" he pleaded, showing me the questions.

"Anything I learn [from the Russians] will be reported."

"Yes, but I must have something to show for my time."

I examined the questions scribbled on the paper. They appeared to have been prepared by a group of intelligence analysts who had spent their last ten years living in a cave; the answers to the rocket engine questions would in no way help Pratt & Whitney, Rocketdyne, or Aerojet build better rocket engines, but they would contribute greatly to the make-work paper mill in Building 828. "God," I said, "don't waste your time on this."

"Can't you give me anything?" he asked pathetically.

"Report this," I replied. "Gennadi Dimentiev told me the Russians plan to develop a hypersonic aircraft that could be used both as the booster in their space shuttle and as a long-range high Mach number bomber weapon system." I provided Soukhanov with technical details such as Mach number and staging altitude, and he diligently wrote the information down on his pad. I knew that the information would be welcomed by the military establishment because it supported its position that the United States lagged behind the Russians in scramjet technology. I was curious how the information would be used and whether it would find its way into a Defense Intelligence Agency report—this was an interesting experiment, because Gennadi Dimentiev never told me any such thing!

Normally after a foreign trip, I would fill out an expense report that covered my hotel and meal expenses. This time, since just-promoted Assistant General Manager Richard Coar had ruled that I was to be responsible for all expenses associated with the trip, I did not fill out any report, in spite of the fact that I was on company business when I met officials of the Bolkow Space Division in Germany. Robert Atherton and Richard Mulready, the senior managers of the company's most advanced rocket engine program, had given me the go-ahead to visit the Germans with the hopes of luring them away from Rocketdyne so that Bolkow could reach an agreement with Pratt & Whitney instead; the objective of this maneuver was to enhance the company's chances of winning a potential one billion dollar contract to build NASA's space shuttle rocket engines. My negotiations with the Germans led to two secret sojourns by company program manager Richard Mulready to Munich in 1970 and 1971, yet it was ordained that I was to pay for all expenses associated with the 1970 trip. This background, and that in the following paragraphs, is mentioned here because it relates to what is later referred to as the "December 1970 blow-up" and it offers insight into Pratt & Whitney's decision-making process, my status during this period, and more significantly, what would turn out to be the most bizarre period in Pratt & Whitney's history in its dealings with the U.S. intelligence establishment.

Tuesday, October 13, 1970: I received a letter from the Germans. The letter said: "We . . . ask you, to examine the possibility that one of your gentlemen, officially entitled to discuss the ideas presented by you, should visit us shortly here in Ottobrunn." The Germans did not sign a contract with Rocketdyne and they appeared to be interested in what Pratt & Whitney could offer on a possible German-American space shuttle rocket engine venture. With the German letter in my possession, I summarized the results of my two-day visit in Ottobrunn before Richard Mulready, senior program manager of the space shuttle engine, and other members of the Pratt & Whitney shuttle team. They were surprised that I had made such inroads with the Germans, and when I volunteered that I had invited members of the Bolkow design team to Pratt & Whitney, Frank McAbee, a member of Mulready's staff, who would later be promoted to executive assistant to the chairman of United

Aircraft Corporation, gasped: "If I know [general manager] Gorton, the closest your German friends will get to the facility will be the Beeline Highway [on the other side of the gate]." Mulready blushed. I had put my job on the line, and there was no turning back. It was company policy that nothing could be done without Gorton's approval—this was no exaggeration—but Gorton wasn't in Germany and the circumstances of the situation dictated that I use my judgment. I asked Mulready to acknowledge the German's letter as soon as possible. He said his hands were tied until he could brief Gorton on the arrangement.

Thursday, October 15, 1970: I called the space shuttle office to find out the status of the German project, and if I still had a career with Pratt & Whitney. I was told that Mulready tried to see Richard Coar, the assistant general manager, but was rebuffed; the Air Force was visiting the facility to attend a quarterly review meeting on the F-15 jet engine, and Coar's time was occupied for the remainder of the week.

Friday, October 16, 1970: I learned that Mulready had made an appointment to see Coar on Monday, October 19. The bureaucracy was stifling! I was amazed that the senior program manager of the Pratt & Whitney space shuttle rocket engine did not have the authority to write or telephone the Germans, and he had to wait almost a week before he could explain the problem and even ask permission to do so.

Monday, October 19, 1970: Mulready discussed the Bolkow venture with Coar, who would not approve the telephone call to Germany unless B. A. Schmickrath, president of Pratt & Whitney at the division headquarters in East Hartford, Connecticut, approved. Back in May 1969, Gorton sent Schmickrath a memorandum stating that at least in the area of foreign technology, the Air Force thought that Pratt & Whitney was doing a good job. On my copy of the memorandum, Lowell Ruby had written across the top that the 1969 foreign technology effort vis-à-vis the Air Force was accomplished practically single-handed by me. Now, a year and a half later, Pratt & Whitney president Schmickrath was being asked to make a decision that would not only affect the company's space shuttle effort, but my career.

The following week I received the expected telephone call from Super Smart. "Pete, we heard you did quite well on your vacation."

"You might say that," I replied.

"Are you going to write a report?"

"Yes, I am."

"Will you let us see it?"

"I see no reason why I should. You weren't interested in my proposals before the trip. Why the sudden change of heart?"

"Pete, we don't control what our neighbors [the Operations Directorate] do." He was talking cryptically about the spooks, as if he had no personal dealings with them himself, which was a farce.

"Well if that's your position, then you have no right even asking, do you?" (I.e., the collection of intelligence is exclusively the spooks' responsibility.)

There was a pause. "You were pretty obvious in Germany."

"I wasn't hiding behind pillars or flower pots staring at you know who, like some of your people, if that's what you mean."

"My people?" he retorted.

"Yes, your people. They wouldn't leave us alone in Rome or Konstanz. Anything I report will be handled by the other organization through official channels. I desire no contact with your people regarding my trips."

"That's your right," James Bartley said, listening on an extension. "I'm sorry," he continued, "there's a lot of politics that we have to fight. Pete, about your letter. We could offer you $10 an hour for up to fifty hours." James Bartley was referring to my letter proposing to do analysis work for them. "I'd have to caution you," he added. "Some people have lost their jobs over it. That happened to a guy on the West Coast."

"Thanks for the offer, Jim, but I'm really not interested. I'm planning to write a book on the intelligence establishment and . . ."

"Don't do that!" he cut in.

"I'll tell you about it in private, if we ever get together again."

"Pete, our time is up. They're timing our calls. We'll call again." They hung up. Under the circumstances, the call may have been taped; I hoped it was.

How things had changed! When I first got involved with FTD I was one of millions of Americans who had been brainwashed into believing that the military intelligence services were highly competent and efficient in collecting, analyzing, and disseminating intelligence relating to the national security of the United States. This myth, perpetuated by a Defense Department public relations bureau adept at Madison Avenue salesmanship—such as the literature the DIA had sent me in 1967, when I was considering employment with them—had been swallowed hook, line, and sinker by an uninformed Congress and public, including people like myself. Having worked and talked with FTD agents, I found competent men overshadowed and outnumbered by incompetent bureaucrats who had secretly abused their position with impunity and complete disregard for the taxpayer and our national security.

October 22, 1970: With H. Norm Cotter and Lowell Ruby's approval, and only after Assistant General Manager Richard Coar had reread the censored version of the second annual foreign technology report, I forwarded a memorandum to Pratt & Whitney's customer communications control and asked them to distribute the report to the personnel approved by the Air Force Rocket Propulsion Laboratory. I reviewed its history: I started working on the report in June 1969; the draft was completed in February 1970; the first version was printed in July 1970; the censored version was printed in September 1970; and it was being distributed in October 1970.

October 23, 1970: B. A. Schmickrath, President of Pratt & Whitney, approved of my Bolkow negotiations, and Mulready's deputy was permitted to telephone the Germans. It was tentatively agreed that Mulready would secretly visit Bolkow in Ottobrunn, Germany, during the first week in November and represent Pratt & Whitney officially. I was privately hoping that I could accompany Mulready on the trip, but those thoughts were snuffed out by Frank McAbee (currently executive assistant to the chairman of United Aircraft Corporation) when he told me in so many words: "Don't call us, we'll call you." This also buried my hopes of getting the company to reimburse me for my expenses, including hotel, meals, and travel. Instead, I was left with the feeling that I should have been thankful that I still had a job. If I needed a stimulus to act more in the national interest rather than only Pratt & Whitney's interest, which I didn't, the Bolkow episode was the icing on the cake.

The conditions were ripe to do something I had wanted to do for about a year. My foreign technology report was finished; I had the Air Force release letter; it was being distributed, and I had no intention of writing another report. I already questioned the competence, integrity, and operations of FTD, and I could no longer prostitute myself for the benefit of Pratt & Whitney or FTD. The policy "Do anything to please the Air Force" was wrong. Accordingly, on October 27, 1970, I wrote a memorandum to Lowell Ruby and Norm Cotter and asked to be phased out of the company's foreign technology program. I recommended that the company do likewise.

Cotter asked me into his office for a verbal explanation. "I no longer wish to act as a buffer between the company and FTD," I said. "And I believe that further association with FTD's espionage agents might endanger Diane. I think it's clear to everyone that they're using the agreement to co-opt engineers to perform spy missions for them. I don't want my name connected with them, I don't want one of their hacks walking around with my name in his briefcase, and I strongly recommend that you take my advice in the memo—they're bad news!"

"If that's how you feel about it," Cotter said, "we'll honor your request. I guess Lowell [Ruby] will have to handle the correspondence now." Cotter handed me my memorandum. "You could write a book about your experiences."

"Yeah, but that's downstream." Cotter was nobody's fool, and though he may have suspected that I had decided to blow FTD out of the water, I didn't want to alarm him and admit that those were my long-range intentions—at least not now.

22

October 29, 1970: I wrote to Justin F. Gleichauf, chief of the CIA Miami field office, and informed him that I intended to incorporate my personal notes into the book I was writing. Because I wished to sever completely my ties with FTD, I wrote:

> In the future, I also request that any notes that I do transmit to you be kept within your organization, and under no circumstances are they to be made available to the military. The reason for this is that as a private citizen, I do not wish to be subjected to the harassment and treatment that I have received in the past for wanting to transmit my notes through your organization only.

Gleichauf visited me at Pratt & Whitney several days later and I filled him in on Russia's interest in reaching a science and technology agreement with the West and the fact that Premier Aleksei Kosygin wanted a US-USSR summit conference; this was information I had acquired from first-hand sources. Gleichauf wanted to run the gist of my discussion with Dimentiev and Riazantsev through CIA headquarters in Langley before I contacted the State

Department, as the Russians had requested. I promised to sit on it until I heard from him.

I told the CIA agent that I was rewriting my secret report for public consumption—I was concerned with Soviet weapons developments and the fact that the company had whitewashed my conclusions—and I planned to attend future conferences with the idea of using the new data in the book.

Gleichauf said that the CIA couldn't comment on the book, but he confirmed that all intelligence I submitted to the CIA in the future would be restricted to its headquarters and the CIA would reject requests by FTD to debrief me. Thus, after almost three years of association with FTD, the spooks in Building 828 would learn through company and government channels that I had severed relations with them.

By November 1970 the battle lines were drawn and my friends in Pratt & Whitney and the intelligence establishment surmised that I was secretly putting together the story on Building 828. In what I thought was an explosive and damaging indictment of FTD, I was sent a memorandum dated November 18, 1970, by the Eagle. He attacked a classified intelligence assessment authored by an FTD analyst named Michael A. Pennucci, in which it was recommended that FTD participate in the exploitation of certain Russian aerospace hardware. *The Eagle noted, however, that he had seen the draft of the Pennucci report in 1968 in a Holiday Inn in the possession of its real author, an engineer affiliated with General Electric.* The Eagle noted that items 2 and 3 in Section VII of the Pennucci report, identification number FTD-CR-20-36-70, were designed to enhance the personal, professional, and financial status of its real author, whose company would benefit from the recommended FTD program. The Eagle concluded that this was another event in which one would be justified in questioning the relative level of ethics and professional integrity allowed in Building 828.

November 20, 1970: Gleichauf called and recommended that I notify the U.S. Department of Commerce about the Konstanz proposal—the U.S.-USSR technical exchange. He gave me the name and address of the man the CIA thought I should contact. "Are you going to pursue the proposal through the Department of Commerce?" I asked.

"Heavens no, Peter. They're very much independent of our shop. Keep me informed."

On November 21, 1970, I mailed letters and handwritten attachments to the U.S. Department of Commerce and the Department of State. The Department of Commerce letter read:

Mr. John S. Shepard
Director, Technical Data Division
Office of Export Control, Room No. 2225
U.S. Department of Commerce
Washington, D. C. 20230

Dear Mr. Shepard:
A U.S. government official advised me to (1) inform you of Soviet interest in a particular technical exchange and (2) seek
your advice and assistance. The attachment is provided for your
retention and contains an account of the private matter in question. As the attachment indicates, your interest and guidance
would be very helpful. . . .
I am looking forward to hearing from you and hope that we can
discuss the matter in more detail in the immediate future.

Very truly yours,

Peter N. James

On December 10, 1970, Diane telephoned me at work and said
that we had received a letter from the Red Baron, the ex-Air Force
officer who had invited us to dinner in Germany. The Baron said
that he would be passing through Miami International Airport on
Sunday, December 20, and realizing that we were only seventy
miles away, invited us to meet him and hit the night spots on
Miami Beach. Under the circumstances, I suspected the Baron's intentions because with FTD officially cut off from me, the agents in
Building 828 may have been trying to reestablish personal contact,
mainly to find out what I was up to. I accepted his invitation; intelligence, whether domestic or foreign, was still a two-way street
and if my suspicions were right, I could learn more about FTD's
long-range plans.

December 11, 1970: The Eagle telephoned from East Hartford
and in very cryptic language notified me that an investigation of
United Aircraft Corporation (i.e., the Pratt & Whitney division, et
al.), employees and FTD was in progress. Because I was still known
as "Mr. Foreign Technology," though I had quietly disengaged
from further involvement with FTD, the Eagle wanted me to know
about the investigation in the event I was drawn into it. He mentioned that the FBI, Department of State, and Charles Mahan, deputy security officer for the corporation, were conducting inquiries
in East Hartford, and the Swimmer was being investigated because
of his "performance" in Brussels. I assured the Eagle that I had
never been involved with any of FTD's overseas operations, and

163

that as early as July 1969 I cautioned the company about getting involved with FTD's overseas intelligence operations.

"They should have heeded your advice, Pete," he said, "because this is one investigation that neither FTD nor the company will be able to sweep under the rug."

I telephoned Supervisor of Plant Protection Leo Faucher's office. "Leo's not in now," Lucille Hoagland, his faithful secretary, replied. Whenever Gleichauf would visit me in Pratt & Whitney, it was Lucille who would call and let me know when the CIA agent was in the building.

"Lucille," I asked. "Does the name Charles Mahan mean anything to you?"

"No . . ." She sounded unsure.

"Tell Leo I'll call back."

Half an hour later, Leo Faucher telephoned me, and after I mentioned my discussion with the Eagle, he asked me to drop by his office so we could talk. Without the knowledge of my superiors, Lowell Ruby and Norm Cotter, I met the security chief behind closed doors in his office. He asked what I knew about Mahan's investigation. I summarized what little I did know, and added: "Apparently one of our managers is being investigated."

"Who?"

"I'd rather not say."

"Would that name be [the Swimmer]?" he asked.

"That would be a good guess. How did you know?"

"[The Eagle] has made allegations to this effect," Leo talked in guarded generalities and I began to get the impression that he did not know the extent of the company's involvement with FTD, nor fully understand its implications. Assuming that he would be asked questions by the FBI and Department of State about the company's dealings with FTD, I said: "Leo, I think it's time we had a long talk. I'd like to tell you about FTD's operations, but I want your promise that anything I say will not reach their ears upstairs [Ruby and Cotter]."

"Anything you say won't leave the room," he replied.

It took me an hour to start from the beginning and describe FTD's foreign and domestic operations: how they were recruiting engineers from the Florida facility to spy abroad; how FTD attempted and finally succeeded in obtaining a list of company engineers; its use of post office boxes to bypass the company's government mail control system and the security department; how it was obtaining company secrets, and the likelihood that the company's competitors were benefitting from the arrangement; how intelligence reports were used as bait to elicit company favors or secrets;

how it manipulated intelligence; how FTD intimidated East Hartford and the Eagle and attempted to get him replaced because his assessments differed with theirs; how Nicholas Post attempted to intimidate me over the telephone because I wouldn't allow two of his people to debrief me; how FTD tried to recruit me, and then after I would not agree to cooperate, how it harassed both Diane and me on our last trip; the fact that it placed Americans traveling abroad under surveillance; how it planned to spy on our European allies; etc.

When it was over, Faucher was speechless. The chief of security for Pratt & Whitney's Florida Research and Development Center sat in his chair, shaking his head, unable to comprehend how all this could have transpired during his tenure, let alone in the United States.

"Would you object if I got this down on paper?" he asked. "Lucille can transcribe it . . . she's my private secretary. I'll keep the record in my personal files." Making a verbal statement to the chief of security was one thing; allowing his secretary to transcribe it was another—I was naming names and dates of memoranda I had written, alerting Ruby and Cotter of FTD's ambitions and the dangers of getting involved with FTD's overseas operations. My recommendations had been ignored, and now, Lowell Ruby, with H. Norm Cotter's approval, was making plans to attend an international conference in Rome during the spring of 1971. Both Capt. Hal Gale and James Bartley had intimated during my last visit to Building 828 that the Operations Directorate was firming up plans to approach both Cotter and Ruby. In fact, in my last FTD trip report dated July 31, 1970, I said that the Operations Directorate was interested in working closer with the Florida division—it was on the record.

Faucher was waiting for my decision. This was dynamite; there was no other interpretation; my superiors would be implicated.

"Okay Leo, let's get it down on paper." I could see four years of college and eight years with the company riding on the solemn word of the security chief.

Using a court recorder and again behind closed doors, Lucille Hoagland transcribed my statement. Leo Faucher inserted his own comments into the record as well. Two hours passed since I had entered his office. My palms were sweaty, reminding me of the time I had taken a lie detector test in the CIA's Langley headquarters. It didn't take a genius to recognize the enormity of the situation, nor that I was describing for the Pratt & Whitney security chief a secret spy complex that had infiltrated private industry.

165

Using the tactics of George Orwell's Big Brother, FTD was expanding its empire by leaps and bounds, and it had successfully avoided detection by law enforcement and corporate security officials because its contacts with private industry seemed legitimate.

"Leo, we've only scratched the surface," I said, as Lucille collected the unedited transcript. "I'll put together more material for your use next week."

"Good," he said. "The Defense Department will be here on a security inspection and Mahan will be here too. Get them here early next week, before his visit. Monday would be helpful." With his Defense Department obligations, I was counting on Faucher to notify investigators in the Defense Department and FBI of my charges so that the matter could be looked into without costing me my job.

I brought my files home to prepare a general write-up for Faucher and handwrote a personal thirteen-page memorandum to supplement the transcribed statement. I transmitted this memorandum, plus letters of company-FTD correspondence, to Faucher via his secretary Lucille Hoagland in a double-sealed envelope on December 15, 1970.

On December 17, 1970, at 9:10 A.M. the caldron boiled over. Leo Faucher and Charles Mahan, the firecracker deputy security manager for United Aircraft Corporation, visited me in my office and asked what I knew about the company's relationship with the U.S. intelligence establishment, and particularly if I knew of any employees who were under private contract with FTD. Both Faucher and Mahan mentioned the Swimmer. I disclosed the encounter I had with the Swimmer in the men's room and later in his office, when he admitted being approached by FTD intelligence agents to spy for them. I also mentioned seeing the Snake and another man enter his office at a later date. The nature of Mahan's questions indicated a gross lack of coordination between the company's management and its security departments.

The meeting ended at 10:45 A.M., and both Mahan and Faucher assured me that Lowell Ruby and Norm Cotter would not be told about the substance of our discussions.

Minutes after they left, I received a call from a man with CIA connections. "Pete," he said. "What's happening in Florida?"

"With respect to what?" I asked.

"The Agency [CIA]."

"It's a private corporate matter," I replied.

"Anything the Agency did?"

"I don't think so, but I don't have all the facts."

"For what its worth," he said, "[The Swimmer] is being investigated for a possible violation of federal statutes. It's already reached the Executive Office! They're trying to pin down whether [the Swimmer] was under private contract with FTD when he was in Brussels. The FBI was brought into the case because there were reports that he allegedly violated export control regulations and the espionage act; he may have divulged classified information to the Soviets." This was strong stuff. And it was ironic! I had advised the Swimmer against getting involved with FTD on a covert operation and urged him to keep Faucher's security department informed. The thrill of a James Bond adventure, however, appealed to him. The Swimmer participated in an overseas intelligence mission—his first and last—and now he was being investigated by the FBI and Department of State, and Pratt & Whitney was in trouble.

The caller continued: "The problem's been compounded by United Aircraft headquarters. Someone told [government] investigators that [the Swimmer] was on company business; but it appears that he either turned in no company expense report or he did not bill the company for expenses!"

My heart leaped: the uncanny condition of my last trip to Europe was that the company would pay for no expenses, even though I was on company business when I visited the Bolkow Space Division; this ruling was legislated by assistant general manager Richard Coar according to my immediate superior, Lowell Ruby. It was getting involved.

It appeared that the FTD connection was about to blow up in the company's face—something that the Eagle and I said would probably happen—and that government investigators had not been told about FTD's role. Was the company involved in a cover-up to protect the "Air Force?" Was that the real purpose of the Mahan visit? Since I had spelled out in no uncertain terms that the Swimmer had indeed been in personal contact with FTD agents, it appeared that Faucher and Mahan were now obligated by law to notify government investigators of both my verbal and written statements, since according to my source the Swimmer was being investigated for a violation of federal statutes and the matter had reached the Executive Office. The seriousness of the problem was growing exponentially by the minute.

With Mahan and Faucher conducting inquiries on the ground floor of the Florida facility, on the second floor Lowell Ruby was firming up his plans to participate in the 1971 Rome conference. I dropped by Ruby's office, and without violating the confidence of the security department, I advised him that company engineers who were under private contract with FTD were being investigated by the government.

"I'll take my chances," Lowell said, having already taken care of most of the conference paperwork. His participation in the Rome 1971 meeting had been approved by H. Norm Cotter. This was consistent with the fact that Cotter, who had to approve all my trips abroad, told me earlier in the year that he had approved the Swimmer's trip to Brussels; Cotter didn't bother asking the Swimmer who was funding it, though he said that he assumed FTD was behind it.

Friday, December 18, 1970: I was called into Ruby's office. Red-faced Norm Cotter had just returned from a meeting with his superiors, and from the short staccato jabs he was giving Lowell Ruby, it appeared that General Manager W. L. Gorton had been admonished by United Aircraft corporate headquarters because the Pratt & Whitney Aircraft Florida division engineers were performing spy missions for FTD. Pointing to the dejected Ruby, who to my knowledge had never spied for FTD, Cotter barked: "And make sure you cancel that trip to Rome!" Ruby glumly stared at his desk top. The head of the systems analysis department then turned toward me and said, "And that includes you too! And no book!" He looked for my response. "Is that understood? NO BOOK!"

"No book," I parroted, realizing that he would have fired me on the spot if I had failed to respond. "I don't understand [general manager] Gorton's position," I finally said, treading on thin ice. "I've never worked for FTD and my contacts with the CIA have been monitored by the security department. Besides, you know how I feel about FTD."

"That doesn't matter!" he shouted. Pointing to my chest, Cotter threatened: "If you ever leave the United States for any reason, you'll place your job in jeopardy!" He paused to weigh the impact of what he had said. "In fact, I'll make it even stronger than that. If you ever leave the continental United States for any reason, whether it's for a vacation, or a weekend, without [general manager] Gorton's permission, you'll be fired!" I had been carrying on a campaign against the wisdom of continuing an association with FTD, and now I was being punished because the company's first overseas venture for FTD had backfired; this was one of the reasons why over the years I had refused to have contact with intelligence agents while attending international conferences. "And you can tell [the Eagle] that if I ever see him down here again, I'll punch him in the nose!" My Lord, I thought. The Florida division was holding the Eagle personally responsible for the investigation.

And why was I being reprimanded? Did Faucher show my statement to the general manager?

"The ruling's not fair," I said. "It was a direct result of my conference activities that Pratt & Whitney is negotiating with the Germans now. Doesn't Gorton know that I was the one who initiated the negotiations?"

"I don't know," Cotter answered. That said a lot. I had risked my career to improve Pratt & Whitney's space shuttle competitive position, and the space shuttle office was taking credit for the German venture. In fact, the engineering department was already giving Richard Mulready credit for the "shrewd" German deal.

"What about the technology exchange the Russians expressed interest in? What if the State Department wants to pursue it?"

"Then work for the State Department!" he replied sarcastically. "And no book!" he thundered. Cotter stormed out of the office leaving Ruby and me in the shadows of his echoes.

I was now in a precarious position. I had blown the whistle on FTD, corporate headquarters was in an uproar, the security department had a lengthy transcript in which I had named names, I had been threatened to be fired by my department head, the company feared my work on the book, and General Manager W. L. Gorton had recently announced that there would be a reduction in work force at the Center. I thought I had done the right thing by cooperating in confidence with the security office, but now I wondered. I didn't know whether the corporate investigation was aimed at getting at the facts, or whether it was an attempt to cover up the company's involvement with FTD by plugging up the leaks. To get an answer to this question, I contacted a source with close CIA connections. He responded both verbally and later in writing. His note read:

United Aircraft management is still hopelessly ignorant of the facts. My CIA friend says that he gave warnings about . . . and the Brussels set-up for [the Swimmer] . . . at the time Charlie Mahan ignored the warning. There was plenty of flack that started right after [the Swimmer's] performance [in Brussels]. When Mahan came to Florida . . . he had been chewed out plenty for his failure to take action, State [Department] and FBI really jumped on him. So the result was a big cover-up to protect Mahan.

I cornered the Swimmer, who was also blaming the Eagle for clipping his wings. "He's jealous, don't you think . . . huh, Pete?" the Swimmer asked me, nervously pacing back and forth, combing his hair. The Swimmer seemed oblivious to the fact that charges had been made against him. I returned to my office and telephoned the Eagle and briefed him on the turmoil in Florida.

"Well, they got caught with their pants down," he said. "Any problems they have, they brought on themselves! They should have listened to us."

A girl from the company's security control station called later in the afternoon to tip me off that Pratt & Whitney security chief Leo Faucher ordered the immediate destruction of the remaining nonassigned twenty-seven copies of my annual foreign technology report. I telephoned Ernie Woleslagle, Faucher's assistant, and was told that the "need-to-know" Pratt & Whitney used to obtain classified information from the Air Force on foreign technology had expired on July 15, 1970, with the declassification of the XLR129 rocket engine program. This was legal mumbo-jumbo. He could not explain why management had waited until December 18—the day of the blow-up and about six months after the rocket engine program was declassified—to enforce the ruling, especially since fifty copies of the report were distributed outside the Center three months after the contract expired. I asked Woleslagle to save the documents. He said that there were a number of ways, all approved by the Department of Defense Standard Practices and Security Manual, that the company could use to retain the secret report.

"Then help me," I pleaded.

"You kidding?" he asked. "The boss [Faucher] made the decision. I'm not going to stick my neck out!"

I telephoned two company security subcontrol stations, and using my authority as assistant project engineer and author of the report, I ordered them not to do anything until they heard from me again. I was trying to buy time, hoping a miracle would save them. Faucher heard about my order and telephoned me again. "Pete, the reports have to be destroyed!"

With my telephone ringing by the minute, Bob Bradie, an assistant project engineer sharing my office, shouted: "Hey Pete, what are you running, a bookie joint? What's going on?"

I was mentally exhausted by the end of the day and enroute home I felt that there were few managers in the Center I could trust. While Les Harrell, my administrative supervisor, said that H. N. Cotter and Lowell Ruby had me rated as "above average," I realized that the rating no longer meant anything. My attempts to get the FTD story out privately and responsibly had boomeranged. From what I could gather, the Florida division management had decided to destroy the foreign technology reports because they tied the company in with FTD, and until the FBI and State Department investigations were completed, the FTD connection was one relationship they could not advertise. They had to keep the lid on and ride out the investigation, but they had a problem: I had made statements to the security chief and I had indicated a willingness to write a book.

On the evening of December 20, 1970, Diane and I met the Red Baron at Miami International Airport. We drank and danced the night through, and when it was over at daybreak in a coffee shop of Miami International Airport, the Baron asked what hotel we planned to stay at for the 1971 space conference in Brussels.

"We'll keep you informed," I said, suspecting that we did not know the Baron well enough to have merited the red carpet treatment, and our night on the town may well have been written off as an FTD domestic operations expense. What would follow remained to be seen, but Brussels appeared to be the key to the Red Baron's Miami visit.

To compound the chaos at the Center, the prestigious Hudson Institute, which performs special studies on national security issues, and a unit at Wright-Patterson Air Force base under contract with the Air Force Space and Missiles Systems Organization (SAMSO) in Los Angeles, requested copies of the foreign technology report. Both were flatly rejected by Pratt & Whitney on the grounds that "all available copies have been distributed," when numerous copies of the report were stored in company files waiting to be burned by Faucher's security force.

I was overcome by an indescribable feeling. Allegedly mature men were following orders beyond belief for fear of losing their jobs. At first the Nazis burned books, then they burned men. The thought of Faucher's uniformed security officers purging files and burning my work—for political expediency at that—sent a chill down my spine. Was the "Air Force" applying pressure on the company? Where would it stop?

January 8, 1971: Bill King, a Pratt & Whitney field representative in Washington, telephoned and asked me to send a copy of the report to personnel from McDonnell Douglas Corporation who had heard about it from Charles Mathews, deputy associate administrator for manned space flight, NASA. I summarized the background of the report and the political turmoil in Florida. "What the hell's going on down there?" he asked.

171

"You can classify it as an attempt to sweep an incident under the rug," I answered.

"Who's making the decisions?" he asked.

"Who else?"

"Look, you guys are in no position to rock the boat with NASA! [because of the forthcoming space shuttle engine contract award]" King said. "Get me a reading and let me know what the hell they decide!"

I telephoned the security department to check on the status of the twenty-seven copies. '"They have been destroyed," I was told calmly. I quickly drafted a memorandum, hoping that the NASA involvement could at least salvage the remaining copies of the report signed out by managers in both the Pratt & Whitney Florida and East Hartford divisions. My memorandum to Lowell Ruby read as follows:

> During a meeting between personnel from McDonnell Douglas Corporation and NASA in Washington, Mr. Charles W. Mathews (NASA Deputy Associate Administrator for Manned Space Flight) recommended that the McDonnell people obtain a copy of our annual report on foreign technology. Our Washington Office would like instructions for following through on Mathews' recommendation.
>
> As I was directed by our security department, et al, not to distribute any additional copies of the document except for those previously promised . . . , I would appreciate guidance concerning any further distribution. To my knowledge eleven copies of the report exist in-house; two file copies and nine internally distributed.

This was my last-ditch effort; I feared another burning exercise with the objective being the complete destruction of all copies, except a file copy. I received Ruby's handwritten reply later that afternoon: the Center would no longer distribute the report.

I telephoned a civilian with close CIA connections and told him that the twenty-seven copies had been destroyed. Minutes after hanging up, to Bob Bradie's amusement, our office telephone rang again. My civilian friend said that his CIA contact was shocked when he heard about the fate of the twenty-seven copies. The word was spreading like wildfire in CIA headquarters that Pratt & Whitney in Florida was engaged in a "Fahrenheit 451" exercise.

23

January 20, 1971: W. T. Dwyer, the former head of security and now director of personnel, telephoned me. "Pete, you'll be receiving a letter from a Colonel Campbell from the State Department. Contact me when it comes in." This was totally unexpected.

"Is the Office of Munitions Control involved?"

"All I have here is a Colonel Campbell. He said something about you planning to visit the Soviet Union. See me when the letter comes in!"

After almost three months, the government's response to my letter of November 21, 1970, concerning Soviet interest in a science and technology agreement, was to contact the director of personnel at Pratt & Whitney!

February 1, 1971: The long awaited State Department letter, written by Mr. John W. Sipes, director of the Office of Munitions Control, arrived at my home by registered mail. The two-page letter was stamped, "Limited Official Use," and written on official Department of State stationery. The Limited Official Use marking was interesting since the State Department thought nothing of calling the Center and informing it of the contents of my private letter to them—especially the fact that the Russians had asked that I visit Moscow in 1971 to propose with official U.S. government backing a technology exchange between both governments. Sipes quoted federal statutes and regulations to discourage me from pursuing further discussions with the Russians. The fact that the State Department had contacted the director of personnel at Pratt & Whitney indicated that they were up in arms over the matter. I had violated no law, and I had kept H. Norm Cotter and the CIA fully informed of the Russian proposal. As if my problems with FTD and the company weren't enough, it now appeared that the State Department was exerting pressure on me to stay away from the Russians, as if it feared that I might learn about the details of the secret negotiations between U.S. and USSR negotiators; SALT I was being negotiated in Helsinki and Vienna, and it was no secret—based on my meetings with high-level Soviet officials in Venice, Mar del Plata, and Konstanz—that the Communist Party of the Soviet Union was intent on making private overtures through lower-echelon representatives to acquire long-term loans and American scientific and technological expertise to uplift a sagging economy which over the years had been mismanaged by Kosygin's Council of Ministers. I saw both a frightening clandestine military arms build-up behind the Iron Curtain and secret negotiations which would ultimately deliver American economic assistance and computers to the Soviets in exchange for their promise to act responsibly in the future and not blow us off the map. The State Department feared that my contacts may have been spilling the beans on the Soviet's negotiations with our government. There was a gap between what the American people were being told by the Nixon Administration and what was really going on behind the scenes in American-Soviet relations, and FTD was playing a decisive silent role in the negotiations. Unknown to almost everyone was the fact that an FTD pawn with the IBM Corporation was providing FTD with intelligence reports on Soviet computer technology while at the same time trying to work out a computer deal between the Soviet government and IBM! In effect, both FTD and IBM would benefit from the computer deal and the American people would pay the consequences.

I telephoned Gleichauf about the State Department letter. "It doesn't surprise me, Peter," he said. "Thanks for keeping us informed."

I waited two days before showing the letter to William Dwyer in the personnel office. He read it: "Are you going to reply to Mr. Sipes?"

"Yes, I intend to assure him that I have always acted in the best interests of the United States and I will keep him informed if I ever travel to the Soviet Union." Dwyer raised an eyebrow.

"Send us a copy of your reply."

Cotter later called me into his office and made it clear that the CIA was not helping the company any, and it was in my interest to reevaluate my priorities.

"What do you mean?" I asked.

"Gleichauf can't award us a contract! No matter how you feel about FTD, they're still a branch of the Air Force. Did you tell Gleichauf you no longer have a reason to see him?"

"He knows about my travel restrictions. If the company lets him through its doors, and he wants to see me, I'll accept." I wasn't about to do the company's dirty work for it. An ominous pattern was developing and the noose was getting tighter; I would be fired if I attempted to write the book; I would be fired if I crossed the Atlantic Ocean; and I placed my job in jeopardy if I cooperated with the CIA. I began to get the feeling that both Gleichauf and I had been made scapegoats for the ill-fated FTD operation. I detected a pro-FTD, anti-CIA policy emerging at the Center, and this placed the December blow-up in its proper perspective; I never did believe that FTD was really out of the picture.

As I was listing for my personal files the cast of FTD and Pratt & Whitney characters who had been in touch with each other, I received the following note from East Hartford:

Pete James. Today's question: Is [the Designer] tied up with the spooks? He and [the Swimmer] were here Friday checking up on things.

A subsequent check on the Designer—the man identified in the note—showed that he similarly covered the 1970 Brussels meeting with the Swimmer!

March 1, 1971: Lowell Ruby rushed up to my desk—I was now working on manpower and budget studies as his personal assistant—and exclaimed: "Just got a call from captain—I mean . . . listen to this—*Major* Gale. He wants you to fly up to the base for two days."

"I'm sorry, Lowell, I'm not interested."

"They want you to critique FTD's latest intelligence assessment."

"I'm not interested."

"They want to talk with *you*," Ruby said.

"I recall last October I sent a memorandum to you and Norm [Cotter] requesting that I be phased out of the company's foreign technology program. My request was granted . . . Lowell, they want my Rome and Konstanz data."

"There's nothing we can do now," he said apologetically.

"What about downstairs [General Manager Gorton and Security Chief Faucher]? I thought they ordered everyone to stay clear of FTD, or was this a hoax?" Ruby shrugged, pursing his lips. "Lowell, FTD is only interested in picking my brains. I don't want to go."

"This will be your last trip," he said. "We still have contracts with the Air Force, and you're our foreign technology expert. If I could send someone else, I would." I had been expecting this. I was disappointed that the request—I guess *order* would be a better word—had come from Lowell Ruby, a man I deeply respected at one time. I really believe he would have gone himself if he could, but FTD wanted to see me, and for reasons only he could explain, Lowell Ruby couldn't tell FTD no.

"Okay," I sighed. "When do you want me up there?"

"Be there Tuesday and Wednesday next week," he replied, very much relieved. Because the company was on an economy program, air travel of any employee had to be approved by a company department head. H. Norm Cotter approved the trip.

March 8, 1971: I flew into Dayton and quietly checked into the Falcon Motel in Fairborn, Ohio, in the evening. This time there was no thump on the door. I was planning to step out for a drink but changed my mind when I saw the television movie *Vanished* on the screen. The script became more realistic with each passing moment, and when an American scientist registered a complaint that the U.S. intelligence community was recruiting American scientists to attend international conferences to spy on their own colleagues, I thought I was seeing a scenario of things to come. I wondered how the spooks in Building 828 reacted to the young man's plea over nationwide television, though it was only a story.

Wright-Patterson Air Force Base, March 9, 1971: I drove to the air base, checked in at the registration desk, obtained a temporary vehicle pass, and drove through Area A to Building 828. I was greeted by Major Gale and escorted to a small conference room which reminded me of the Viet Cong interrogation rooms simulated on television; it was about the size of a bathroom and the walls were cracked. This was the third time that I had been in this particular room, and under the circumstances, FTD had plenty of reasons to record my conversation. Major Gale opened: "This is our latest intelligence assessment, Pete"—he slid a secret report across the table toward me—"and we'd like you to give us your comments. Naturally, we have nothing from your meeting in Konstanz."

"I'll give you my personal opinions. But I won't divulge anything I learned in Konstanz."

He grunted. "Well, if you want to give me your opinion, and include anything you learned as your opinion, it's fine with us."

He allowed me to read the assessment. I read a section on the Soviet space shuttle, an abridged version of my last foreign technology report; about 90 percent of the section had been extracted and rewritten from the report. "Is this document going to be released by FTD?"

"No, by the Defense Intelligence Agency."

"Then you're saying these views now represent an official assessment by the Defense Department?"

"That's right. You're the national estimate on the Russian shuttle." If I represented the national estimate, it said a great deal about the allocation of intelligence resources. I should have been elated that the Defense Intelligence Agency blessed my analysis, but I wasn't. All the agony of subsidizing my trips abroad and preparing an 800-page two-volume foreign technology report was coming to light, but something was missing. I continued reading the report, making a few corrections here and there on the spelling of Russian names, but I could make no significant changes because the assessment was already my own, and I had no intention of updating their report with what I had learned in Rome and Konstanz; that was for my book. As I flipped through the pages I realized that they not only accepted my analysis of the Russian shuttle effort, but some of my notes from the 1969 conferences—the ones the systems group in Building 828 wanted to discredit!

"Where's your other data? This report is based on my contacts in Mar del Plata."

"That shows how important your material is, Pete." I continued reading the assessment, finding nothing that I did not report a year earlier. It was now clear why they were so desperate for my latest input: since I was giving my data exclusively to the CIA, then the publication of its report would make it appear that the DIA lagged behind the CIA in the Russian shuttle assessment by about a year. I handed the report back to Major Gale.

"Hal, tell me, why is my name mud around here?"

"Jealousy. The operations people have been content to work with the lower level Russian engineers. But you've changed that. You have some people asking: 'Why are the directors, members of the presidium [of the USSR Academy of Sciences], and now, the assistant to the deputy premier of the Soviet Union [i.e., Georgiy Zhivotovskiy], willing to talk with you? What secrets are you giving away?' "

"You're talking about loyalty."

"Not me. But *some people* are! Maybe they're jealous because they're not the ones talking to these people. Why are you successful with the Russians?"

"If you want to learn something, you go to the top—to the men who know the answers. Your people aren't sincere in dealing with the Russians. You're really out to spook them. You hate Russians and they know you hate them. I might disagree with their form of government, but I like the Russian people and I always will. Yes, I've developed very good rapport because I've kept my word. And when they asked me something that required a classified answer, I told them the answer was classified, so I couldn't discuss it. Your people have lied to them left and right, and they're on to it. Ask yourself: how much can you learn if the Russians won't even give you the time of day, or if you have to spook them from behind pillars or flower pots? I'll stack up person-to-person contact against all your electric gadgetry and leeches."

"Some people think there's more to it than that."

"What would you say if I brought up this loyalty business with the CIA?"

"I wouldn't do that. You wouldn't want your name associated with an investigation of this nature." Gale was probably thinking of himself, since the CIA would ask who was challenging my loyalty.

"If a charge has been made, I'd like to clear it up."

"You've got a lot to learn about the operation of our government, Pete."

"I'd like to write a book on how your part of the government operates," I said, irked at his "I know something you don't know" attitude.

Gale jerked his head. "You tell this to anyone else, and they'll have your job!"

"Nonsense."

"If you want to get things stirred up around here, just tell them you're writing a book."

"It's been done before."

"Are you serious?"

"Yes." The major picked up the intelligence report from the table.

"Well," he mused. "Make sure I'm not here when it's published."

"I'll be responsible." Major Gale shook his head. As a group leader in FTD, he was obligated to inform his superiors that I was going through with the book.

I drove Major Gale and James Bartley to the Officers Club for lunch. "Have you written your Konstanz report?" Bartley asked.

"Yeah, it's about an inch thick, and it's in a safety deposit box," I replied, remembering that FTD had a special Mission Impossible team of thieves who believed that the end justified any means.

Gale smirked. "You're not taking any chances, are you?"

"You might say I learned from experience."

"You've got a lot to learn," Gale said.

"How long can you keep going to these conferences?" Bartley asked.

"I really don't know. Cotter threatened to fire me if I crossed the Atlantic. I hope to get around that. It's unconstitutional, you know."

"Unconstitutional! Ha!" Gale blurted, almost spitting out his food. "Pete, you're a hopeless case!"

"I've got some questions I'd like answered before I leave. I'm getting out of the business. I was never really in it, you know."

"No one will believe you!" Gale said.

"How long are you going to be here?" Bartley asked.

"Till three tomorrow."

"We'd better get together before you leave."

Later in the afternoon, before I returned to the Falcon Motel, I read a Defense Intelligence Agency report and ran across the item I had set up in Konstanz: erroneous information similar to what I verbally gave Ivan Soukhanov, the Library of Congress supervisor, appeared in the report as if it were factual; no attempt was made to indicate the data came from secondary word-of-mouth sources. The Defense Intelligence Agency assessment was worded so that the military could justify a related research and development effort in the United States, presumably to be managed by the military.

24

Wright-Patterson Air Force Base, March 10, 1971: I showered, dressed, and checked out at 8:00 A.M. This would be my last stay at the Falcon. I passed the Air Force Museum on my right and entered Area A at 8:10. After registering, the officer guarding the gate waved me through, not bothering to get outside his warm hut to check my visitation pass. I signed in at the reception desk, showed my identification and visitor's passes, and asked the receptionist to call Bartley. The conference rooms were all being used, but in the basement of Building 828 was a poorly lighted boiler room, perhaps the safest place to hold a meeting. Bartley closed the door. "Well, where do we begin?" he asked, his voice being barely audible over what appeared to be the hum of a distant fan.

"I'll let you carry the conversation."

"What did you think of our latest product?" he asked.

"Looks like you made good use of my work in Mar del Plata."

"We did . . . What do you want to know?"

"If the DIA is using my work in their finished intelligence assessments, why are there questions concerning my loyalty?"

"It's a long story," he said, offering me a cigarette. "First, we don't question your loyalty. You don't understand how the government operates. Let me start from the beginning." He paused to collect his thoughts. (Note: The paragraphs below contain a paraphrased version of the main thrust of the story I was told, written as if Bartley were speaking.)

"In the early sixties, a number of intelligence analysts responsible for assessing Soviet military capabilities were proven wrong when more tangible evidence on the Soviet posture came to light. Heads rolled, promotions were lost, and resignations followed. In the intelligence business, you're expected to do your job right, and you're hauled over the coals when you do it wrong. Over the years, the DIA and CIA made assessments which they later regretted. To take a position one year, and then, when more evidence comes to light, to completely reverse a position the following year, is not easy to do under our system. This makes everyone, including the brass, look like they don't know what they're doing. Some people can't rock the boat because their jobs are at stake, they have mortgages, and they have wives and children. If they make a bad assessment, they jeopardize everything. Assessments can be changed from the previous year, but they are seldom reversed.

"In the early-middle 1960s we were asked to take positions on a number of rocket-related areas. In some cases, we had only weeks to make assessments. Toward the latter part of the 1960s these assessments were cast in concrete. Then in the latter part of 1969, a man named Peter James attended a conference in Mar del Plata and came up with tons of intelligence that was diametrically opposed to the official positions taken by career intelligence analysts. The CIA reported you weren't working for them, but they had obtained your private notes. When the CIA reports reached us, it stirred up a hornet's nest. It didn't take long for things to get hot around here . . . Then your red report [second annual report] arrived, and it included the Argentina coverage. You never saw such a stir. The systems group wanted to discredit you. They got their copies and went behind closed doors to review it word for word. As their evaluation of your work progressed, reports started to trickle in from reliable and sensitive sources. The information corroborated your reports from Mar del Plata and the analysis in the red report. The CIA said your report had a great impact on their effort. You can't imagine what an impact the reports have had. The CIA distributed interdepartmental memos to this effect. As more reports came in, someone gave the order—it came from the top—to stop all efforts to discredit you. This was a blow to the systems group.

"Then you went to Konstanz and everyone here knew you were attending the meeting. We learned you were making the usual contacts. We waited for the CIA's coverage of your notes. In November, we got the word: You had nothing to report! This raised

181

cries: What happened? Impossible! The CIA is holding out! We asked the CIA for your notes again. They repeated you had nothing to report. Well, you can guess who started to raise questions about your loyalty. That's the status now," Bartley said, taking a puff from his cigarette.

"Under the circumstances, being an Albanian doesn't help my situation any."

"You Albanian?" he asked.

"First generation American. Both my parents were born in Albania."

"That's interesting."

"I know. With my Eastern bloc connections, the security people could have a lot of fun if they wanted to. You've cleared up most of my questions. This infighting shouldn't be permitted. It's destructive to your overall objectives. In theory, you shouldn't be concerned with what I give the CIA."

"You've got to remember our people are trying to do a job too. Are you going to keep working in this area?"

"I'm getting out. I want to work on a book. I think the public should be told what's going on and a few other things."

"Pete, there was one thing reported on you by our intelligence that caused concern. It even went up to the top."

"What's that?"

"You once told one of our people: 'Well, if the government won't support me on this, I'll do the damn thing myself!' Something like that. Anyway, the report said you're not willing to take orders."

"Oh, hell, Fred [the Pisa proposal] wouldn't play the game my way, so no agreement was reached. I'm not obligated to play by your rules. That's why I refused to see the two men in Florida."

"You were entirely within your rights."

"I know I was!"

"But that remark worried a lot of people."

"I'm bound by the laws of this country, not the espionage establishment."

"Laws in this business don't mean much," he said, knocking ashes to the floor.

"On your side of the fence, maybe not. But on my side, that's all we have."

"I could tell you stories that would make your hair rise. You understand why some people have raised questions, don't you? We were waiting to see the results of your last trip. No one believed you had nothing to report."

"I asked the CIA to restrict my future input to their Langley headquarters; they kept their word."

James Bartley and I talked in the boiler room until noon.

At the Officer's Club I broke bread for the last time with Major Harold Gale and James Bartley; they knew I had washed my hands of FTD. "After three years of association with your organization, I'm glad I'm independent of it." I opened, addressing Major Gale.

Bartley laughed as the major smiled wryly. "It's not all that bad. What's on your mind?"

"I'd like to voice some personal opinions independent of Pratt & Whitney's position. May I?" They both nodded. "The intelligence community needs to be reorganized. First, you're not getting the most out of your expenditures. And second, the users of the technical intelligence are not getting the data in time to be useful."

"We've sent you reports," Gale said.

"Let me be blunt. The company has yet to use in its rocket or jet engine programs anything you've sent us."

"I doubt that," Gale replied.

"I'm being candid. You won't get anyone in the company to tell you this officially. Look at our two major programs: the F-15 and space shuttle engines. Our engineers have not used any of your information in the design of those systems; that is saying a hell of a lot."

"Why?" Bartley asked.

"Because you can't design advanced engines using old Russian textbooks censored by the KGB."

"We're working on getting the material translated faster!" Gale said.

"That's not the answer. The industry needs modern foreign *hardware*, not high school translations."

"You're not taking advantage of the system, Pete. We've sent you reports. If Pratt chooses not to use the data, it's not our fault."

"You've sent junk! Answer this, Hal: why is it that when our country embarks on a major space shuttle development program— a program that will cost the taxpayer billions—the U.S. intelligence community has done nothing to support us with input on the Russian program? It's been over six months since my report was released; I identified Russian institutes, facilities, ministries, and personnel who are working on it. We've received absolutely no feedback. We're asking for your help. Aren't you working on it?"

"Yes," the major said, "but you know you represent the national estimate on this program."

"Baloney! It's a matter of stopping some of your unproductive in-house programs and reordering your priorities. You can stop translating almost all of the foreign publications you do translate. That's another area that would give the taxpayer a break."

"What's this taxpayer kick you're on?" Gale exclaimed.

"I believe it's our tax dollars, mine too, that pay your salary. How can you justify FTD's existence if the users of the intelligence collected never get to use it?" The major tapped his spoon on a saucer. "If there is good data around, it's being pigeonholed like my first report. Here's another one: why does the aerospace industry need you? It seems to me that if the military intelligence services can't give the industry the type of data it needs, we're better off setting up our own intelligence organization. Some companies are already doing this."

"You forget," Gale began, "our mission is to keep the *Pentagon* apprised of the Soviet military capability and threat. The aerospace industry is third on the totem pole."

"If we're third, then why must we play ball with you to obtain intelligence reports?"

"You don't have to."

"Yes, we do. You won't send us anything unless we promise to perform an analysis in return. Isn't that right?"

"Well, you don't expect us to perform a service without getting something in return, do you?"

"You are already getting paid by the taxpayer. He's not paying your salaries and subsidizing your covert programs so you can pigeonhole the results and build an empire. There's no reason why the aerospace industry can't use the results of your work with no strings attached."

"You've got it all wrong. We're not pigeonholing the data!"

"Then what happened to my 1969 report? It never got out of [Building] 828, even when we supplied the names of Air Force officers in the Pentagon we thought should see it. For the amount of money you're given, you're not doing the job that could be done, and the aerospace industry, other users of foreign intelligence, and the taxpayers are paying for it dearly."

Bartley took a bite of his sandwich. The major was being pushed into a corner to defend the military intelligence services and he looked as if he were ready to unwind.

"Pete, you do have access to intelligence with no strings attached. We're not a library service!"

"I don't think so. First, FTD approaches Pratt & Whitney. You promise to send us foreign intelligence if we promise to send you a yearly report in return. We agreed to cooperate in the area of liquid rockets. Then you approach the company and make a similar proposal in the area of airbreathing technology. When we say

184

we would like to receive the data, but don't have the manpower to prepare two yearly reports, you balk and take the position you won't send any airbreathing data; a position that is absurd since we're developing the engines for the Air Force's next air superiority fighter!"

"You could get the reports from other government sources," he replied.

"That's right. We've gone that route too. We get approached by ASD [Aeronautical Systems Division of the Air Force Systems Command] and they propose to send us intelligence in exchange for a report in return. Then the Army got involved. They were willing to send us foreign helicopter data, again in exchange for a contractual response. Each military agency promised to send us better intelligence than the other, but each would send the intelligence only if we promised to respond with a report. Where in the hell are all you guys getting the money to subsidize these ventures?"

"Look, if you establish the need-to-know, you can get DIA assessments from your contracting officer."

"That route doesn't work either, because no one will volunteer the names and identification numbers of the DIA reports on file for us to order. You won't, because then I could receive the same data elsewhere and no longer be obligated to prepare a report for you. And that applies to the other groups who want their own special deal. On this point, everyone plays dumb, as if a list of documents doesn't exist. You all have us at your mercy."

"I wouldn't say that," he replied.

"Well, I've done a great deal of thinking about this, and I've concluded that under the current system, you're forcing the aerospace industry to either get into the intelligence business, because you're not doing your job, *or take other action*. I'm speaking from a national position now. If your organization exists, it must be, as you say, for another purpose."

"Other members of the [aerospace] industry don't feel this way," Gale responded angrily.

"Like hell they don't. I know people in industry who would support a joint industry-government intelligence panel. I've already looked into it!"

"What?" the major cried. "You could be charged with collusion!"

"Baloney. I've looked into that too. Not if we deal exclusively with *foreign intelligence* and act in the *national interest*. I'm aware that such a plan would lessen the importance of FTD and other redundant intelligence activities that are unfortunately subsidized by the taxpayer; but if it makes useful intelligence available to the user, without a middleman, without the massive bureaucracy, without the private deals between the military and industry, it's got to be better. Accept it, Hal, the people who design, develop, test, and evaluate aerospace systems—the American aerospace industry—can evaluate foreign aerospace hardware and data more effectively than the intelligence community. The Russians reached this conclusion years ago. It works."

Major Gale sipped his coffee and cast a glance at Bartley. I continued: "If there is a coordinator of this work, it should be a non-military organization. Right now there is a conflict of interest. You have the power to assess the Soviet capability so that our country must develop the aerospace weapons systems that you also have contractual and management responsibility over. If you want the responsibility for developing new weapons, that's one thing, but let the civilians with guidance from the military prepare the intelligence assessments to determine whether we really need the weapons. That's something I intend to change."

"You'll never get it through!"

"I will, once I convince the decision-makers that you're smothered in bureaucracy, interoffice competition, jealousies, people who are more concerned over keeping their jobs than they are in doing a good job, a high turnover rate, poor security procedures that invite compromise, and other things that contribute to erroneous assessments. There's nothing wonderful about a big budget and a tremendous number of spooks. If the man-in-the-street were given a tour of Building 828 and seen what I've witnessed—on both the analysis and collection sides of the house—you'd all be out of business. Congress would close you down!"

"What do you intend to do?" The major was interested in my response, though he tried not to show it. He stirred his coffee with eyes on the table. James Bartley, the diplomatic analyst who was digesting more than his sandwich, looked in my eyes, as if to say: "Keep your mouth shut."

"I plan to write a book; I also plan to go to Congress with the problem." It was as if someone had spread a black veil over the table. The seconds passed.

Major Gale finally spoke: "We're all looking forward to seeing it." I dropped the major and James Bartley off at Building 828 and bid my other contacts good-bye.

As I was leaving Building 828, I met a former FTD intelligence analyst who was now assigned to another division. "Pete, you been talking with FTD?" I nodded. "Are you going back to Florida?"

"Yeah, what's up?"

"FTD blew the thermodynamics cycle on the FOXBAT [i.e., the Russian MiG-25 fighter and interceptor]; it's all wrong."

"Are they going to tell anyone officially?"

"No . . . That's why I'm telling you! They don't even know what kind of compressor the Ruskies are using."

"Thanks for telling me." What a fitting conclusion, I thought, to my now-strained relationship with FTD. When their assessment is proved wrong at a later date, their mistake will be covered up under the shroud of national security, and with the support of a few misguided newspapers they will pin the blame on the next crop of patriotic pilots—the way it was done to Francis Gary Powers.

As I approached my car an FTD agent caught up with me. "Pete, before you leave," he whispered, "I want you to know that we heard about the changes you want to make in the community. The whole place is buzzing. I agree with you, and I hope you can do it, and there are people here who support you too, but we can't go on record or they'll have our hide. Just be careful. I'm afraid you don't know how some people feel about it, or the extent the brass runs things here. Be careful!" The agent wished me luck and left. The clandestine exchange indicated that my plans to write a book were interpreted by the brass to mean that I intended to blow the Foreign Technology Division out of the water. The agent was encouraging me to press forward, yet he was also warning me, as if he had heard something in Building 828 that I should know about. I drove to the airport and boarded a jet for Palm Beach, leaving the groundswell behind.

25

Word about my writing plans spread like wildfire. FTD had a tiger by the tail and the U.S. intelligence establishment personnel who knew about the "James case" were polarized into two camps; either pro-CIA or pro-FTD. On March 23 a reliable CIA source tipped me off that FTD was generating a dossier on both Diane and me. "Pete," he said, somewhat concerned, "they're throwing Diane's name around carelessly."

"Thanks for the information. What else have you heard?"

"They've identified all your contacts in Rome and Konstanz. They have each meeting broken down by date, time, and place."

"Sounds like someone turned them loose in 1970. What the hell are they setting up . . . a police state?"

"Some people in Langley are worried over just that."

"You're joking."

"No I'm not."

"Who gave them the green light?"

"I don't know." I was worried about the unknown. I had enough on FTD to launch congressional investigations in a number of areas. But there was something else about the 828 operation that haunted me. Covert programs like the Hughes plan, military spying on Americans both at home and abroad, and now the comment that some persons in the CIA headquarters feared a drastic erosion of our individual freedoms by the federal government. I could handle FTD, but if the problem involved other branches of the government . . .

March 25, 1971: I received a telephone call from the security department notifying me that Justin F. Gleichauf was in the facility. I had with me a vinyl folder from the 1970 Rome conference. Inside were letters sent to me in January 1971 by two prominent Russian officials. I was reluctant to disclose their contents to the company's security department—the December blow-up and Fahrenheit 451 exercise cured me of this "moral obligation"—but with FTD embarked on a super-spook operation both to discredit me and to protect its own interests, I wanted the CIA to have a record of *The Kremlin Letters,* as Diane called them, just in case.

"Peter, it's been several months since I last touched base with you," Gleichauf said.

"Yes, a lot has happened since then. I've received several letters from the professor's friends [i.e., the Russians]," I said cryptically. "It appears that they are still interested [in having me visit the Soviet Union to propose a science and technology agreement]."

Leo Faucher and H. Norm Cotter joined us. The last time the company's security chief rode shotgun on a meeting between Gleichauf and me was in 1966. Gleichauf explained the nature of his visit. The CIA needed the company's cooperation to acquire information via overt means. Though Gleichauf's request was harmless —he asked me to write a letter to one of my contacts in Moscow— the chief of the CIA Miami office needed both my assistance and the company's approval. The difference between FTD and the CIA's methods of dealing with private companies was most apparent. As Gleichauf explained the problem to Faucher, Cotter interrupted him: "Mr. Gleichauf, you should know that Pete is placing his job in jeopardy if he continues his association or correspondence with his foreign contacts."

Gleichauf stopped, glanced at Cotter, and slipped the paperwork back into his briefcase. "Very well," he replied courteously. "That is why I am asking your permission. The matter is closed as far as our shop is concerned." The events of the past year had polarized Pratt & Whitney into two camps: East Hartford was pro-CIA; Florida was pro-FTD. With Norm Cotter's approval, Lowell Ruby had ordered me to cooperate with FTD against my wishes; thus I entered the lion's den in Building 828 only two weeks earlier. Now, Norm Cotter was ordering me not to cooperate with the CIA, and he made this abundantly clear before Faucher and Gleichauf. And

I placed my job in jeopardy if I maintained any contact with foreign scientists; this ruling was both an anti-CIA, anti-book position, and there was no other interpretation—it clearly benefited FTD. I said good-by to Gleichauf in the security department in the most formal surroundings ever, and I never did show him the Kremlin letters.

At 4:30 P.M. it was time to go home. The chances that the security guards would stop me for a search were remote, since I had a "number one" insert on my identification badge. During the past nine months, since my promotion to assistant project engineer, I had been stopped only once for such a search. I walked down the stairwell trying to beat the other engineers to the parking lot. At the door the security guard's eyes drifted down to my folder. I gave him the usual smile, and showed the badge clipped to my left breast shirt pocket. "Number one check today, Mr. James," the words rang out. Good grief! I looked into the guard's eyes and somehow maintained my smile. Not now, I was telling myself.

"Number one check!" I announced after him, using as definitive a tone as I could muster. Suddenly everything went through my head—my God; the Kremlin letters. If he sees the letters, I'm through. It was only a few hours earlier that Cotter had told Gleichauf: "You should know that Pete is placing his job in jeopardy if he continues his association or correspondence with his foreign contacts." There was no possible way I could explain the letters to management. I passed the folder to my right hand. Engineers were starting to pile up behind me. I reached for the zipper and said, "Ohh Kayee," imitating Astronaut Alan Shepard's Apollo 14 moonwalk jargon. I pulled back the zipper, wondering if the colorful Russian postage stamps were exposed or if the Cyrillic lettering of "Moscow" would catch the guard's eye. The edges of the letters were exposed. Would he pull everything out? Why was I singled out for a number one check? Was it related to Gleichauf's visit? Was it a trap to justify their new anti-CIA position? Did Faucher see my folder in the meeting with Gleichauf and wonder what was in it? The security guard started to part the folder with both hands; he was going to remove the material for examination. "Here . . . take your time," I said, thrusting the folder into his left hand. My heart was beating so hard that my badge seemed to move with each throb. With his free hand the guard began parting the sheets.

"Anything classified?" he asked.

"Nothing classified."

He spread the folder even more. The Russian postage stamps were exposed. The edges of the letters still faced him. He looked up at me. "Okay, Mr. James." I took the folder.

"See you tomorrow," I said, walking past the secured doors toward the parking lot. I came within inches of losing my job and the security guard came within inches of being a hero.

April 5, 1971: Leo Faucher reminded me that the company was still waiting to receive a copy of my reply to the State Department. I ignored his request. Then W. T. Dwyer, director of personnel, joined the chorus and similarly asked me about the "company's copy." It had been well over a month since I had written to the State Department, and I could have continued to refuse its requests on a constitutional basis, but I would have been looking for a job as well. I sent a copy of the letter to Faucher and defused the issue.

April 26, 1971: Lucille Hoagland, Faucher's secretary in the security department, called me. "Mr. Gleichauf would like to talk with you. Would you consent to see him?" she asked.

"Of course I would consent to see him," I answered. In the almost six years I had been dealing with the CIA, Lucille had never before raised the issue of whether I would *consent* to see Gleichauf.

I met Gleichauf the following day in the security department. One of Faucher's assistants escorted us to another conference room, and this time we were left alone. "It's good to see you again," I said.

"You're looking good, Peter. The reason why I'm here is that I want to invite Diane and you to dinner. I have been given a new assignment and I want to show my appreciation for all you have done for us over the years." His words rang in my ears. After six years, I couldn't believe that our relationship was coming to an end. He was just as professional, polished and mannerly as when I met him after the Athens trip in 1965. "Peter, I want you to know that words can't describe our appreciation of your work. You have contributed significantly to our national security, and you've helped me personally in the performance of my assignment."

Gleichauf handed me three sets of 8½ x 11 sheets: questions on the Rome and Konstanz conferences. I read the questions carefully and placed the material back on the table. "I don't want to do this to you," I began, "but I've got to . . . I'm not going to answer those questions, and I'll tell you why." He repositioned himself in his chair and waited for me to continue, not giving me any sign of approval or disapproval. "In the first place, those questions originated from FTD. I recognize the style and I can name the officers behind them. I was asked these questions at FTD last month. And I'm aware that you are following instructions; I doubt that you are even told who requested the information. My other reason is more important. I'm torn between withholding information that might be vital to our national security and transmitting this information to the proper authorities with the full knowledge that my contribution will also be used to justify future military intelligence operations. I've collected intelligence, while at the same time I've analyzed intelligence. Not many people have done this simultaneously. I've seen the results of this massive expenditure of resources and the results are not flattering. I am a taxpayer and I've tried to correct this situation internally. This included suggestions to you, to the proper military intelligence authorities, to members of the Executive Office, and Pratt & Whitney management. I have yet to see the results. Another option I have is to withhold information from the intelligence community until someone starts asking the right questions. If I answer those questions, the data will be cannibalized and incorporated into the military's human intelligence program, and used for a purpose that would not serve this country's interests. I'm through helping them build up their empire. I've been told that just one of their conference operations costs around a quarter of a million dollars, if not more. You can tell FTD that I will no longer support their boondoggles and if they want to challenge my loyalty, let them. I know that I've done my duty, and they know it too, or they wouldn't be quoting my work in their finished intelligence assessments. I believe that my position is in this country's best interest. As far as the information is concerned, I'll get it out and I'll use my book as the instrument."

"How is the book coming along?" he asked curiously.

"It's about one-quarter done. By the way, I was told by Cotter that I would be fired if I attempted to write a book that was even remotely related to foreign technology."

"Oh, no!" he gasped. "Then you should look after your job, especially these days, Peter. I've traveled throughout the South and West. The [aerospace] industry is in trouble. California looks like a disaster area. At least, if you do anything that might affect your employment status, make sure you know where you land. Don't act hastily! I hope my replacement gets a chance to know you. This has been the best working relationship that I have encountered in this business, and I'm speaking for the government, my colleagues at the home office, and personally." He paused to reminisce. "After all you and Diane have done, and with your own money, and now . . . I can't understand what goes on in the minds of some people. They know that you've done this voluntarily for dear old Uncle Sam. What do they expect?" He gathered his notes on the table. "Peter, it has been a great pleasure working with you. I can't believe this is coming to an end, my transfer and all."

"I still value the paychecks," I said, "but I've reached the point

192

of no return. There comes a period in your life when you can no longer prostitute yourself. If there is one message I'd like you to relay to your home office, it's this: I am appalled at the massive waste and misuse of public funds and have lost all confidence in the ability of the community to provide a reliable intelligence assessment. I will no longer cooperate as long as my efforts are used to build empires and provide havens for incompetent officers who couldn't hold a job if their conduct was properly monitored and their programs placed under the watchful eye of an informed Congress. Additionally, I wouldn't mind it if your organization could keep FTD from harassing me. That's basically what I have to say. I'm glad that I live in the United States and can say it."

"Peter," he said shaking my hand, "you remind me of myself in my earlier days. Just make sure you know where you land." The official Gleichauf-Pratt & Whitney-James relationship, which began one day in October 1965, was terminated at 11:00 A.M. on April 27, 1971.

I finally tired of the charades between the Florida management and the agents in Building 828. Accordingly, in early May 1971 I asked Lowell Ruby and Norm Cotter for a two-month leave of absence without pay. My cousins in Greece had invited Diane and me to their home on the Aegean Sea, and this seemed like an ideal place to get away from it all. "Gorton will have to approve your request," Cotter said. This indicated that I was still restricted to the continental United States, unless Gorton ruled otherwise. "Your request must be in writing," Cotter added, "and the condition of the leave is that you cannot accept an invitation to visit or lecture in the Soviet Union, even if you're invited officially by the Russians. If you do lecture, you're fired. And if you participate in any technical activities or hold discussions with any scientists or engineers you place your job in jeopardy." Since I needed first-hand contact with scientists and engineers whom I knew since 1965 to work on the book, the ruling meant that I could not successfully complete the book without placing my job in jeopardy. Whereas the company's travel ban had prevented Diane and me from taking a short trip to the Caribbean during the past Christmas, the company in effect was willing to lift the ban under the condition that I had no contact with my friends. The idea not only seemed preposterous, but I questioned its legality. A final outrageous condition was added: if I wished to continue working for Pratt & Whitney Aircraft, I had to terminate all official, personal, or friendly contacts with representatives of the United States government—under no circumstances was I to provide any branch of the government with information that resulted from this or future trips. There was no other interpretation: the company had sold out to the "Air Force." My FTD contacts knew I intended to approach Congress with the foreign technology problem and write a book; the ruling prevented me from doing so without placing my job in jeopardy.

The company's phobia of alienating the "Air Force" was now reflected in a ludicrous memorandum I had to write which I doubted had been asked of other engineers who had traveled abroad. As if this were a melodrama of exaggerated proportions, accommodating Lowell Ruby asked me to write a draft of the memorandum first; he wanted to approve it before it got to Cotter, who similarly wanted to approve it before Gorton saw it.

An hour later I submitted the draft to Lowell Ruby. In the upper right hand corner of the memorandum I wrote: "Lowell, here's my draft; please add or make deletions." The draft was reviewed by Ruby, then Cotter, and returned with the following changes:

In the sentence: "I understand that if I participate in any technical discussions (i.e., international conferences, discussions with foreign scientists or engineers, etc.) my employment with FRDC will be terminated with prejudice," Cotter changed the word "will" to "could" and Ruby with the softer lead pencil, crossed out the words "with prejudice," indicating that they wanted to tone down the extent of the threat in the event the memo fell into the wrong hands.

I submitted the draft to my secretary and she typed the final. H. Norm Cotter ordered me to send it to my immediate administrative supervisor, Les Harrell, who was not aware of the company's covert dealings with FTD. Cotter directed Harrell to expedite the request personally and to obtain W. L. Gorton's approval. The private memorandum was being treated like a multi-million dollar contract, and since Harrell worked indirectly for Cotter, he followed orders like a good soldier. This was the first time I could get the general thrust of the company's December 18, 1970, decree—the day of the blow-up—down on paper, and I welcomed it. Considering the Florida division's pro-FTD stance, it would not have surprised me if a copy of the memorandum secretly found its way to Building 828.

26

In the privacy of our apartment a CIA source briefed me on the Brussels affair involving the Swimmer.

"What triggered it?" I asked.

"[The Swimmer's] performance. It was enough to get the State Department and FBI all hopped up. They went after the corporation's [Defense Department] security clearance."

"Hell, that would close us down."

"Yes, it would."

"So what happened?"

"The company appealed to the Executive Office."

"The Executive Office? Who in the Executive Office?"

"The top."

"You mean the President?" Our visitor nodded. "Nixon?" He nodded again. "You mean Nixon personally overruled the State Department and FBI?" He swayed his head. "What's Nixon's connection with FTD?"

"It was a national security matter."

May 20, 1971: I received a telephone call from a civilian with CIA connections. He said that several higher echelon members of the CIA were very upset over the corporation's handling of my case,

195

since they felt my conduct was entirely legitimate and above the table. While words couldn't undo the damage already done, the civilian paraphrased a message to me from CIA personnel I did not know:

> We sympathize with your problems, and while we are in no position to do anything about them, without intimidating a private corporation, we want you to know that your secret report is being put to good use and it has had a tremendous impact on our effort. You have the right to feel that you have greatly contributed to the security of the United States.

Les Harrell, my administrative supervisor, notified me that my leave of absence had been granted. At Lowell Ruby's request, I prepared a letter to Major Harold Gale, thanking him for permitting Pratt & Whitney Aircraft to review FTD's latest report on foreign propulsion technology. In another attempt to involve directly the aerospace industry in the evaluation of Russian technology and weapons systems, I concluded the letter with the following statement:

> We feel that the task of evaluating foreign airbreathing propulsion technology is extremely complex and requires the combined efforts of a team of U.S. government and private industry experts. In this way foreign technology can be exploited by taking advantage of industry's engineering experience and government's resources; the overall objective being—make the best use of the foreign data that is available at the least cost. We would be interested in exploring this idea with the Air Force and, as always, would welcome any foreign airbreathing data that might help us improve our product.

I submitted the letter to Ruby. An hour later he diplomatically told me that he would personally respond to FTD on behalf of the company.

The next morning I received a carbon copy of his response to FTD. No mention was made that in a memorandum to Lowell Ruby by senior project engineer Hal Tiedemann—Tiedemann was now Ruby's new boss and he too reported to H. Norm Cotter—it was concluded that the FTD report was mainly speculative and offered nothing new in Pratt & Whitney's area of interest. My recommendation of permitting an industry team of experts to conduct assessments was deleted in Ruby's response. Even though the FTD technical translation program and unclassified five- by eight-inch cards were worthless, Ruby's response to FTD implied that if Pratt & Whitney's budget situation improved in 1972, the company would spend more time on this "worthwhile activity." I was greatly disappointed. The unclassified cards were a complete waste of taxpayer's money and Ruby knew that I had stopped sending the cards to company engineers in late 1968 because the effort was a waste of company resources. In fact, *both Cotter and Ruby concurred with my decision.* Now, FTD was being sent a letter on Pratt & Whitney letterhead lauding the worthless activity, thereby giving FTD more ammunition to perpetuate this unwarranted program. I had lost the battle to correct the system from within; the bureaucracy had its own built-in system of checks and balances.

I reviewed the Tiedemann memorandum in more depth. It was his expert opinion that Super Smart lacked the experience for conducting an evaluation of Russian scramjet technology. Tiedemann gave specific examples and suggested that a gap existed between what the Russians were actually doing compared to the Russian advancements that Super Smart wanted the readers of his assessment to believe. This was an important point because Super Smart was behind the secret proposal sent to my home, in which he attached an abstract of a paper he had written for me to present at a meeting in Rome; the subject of the paper involved scramjets. This tied in with my earlier analysis of how FTD was manipulating intelligence both at home and abroad. Tiedemann's memorandum was significant because it identified a leading intelligence specialist in FTD as lacking the expertise to analyze scramjet propulsion systems—yet qualified or not, Super Smart was responsible for FTD's assessments in this area.

June 21, 1971: I received a letter from David Franke, senior editor of Arlington House Publishers in New Rochelle, New York, which stated that Arlington House was very interested in my book concept on the Soviets. Because I accepted no money from the CIA for my services, the agency granted me permission to use my personal notes (intelligence reports I had submitted to the CIA) in the book.

June 25, 1971: I received a disturbing telephone call from a man who risked his career to give me a tip. He wanted me to know that FTD had a massive dossier on Diane and me, and this dossier was being used by FTD agents to justify before the CIA the Air Force's need to debrief me. According to the tipster, FTD made eleven requests to debrief me between October 1970 and June 1971; all requests were denied by the CIA. FTD's last request contained a voluminous listing of all my Russian contacts in Rome and Konstanz and it was presented in the form of a demand that FTD be allowed to submit its questions to me personally. "Pete," he said, "there is something you should know. The publication of the *Pentagon Papers* has given the clowns [FTD] a new project; prevent news leaks that might affect the national security." I mentioned my forthcoming trip and he replied, "You personally should keep your distance from them. Don't give out your itinerary to anyone, including your supervision. They're incompetent and untrustworthy. They're out to discredit you. If you go to Brussels, watch out, they'll be waiting for you. The spooks have something planned if you make the trip." He hung up.

I had alerted the brass in Building 828 three months earlier that I intended to write a book and notify Congress. There was no question that the forthcoming book was creating havoc. And both the company and FTD feared that I would transmit my files to a congressional investigative committee; the May 12 memorandum restricting my activities was the company's way of making sure that it could prove to the "Air Force" that all possible steps had been taken to keep me in line. And it made me wonder about the Red Baron, the ex-Air Force officer who asked us to keep him informed of our accommodations in Brussels. There was obviously a concerted effort to stop me from exposing FTD, and the company was a willing participant. The scenario was coming to a climax, and if I chose to make it so, an involved confrontation was in the making in Brussels in September.

July 16, 1971: I said good-bye to my colleagues and wished them luck in the ensuing company layoffs. Lowell Ruby told me not to worry about getting laid off and to enjoy the summer. Before leaving the Palm Beaches, I dropped off my files in safety deposit boxes in the First National Bank of Riviera Beach and the First American Bank of North Palm Beach. Excerpts from an eleven-page statement I left behind, in the event we failed to return, read as follows:

. . . The needed changes [in the intelligence establishment] should be made by Congress, where budgets and divisions of authority and responsibility can be clearly defined. A good private investigation of the United States intelligence community by people who know what to look for—that's the important criterion—by people who know what to look for, coupled with a severe cutback in the military intelligence budget, and either the return of this money to the taxpayer, or the allocation of a small portion of this money to the intelligence activities of other government organizations that are doing an effective job, would help straighten out this mess. . . .

Appendix to Statement: The CIA prepared approximately

twenty-three sets of raw intelligence reports from my notes of the Mar del Plata IAF Congress in October 1969. The listing below shows the code numbers for nine of these reports, which number two to eight pages each:

I70001141S	I70001465
170001197S	I70001221S
I70001336S	I70001848
I70001465S	I70000767S
I70001336	etc.

Some reports on the Mar del Plata IAF Congress were the result of U.S. Government funded [i.e., FTD] operations. Representative reports funded by the taxpayer for this event include the following among others:

I70000716S
I70000348D
I70000294D
I70000320D
etc.

I suggest that (a) members of the Senate Armed Services or Appropriations Committees subpoena officials of the CIA, USAF, and/or FTD and by *subpoena duces tecum* ask these individuals to produce behind closed doors all raw reports generated for the IAF Congress in Mar del Plata, and (b) a comparison be made of my "no cost" effort versus the taxpayer-funded government effort.

Similarly, the following is a listing of report numbers for the II International Conference on Space Engineering, held in Venice, Italy during May 1969:

NO COST REPORTS P. N. JAMES (VIA CIA)	TAXPAYER-FUNDED REPORTS
139005666S	I19007001D
139005677S	I70000134D
139005914S	I19004805D
I17000176I	I19004904D
etc.	I19005172D
	etc.

A private Congressional investigation of these and other activities is warranted.

Book II
The Odyssey

27

July 17, 1971: In Moorestown, New Jersey, I disclosed to Diane's aunt and uncle that I was writing an exposé on the Air Force Foreign Technology Division and there was a possibility that we would encounter difficulties in Europe. They accepted responsibility for the keys to our safety deposit boxes. I gave them the names, telephone numbers, and addresses of people to contact in the event we did not return to the States by October 12, 1971. The list included Justin F. Gleichauf of the CIA, an FBI agent, and a trusted friend. If anything happened to us, the news media would have been handed on a silver platter an abridged version of the FTD story and a blueprint describing the embryo of a police state whose worldwide headquarters were in Dayton, Ohio.

On July 26, 1971, after a week and a half of visiting friends in my home town, Jamestown, New York, we drove to Woodridge, New Jersey, and dropped our car off at my uncle's home. It was a warm and windy evening at John F. Kennedy International Airport when Diane and I boarded Sabena Flight 548, a Boeing 747 jumbo jet, for a European adventure which would thrust us into the middle of an espionage jungle and a frightening international conspiracy. At 10:30 A.M. the following morning, our jet cut through a thick cloud layer and landed in Brussels in the middle of a rainstorm. This would be the first leg of a two-month trip which would end back in Brussels amid swarms of FTD intelligence agents at the International Astronautical Federation Congress.

A few days later we bought a new Volkswagen from the factory in Wolfsburg near the East German border, and toured the Kiel Peninsula, Denmark, and Sweden, before settling down in Bad Gandersheim, a quaint out-of-the way village in northern Germany surrounded by golden fields, rolling hills, and dense forests. It was on August 2, 1971, beneath the weeping willows of Bad Gandersheim that we made the final decision to attend international meetings in Yugoslavia, France, and Belgium. I wrote to Gleichauf and notified him of my decision in the event the "government" later charged that I did not keep it abreast of my plans as I had done in the past. To ensure that I abided by Defense Department security regulations, I visited Mr. Edward Kreuser with the U.S. embassy in Bern, Switzerland, on August 5, 1971, and notified him that I planned to attend the three international meetings. Kreuser advised me that I could fulfill my security obligations by filling out a company debriefing form when I returned to work.

Venice, Friday the 13th, August 1971: We drove to Venice via the Italian Autostrada, parked our Volkswagen in a filled-to-capacity garage on the mainland, and took a water taxi to the Ala Hotel, the Russian delegation hotel during the 1969 Venice conference. In a nostalgic photographic tour of Venice—I could still see Zhivotovskiy seated on the terrace of the Monaco and Grand Canal Hotel—I revisited San Giorgio's Isle, St. Mark's Square, the Palace of the Doges, the Ala Restaurant and lounge, and the Europa Hotel, where Zhivotovskiy and KGB Col. Nikolai Beloussov played their roles. I mailed a post card of the Ducal Palace to Zhivotovskiy in care of Vladimir Kirillin, the Deputy Premier of the Soviet Union, before leaving Venice and driving down the longest and most beautiful coastline I had ever seen—the Dalmatian Coast of Yugoslavia. The picturesque drive between Trieste and Dubrovnik, about fifteen hours long, took us through seaports, Croatian fishing villages, ancient Turkish and Venetian towns, fortresses, harbors and coves, old ruins and monuments, sandy and pebble beaches, sunny resorts and seaside promenades, pine woods, and reddish brown and white arid cliffs. After checking out Dubrovnik for five hours, and satisfied that Zhivotovskiy and his cohorts were not in the Old City preparing for the September meeting, we continued southward to Sutamore, in Montenegro, a small town just north of the Albanian border. An Albanian herdsman in his seventies—he reminded me of the Balkan pinochle players who frequented the coffee house above Osman's Victory Restaurant in Jamestown—watched our car for the night while we slept in a modern hotel for a very reasonable six dollars.

On August 17 we drove through Titograd and around the northeastern corner of Albania into the Kosova province of Yugoslavia, where the predominantly Albanian children who threw sticks and stones at our car reminded me of the Greek and Albanian devils of my neighborhood in the 1940s. Driving through the rugged mountainous terrain on President Tito's new highway, where twentieth century automotive traffic contrasted with the donkey, horse, and gypsy traffic, I was left with the impression that if it ever came to pass, Russia's modern weapons were unsuitable against a guerrilla environment and people whose ancestry dated back thousands of years, and whose knowledge of the terrain surpassed that of modern-day geodetic surveyors. How unpredictable life was: I could have been a hot-blooded Albanian Orthodox herdsman concerned over the unity of my people instead of an aerospace rabble-rouser bent on revamping the U.S. intelligence establishment.

Diane and I spent the last two weeks of August in Greece and visited the islands of Corfu and Mykonos. I worked on the nonsensitive portions of the Russian manuscript during the day, and in the late afternoons, while my cousins skin-dived for octopus, we swam in a cove frequented by Greeks who lived each day as if it were their last. Lying on the pebble beach below an olive grove, I seriously considered staying in Greece for the remainder of my leave. But this was the land where the worthiness of the individual had been instilled in the hearts of young and old, and where one man, Alexander of Macedonia, had set out to conquer the world. If I ever needed the stimulus to take on the Foreign Technology Division and reassert my rights as an individual, I had chosen the right country in which to begin the odyssey. It was an indescribable feeling, but it was as if the Goddess Circe herself were beckoning me to return to Dubrovnik and confront my antagonists.

Piraeus, Greece, August 31, 1971: The Piraeus port authorities granted me permission to drive our car to the port side of the Adjaria, a glittering white cruise ship, most noticeable because of its bright red star painted on the bow. At two o'clock Diane and I walked up the ramp of this one-class Russian ship and were met by the purser. He collected our passports and welcomed us aboard.

I was not the pawn of a clever controller in Washington, nor was I a spy. I was an American who had eluded the tentacles of the espionage establishment and wanted to live his own life. Travel was our first and last love, and now I wanted to write. I was not violating any laws, nor did I intend to. If H. Norm Cotter et al.

wished to terminate my services with Pratt & Whitney because I would not subscribe to the company's questionable policies, then the decision would be theirs to make. I was not about to obey orders blindly without weighing their moral and constitutional implications or their impact on the United States. An uncontrolled cancer was spreading throughout the clandestine branches of our government, it had already contaminated the free enterprise system, and it was now attacking the isolated cells that resisted its metastasis—the American people. From knowing how the Building 828 controllers operated, I understood Americans traveling behind the Iron Curtain or boarding a Russian ship were automatically suspect; after all, their pawns wouldn't operate without the cover of a space conference or something like an official written invitation from a foreign government.

We cruised the Adriatic—it was delightful, with stops in Corfu and Venice again—and at 2:00 P.M. on September 4, 1971, the Adjaria docked in Gruz, the mercantile port on the north side of Dubrovnik. I loaded our luggage in our car and washed off the Mediterranean salt crystals which were sprinkled from bumper to bumper. At 4:00 we disembarked, gave the Adjaria a last look, and drove off. It was our first cruise and worth every penny; the Russian hospitality was tremendous, the ship was spotlessly clean, and as I expected, we encountered no difficulties. I gained more first-hand impressions of the Russian people, and more importantly, the cruise on a Russian ship was a sanitizing process—I could deal with my Russian friends as an American, not as a suspected member of a third-rate intelligence unit.

Dubrovnik, Yugoslavia, Sunday, September 5, 1971: We stayed at our favorite hotel, the Excelsior, which overlooked the Adriatic and the lush Isle of Lokrum, where Richard Coeur de Lion was shipwrecked in the twelfth century on his way back to Britain from the Crusades. The Dubrovnik fortress in full view of our window created an ideal setting for an international conference. We walked to the Old City, through a gate overlooking the white stoned quay, and down the winding footpath, past the entrance of the harbor to the Plaka, the immaculate main street of the fortress. As we approached a cafe, a middle-aged man accompanied by a lady in a green dress watched us for about a minute and then took our picture from about thirty feet away. He wore cuffs on his trousers, he looked like an engineer, and I would find out later that he was part of the American delegation to the conference.

On the west side of the Plaka, a small group of hippies were strumming their guitars near an ancient fountain in front of the Syndicate Hall. Conference signs pointed to an office overlooking

206

a courtyard. I registered for $60 and was given an elaborate light green conference folder imprinted as follows: *The Fourth IFAC Symposium on Automatic Control in Space; September 6-10, 1971, Dubrovnik, Yugoslavia.*

Dubrovnik, Yugoslavia, September 6, 1971: Two men in their twenties leaned over the railing of the Syndicate Hall courtyard; they were Russians. "Pardon me," I said, "do you speak English?"

The dark-haired man with trim sideburns and an open collar white shirt stepped forward and answered: "Yes ... are you American?" I introduced myself. "I am Victor Antonov.* I am with the Institute of Space Research," the young Russian said.

"Oh, then you must know Professor Khodarev."

"He is my chief," Antonov replied. "Do you know Dr. Khodarev?"

"Yes, I hope to see him in Brussels later this month." Antonov's colleague stepped closer to us.

"This is Anatoly Zharkov, my friend," Antonov said. "He does not speak English." The light-haired, heavyset Zharkov shook my hand, bowed, and stepped back again.

"Call me Victor," Antonov said. The Russians normally sent more young scientists and engineers to conferences in Yugoslavia than any of the Western countries. In Belgrade in 1967 I had developed rapport with two young Russians, and in Dubrovnik, it appeared that I would have the same success with Victor. The Dubrovnik conference was on automatic control in space, and I knew very little about automatic control, but I was counting on the Russians to send specialists in the rocket and space field, and they did.

At 8:30 P.M., with a storm brewing at sea, we congregated with the delegates on the open air terrace of the Excelsior Hotel and drank champagne as guests of the mayor of Dubrovnik. Victor introduced us to other members of his delegation, including a Russian named Valery Sokolov, who wore Italian-style glasses and spoke better English than most Americans. I learned that Sokolov had arrived in Dubrovnik several days before his delegation, had a flat to himself in the Old City, was a translator during the technical sessions, and knew Georgiy Zhivotovskiy quite well. Sokolov's eyes lit up when Diane told him about our cruise on the Adjaria. As we talked, a gust from the Bora came off the Adriatic and knocked dozens of cocktail glasses to the concrete patio, shattering them into thousands of pieces. It began raining and the delegates ran for cover into the protected dining room. We talked with the Russians about Florida and Moscow, but our discussion always returned to science and technology. As in the past, these were interesting

*Pseudonym

and cordial exchanges; a chess game with each person attempting to learn the other man's secrets.

About an hour later, the Russians invited us to join them at their hotel. "We have vodka from the Adjaria," I said.

"Good," Victor said, "I brought caviar from Moscow."

"And I have cookies and fruits at my flat," Sokolov added. It was interesting that Sokolov had a flat in the Old City: while the other Russians including Victor were staying at the Adriatic Hotel near Gruz, where the Adjaria docked, almost two miles from the Old City, Sokolov appeared to be running a *quarterback operation* from his flat; after the sessions the Russians could walk over to his flat and be debriefed, before catching the bus to their hotel. The questions he asked Diane earlier, her likes and dislikes, mostly dossier-related, were similar to the questions Gleichauf routinely asked me about the Russians. It was this type of diligent work that alerted the British to the potential of KGB Colonel Oleg Penkovskiy, who turned out to be the best spy "in place" for the West, and Sokolov, not passing up an opportunity, and apparently not aware that the KGB already had a massive dossier on us, was starting from scratch and asking basic biographical questions already covered by Zhivotovskiy in Venice several years earlier.

Diane waited in the lobby with the Russians while I went up to our room for the Kristal vodka, the car registration papers, and my international driver's license, in the event we were stopped on the road. I exited from the lobby elevator and saw an American seated with a newspaper folded across his knees, looking at Diane and the Russians. When he saw me, however, he quickly looked down at the newspaper; strange behavior I thought, for someone I was not supposed to know.

I joined them and we walked through the lower lobby to the hidden driveway overlooking the rough Adriatic waters. While backing out of the driveway in our Volkswagen, being careful not to test the frail railing and the steep drop to the sea below, I thought of a possible *Palm Beach Post* headline: "Local Couple and Two Russians Plunge to Mysterious Death in Mountainous Yugoslavia."

We spent the evening with the Russians at the Adriatic Hotel. I had the opportunity to learn every minute detail about their personal lives—information that could be processed and filed at the Air Force secret facility, thereby justifying the jobs of hundreds of intelligence analysts and support personnel—but I chose instead to research material for my forthcoming book on the Russians.

At 12:45 A.M. we dropped Sokolov off at the west end of the fortress and returned to the Excelsior.

Dubrovnik, Yugoslavia, Tuesday, September 7, 1971: Diane and I joined Victor, and we left the fortress by way of the west side draw-bridge to the small commercial part of Dubrovnik called Pile. The Russian selected a table at an outdoor cafe overlooking both the sea and the busy bus terminal, where incoming German tourists and peasants carrying baskets filled with fruits hustled to and fro, oblivious to the fact that an international conference was being held. We treated Victor to cake and Coca-Cola, his favorite drink since arriving in this Western-style resort, and when the bus to his hotel appeared, we agreed to get together at the harbor for the Wednesday excursion. As he was boarding the bus, within twenty yards of us was the man who took our picture the previous Sunday in the Plaka district. He was accompanied by an American professor who had attempted unsuccessfully to strike up friendly conversations with the Russians earlier in the day. Were they monitoring my meetings with the Russians as FTD had done in 1970? Did the Pratt & Whitney security department tip off the military that I had been granted a two-month leave of absence and would be in Yugoslavia in September? That much Pratt & Whitney knew.

Dubrovnik, Wednesday, September 8, 1971: Diane stayed at the Excelsior as I joined Victor in the aft compartment of a chartered passenger ferry in the harbor of the Old City. About twenty minutes later an American entered the cabin and sat behind us, attempting to monitor our conservation. Victor eyed him and suggested that we go up front and photograph the mountain range from the starboard side. When we were alone, he said, "Peter, you must be careful. That man"—he tilted his head toward a group of four Americans seated on the port side of the ferry—"has been watching you."

"Which one, Victor?"

"The man with the white shirt talking to the man with the beard."

I looked at the men Victor singled out, but I couldn't place their faces, and this was the third day of the conference.

"Thank you. I don't know him. Have you seen him before?"

"One of his friends was asking about you yesterday. I do not know his name."

"What did they want to know?"

"The name of your company . . . I told him I did not know."

"Good."

Our boat was moored at the landing in Lopud, an isle north of Dubrovnik which looked like a fishing village, though it would have been an ideal resort for writers. I glanced at the man Victor pointed out and our eyes met for the first time. He quickly looked away. The situation was unique: in the States a friend with close ties with the

CIA tipped me off that FTD would cause me problems in Europe if I attended any conferences. Several months later, on a chartered Yugoslav excursion boat on the Adriatic, Victor Antonov, whose friend Valery Sokolov appeared to be tied up with the KGB, was tipping me off that I was being watched by a white-shirted American. I thought I had detected miniscule surveillance earlier: the photograph taken of us in the Old City on Sunday; the man in the Excelsior Hotel lobby; the man near the Pile gate after Victor boarded a bus; the man who sat behind us on the passenger ferry. But this was still nothing to get excited about.

The excursion organizers passed out prepacked box lunches of lamb, bread, cheese, and wine. Most delegates separated by national groupings. Victor picked up two bottles of wine and asked me to join his delegation so we could talk in private. I joined the Russians on a twenty minute walk to the other side of the island, and we settled down on a desolate sandy cove sheltered by rocks and cypress trees. Victor submerged the wine bottles in the salt water. We swam and talked throughout the afternoon under the watchful eyes of American professors stationed about fifty yards away. I returned to the passenger ferry with the Russians, noting that the man in the long-sleeve white shirt and his bearded friend seemed to be particularly interested in the fact that I was still accompanying the Russians. Victor saw the men again. "Peter, be careful. Perhaps we should not sit together."

"Nonsense," I replied, taking a candid picture of the duo before boarding the boat. This photo now rests in the CIA files in Langley, Virginia, and while the ideal caption should read "From Russia with Love," it reads: "Men fingered by Antonov." We disembarked at Gruz, and a member of the Russian delegation privately asked me to be at the old harbor of the fortress at 9:30 sharp in the evening.

In a movie-type scenario that evening Diane and I waited in the Dubrovnik harbor in near pitch blackness as the water thrashed against the quay and the fierce wind of the Bora blew through us. A shadowy figure with his collar turned up approached. It was the Russian whom my CIA contacts suspected of being a KGB agent. With the finely atomized salt spray raining down on us, the Russian made it clear in no uncertain terms that I was under surveillance. "You have been watched by your own kind. You will have many troubles," he said. With the KGB using a flat in the Old City as its headquarters to spook the Americans in Dubrovnik, it apparently had learned about an FTD operation in which Diane and I were targets, and now it was passing this information off to me.

It has always been my belief that persons holding a Defense Department secret clearance should expect some surveillance, especially if they have been in contact with the Eastern bloc.

Therefore, as a rule, I did not mind photographic or physical surveillance. I was concerned, however, because in the 1970s the U.S. military intelligence services had been turned loose on Americans traveling abroad, and in Rome and Konstanz, FTD agents went beyond what one would call normal surveillance. This was one reason why I complained about the harassment to the CIA in writing—agents should neither be seen nor heard, and above all, they should never disturb the normal routine of persons placed under surveillance. The FTD operatives consistently violated this accepted code, mainly because their superiors operated under the assumption that laws and ethics have no place in the intelligence field.

I thanked the Russian for the tip and talked him into walking us back to the Excelsior for a drink. A man reading a newspaper watched our every move in the Excelsior lobby. At midnight, before I dropped the Russian off at his hotel, the interested observer tailed us through the hotel lobby to the side entrance of the Excelsior where my car was parked; he watched us drive off.

Diane and I left Dubrovnik secretly the following morning in the middle of a treacherous rainstorm, three days before the end of the conference. Unbeknown to us then, we had not been the only Americans who had been targeted in Dubrovnik by the *super-team*, as the Eagle called them. United States intelligence files show that Dr. John Skull, a manager of the Astronics Division of the Jet Propulsion Laboratory in Pasadena, California, had been similarly spooked by FTD. In Dubrovnik, Dr. Skull was befriended by pawns who had been unable to make their own contacts with the Russians. To compensate for their own failures, the pawns leeched on the technical exchanges between the space expert and Russian engineers. Because of the pawns' presence, the KGB apparently concluded that Dr. Skull was a willing participant in a U.S. government-sponsored intelligence operation. Several weeks after the Dubrovnik meeting, Dr. Skull was in London's Heathrow Airport enroute to Moscow when he received notification that the Soviet government had cancelled his visa to enter the Soviet Union. Though State Department officials have offered him a number of reasons why they believe the Soviets withdrew his visa, the answer to his dilemma is buried in the files of Building 828, whose clumsy agents have turned international conferences into circuses in which even the KGB has on occasion felt obligated to finger the clowns for the protection of other conference attendees.

After spending the night in Rijeka, Yugoslavia, we drove across Northern Italy by way of Milan and Genoa to San Remo on the Italian Riviera, where we checked into the Grand Hotel Londres for a two-day stay. Next stop—Marseille.

28

Southern France, Sunday, September 12, 1971: We took a leisurely ride through the French Riviera, Nice, and Cannes, and along the Mediterranean through rugged coastal mountains that resembled parts of Arizona. At 5:30 P.M. we arrived on the outskirts of Marseille, a major seaport, the second largest city in France, a center for drug traffic, and one of the roughest districts in the world. While I was certain we would have a confrontation in Brussels, I was hoping that we could breeze through Marseille like we did in Dubrovnik, without any incidents. I hoped that FTD was still trying to put the Dubrovnik story together.

We checked into the Grand Hotel Noailles located on a street called La Canebiere and registered for the conference on gas dynamics and explosive reaction systems at the University of Marseille. The French mistakenly reversed my name from Peter James to James Peter, and I let the error stand, hoping that the error would buy us a day or so in Marseille before being identified by FTD agents, who would probably be in Marseille; with money being no problem, they'd attend a conference on the moon if someone would build the transportation system to get them there.

We window-shopped in the evening near our hotel, and as we passed a small cafe around the corner near the Hotel Astoria, I saw

a man drinking coffee, dressed much like a retired indigent Frenchman in need of a fix. That man had attended the 1970 Konstanz
conference, but then he was wearing a suit and tie; his role in Germany was white collar American engineer. So, Marseille, already
saturated with narcotics agents, had attracted FTD agents as well,
at least for the week of September 12. We had to avoid them at all
costs.

Marseille, France, Monday, September 13, 1971: In the daylight
the university looked impressive, though practically every building
had been sprayed and painted by student activists. Diane and I sat
in the back-center of the lecture hall for the opening ceremonies as
Dr. Charles Stark Draper, president of the International Academy of
Astronautics, delivered the opening address. The French sponsors
of the conference announced that 154 delegates had registered for
the meeting. Their declaration that 55 Americans were present was
believable, but 45 Russians? No. From what I could see, there were
no more than 10 Russians in attendance at the opening ceremonies.
As usual, the Russians had withdrawn part of their delegation.
Knowing how the agents in Building 828 operated, the meeting
would be covered overtly and covertly by a super-team of spooks
selected on the assumption that all the Russians would attend,
which never was the case.

After the morning session we joined several Frenchmen for
lunch at the university cafeteria, and then Diane and I strolled on
the east campus. I sized up the American delegation and named the
men I wanted her to avoid. I didn't need any leeches moving in because they "just happened" to know us. This strategy worked so
well in Dubrovnik that I couldn't name more than a handful of
Americans who had attended the meeting; no one interrupted my
discussions with the Russians. The best the leeches could do in
Dubrovnik was to place us under surveillance, though they apparently were about to cause us problems.

We returned to the lecture hall and sat in the back again. This
time, there was a noticeable change in the delegate seating arrangement. The Russians were still in the front left corner of the
lecture hall, but they were surrounded by more Americans, yet no
American, with one exception, was seated with a Russian. It seemed
that no spook had made a move, and this was after the previous
evening's welcome reception, a morning session, a morning coffee
break, and lunch. It appeared to be another case of "how do you
break the ice?"

The afternoon session dragged on until 4:00 P.M., when a short
coffee break was announced. Most of the delegates congregated in
the hall, with the Americans and Russians still keeping to them-

selves. A tall Russian to my left—his name tag read "Smirnov"—
saw the Mars 2 and 3 pins on my lapel. These were gifts from the
Russians in Dubrovnik. As Smirnov poured himself another drink,
Topchian, a short bald-headed Russian with a pronounced black
moustache, approached me, and in a coated accent said, "Mr. Peter!
That is a Russian pin. Do you have Russian friends?"

"Yes . . . my wife and I have many Russian friends. Let me introduce you to Diane." We were joined by Smirnov and both Russians
stood at attention and very politely shook her hand. As was the case
in Dubrovnik, though we didn't know a single member of the Russian delegation, they were close colleagues of men we knew well,
and within minutes, to the noticeable displeasure of the California
contingent of combustion specialists, it was like "old home week"
in Marseille with the Jameses and Russians exchanging jokes as if
they were long-time friends.

In the evening we attended a reception at the Hotel de Ville. The
mustached Topchian joined us on the balcony overlooking the old
port and introduced us to his best friend Vladimir Mitrofanov and
Professor Valery Pazelsky, whose mannerism reminded me of
Zhivotovskiy.

"Mr. Peter," Topchian said, "Professor Pazelsky is with the
Presidium of the Academy."

"You mean the Presidium of the Academy of Sciences of the
USSR?"

Pazelsky chimed in: "I am with the Presidium of the Siberian
Department of the Academy." His English was good, and it even
had that Zhivotovskiy ring to it.

I had to ask it: "Then you must know Professor Georgiy Zhivotovskiy." I looked at his face, hoping that the middle-aged Pazelsky
would give me a sign of recognition, in the event he denied it.

"Yes, Professor Zhivotovskiy and I are friends. I will see him for
a week after this meeting. Do you know Zhivotovskiy?"

"Yes, we have met in Belgrade, Venice, and Argentina. I learned
that Zhivotovskiy is now assistant to deputy premier Vladimir
Kirillin." Pazelsky nodded that this was the case. Pazelsky was not
only the head of the Russian delegation in Marseille, he had to be
KGB. The fact that he would be seeing Zhivotovskiy in Moscow before going to Novosibirsk meant that he was responsible for drop-
ping off the intelligence pick-up for this conference to the KGB. And
Valery Sokolov, the Russian *quarterback* in Dubrovnik, was seeing
Zhivotovskiy after the Dubrovnik conference for the same reason;
the KGB seemed quite organized at these meetings and Pazelsky
was their man in Marseille. As I conversed with Pazelsky, Topchian
escorted Diane to the hors d'oeuvre table to join the rest of the

214

Russian delegation. She was wearing a pin of a Matryoshka, given to her by Victor Antonov in Dubrovnik. As she described our stupendous cruise on the Adjaria, a short obese man appeared before the group. He was K. Scheller of Wright-Patterson Air Force Base.

"Look, there she is surrounded by Russians!" he shouted. "I think I remember your husband from another conference. His name's Peters, right?"

"That's right," she answered.

"What's your name?"

"Diane."

"Yeah, yeah, but the other one, the last one. Peters? Your last name is Peters?"

"That is correct. The same as my husband's."

"What da ya do?" he asked forcefully.

"Nothing in particular."

"Where ya from?"

"I was born in New Jersey."

"Whose ya husband with?"

"He's with no one. He is not working now."

"Yeah, but who *was* he with? Where do ya live?"

"We've been traveling through Europe for two months. What conferences do you remember my husband from?"

"It was one in Los Angeles."

"That's impossible. We only attend international conferences." The obese Scheller walked away, annoyed at Diane's evasiveness. The Russians appeared puzzled.

"Professor Topchian," she asked, "do you know that man?"

"No, I have only seen him once," Topchian replied.

As my conversation with Pazelsky progressed, a civilian from another Air Force facility—I had met him for a brief second at the university earlier in the day—came out of nowhere and interrupted us. "Oh, there you are Mr. Peter," he said. "I didn't think you and your charming wife made it." I decided not to introduce him to Pazelsky. His tactics were uncalled for; I had run across his type in Mar del Plata, Rome, and Konstanz, and I was sick of it.

With a cocktail glass in his hand, the civilian turned toward Pazelsky, stepped half way in between us, and introduced himself. Fred Astaire couldn't have done the two-step any better. The two men stared at each other, but neither said anything. Ten . . . fifteen . . . about twenty seconds passed. "I don't believe I got your name," he said, leaning over and trying to read Pazelsky's tag.

Pazelsky looked at his own tag and volunteered, "Pazelsky, Valery Pazelsky. I am with the Presidium of the Siberian Academy." The civilian pulled out a small pad, drew a sketch, and asked Pazel-

215

sky a question on combustion processes. I'd never seen someone come on so strong to a stranger before. The man should have known better: the Beloussovs, the Zhivotovskiys, and the Pazelskys—the scientific secretaries, the interpreters, and administrative officials with the Presidium of the Academy of Sciences—were not interested in answering detailed technical questions; that was not their specialty. They were trained KGB senior intelligence officers who were responsible for coordinating perhaps the best intelligence collection network in the world. When approached, these men always sent the questioner to one of their delegates, also co-opted by the KGB, whose responsibility it was to report the type of questions that were asked. This and other information would then be processed by the KGB in Moscow, where an analysis would determine what the United States (i.e., FTD) did not know about the Russians.

Pazelsky interrupted the civilian and said, "Mr. Peter, I do not understand your friend!"

I repeated the question for the civilian. "Why can I understand Mr. Peter, but not you?" Pazelsky asked him.

"Maybe it's because of my accent," the civilian replied. He continued drawing in his note pad, and asked Pazelsky another question, this time talking so slowly and enunciating each syllable, that both Pazelsky and I forgot the first part of his sentence. At the rate he was going, the world would come to an end. Pazelsky, who was more interested in filling his glass with vodka than listening to the technical interrogation, interrupted him and said, "I think you should ask Professor Soloukhin this question."

"But I asked Professor Soloukhin earlier and he sent me to you!" the civilian exclaimed. Soloukhin had sent him to Pazelsky, because Soloukhin wanted Pazelsky to "red flag" the man. Pazelsky was not a combustion expert, and Soloukhin knew it. Evidently, the super-sleuth didn't know it.

"I'll try Professor Soloukhin again," he said.

What a routine: Pazelsky and Soloukhin were playing ping pong with the civilian. Another classic lesson of how to spook the Russians.

Pazelsky and I joined Diane, who was showing her Konstanz photo album to the Russians. They shouted each time they recognized a colleague, and when Diane flipped to Yuri Riazantsev's picture, Topchian let out a bear-like groan and grabbed his forehead. Pointing to the album, he staggered back laughing and yelled, "Riazantsev!"—pedestrians on the street below heard him shout—"Riazantsev almost married my sister!" What a strange coincidence: Riazantsev, the scientific-KGB intelligence officer, friend of Georgiy Zhivotovskiy and the man who monitored my State Department discussion with Gennadi Dimentiev in Konstanz, almost married the sister of Topchian, close friend of Pazelsky, who knew Zhivotovskiy, etc. It was indeed a small world.

The lights in the hall flickered, signalling the end of the reception. Topchian asked us to accompany the Russians to a cinema and we accepted. He held Diane by the arm as we walked down the stairs of the de Ville, making sure she did not stumble in the poorly lighted surroundings. Walking along the port toward the Hotel Noailles, we were joined suddenly by the civilian and two of his colleagues. When we reached the street corner, Topchian's friend Mitrofanov, who could have passed as an Allied agent from the Office of Strategic Services in the World War II theater, darted out ahead of us and got lost in the pedestrian traffic. We crossed the street, with the three Americans on our heels, and about half way up the block, Mitrofanov rejoined our group and whispered to Topchian. The civilian's colleague, Dr. S. A. Waiter of the North American Rockwell Space Division, recommended we eat together, but Pazelsky told them that we were going to the cinema. We walked for another block, and Mitrofanov, who had disappeared again, joined us for the third time. On La Canebiere, the civilian insisted that Diane and I join his group for dinner instead.

"We've already accepted Professor Pazelsky's invitation to join them at the movies," I said, hoping they would cool it for the evening. He nodded and left with his cohorts.

Topchian said he was the scientific secretary of the gasdynamics conference held two years earlier in Novosibirsk; that shed more light on his status. All the Russian scientific secretaries I knew were competent KGB intelligence officers. And since Topchian was Pazelsky's friend, it seemed probable that Topchian was at least a scientist co-opted by the KGB, if not more. Mitrofanov, lagging behind by about twenty yards, was not taking any chances; he was watching our group intently, and more importantly, the people around us, including the patrons at a nearby outdoor cafe. Mitrofanov rejoined us when we reached the theater. I couldn't tell whether this serious-minded Russian was armed.

We saw a raunchy low-grade Hell's Angels film. The Russians were in good spirits: when the lead actress removed her bra, Topchian whispered, "I think it is too hot for she." After the film was over, the Russians walked us to our hotel and asked us to join them for breakfast at the university in the morning.

Only seconds after the Russians left, Diane and I were confronted at the Noailles Hotel entrance by Dr. S. A. Waiter of the North

American Rockwell Space Division and his friend. It was odd that they would accidentally bump into us again at 11:15 P.M., just after we parted with the Russians.

"How did you make out with your friends?" Waiter asked.

"We enjoyed the film," I replied.

"Join us for dinner at the port, will you?"

"We're no longer hungry," Diane answered.

"Well then we can have drinks. I know a couple of places at the old port. Come on."

"I'm tired," Diane replied. "We've got to get up early."

"One drink won't hurt," Waiter insisted. "Come on."

"Maybe next time," I said. "Good night." We went to our room, possibly averting an unnecessary confrontation.

29

Marseille, France, Tuesday, September 14, 1971: We awoke early and walked to the university by way of the St. Charles station. It was impossible to get used to the smell of urine along the walls of the train station. Some of the sleezy characters sleeping on the benches at the foot of the stairway looked like they would cut your throat for any loose change in your pocket. We passed the security guard at the main gate and met Topchian and Pazelsky outside the cafeteria. Presenting Diane with a large hardback book, Pazelsky said, "This is for you. A book on science in Siberia." Flipping through the colored illustrations, he added, "You can study Russian with this book." Topchian invited us to sit with the Russian delegation for the morning session, and with the speaker showing slides in the dark lecture hall, the mustached Armenian escorted Diane down the stairs. During one of the American paper presentations, Topchian nudged me and said, "These are old results . . . the work is ten years old."

Pazelsky laughed and chimed in: "Peter, the man who did this work in Siberia has been dead for four years . . . four years!" Both Russians laughed when the speaker pretended to introduce "new results."

Topchian leaned toward Diane and said, "He should be ashamed to present such work here!" Later during the same session, when the obese K. Scheller of Wright-Patterson Air Force Base presented his paper, Pazelsky cried, "These results are old too!" When Scheller's paper was challenged by a Russian named Korobeinikov, a college-age American seated directly behind Pazelsky laughed hysterically. The boy kept shaking his head and continued laughing, as if he were privy to an inside joke.

Vladimir Baev of the Russian delegation asked if I wished to discuss propulsion technology with him. We conversed for about fifteen minutes outside the lecture hall when I noticed a man standing nearby, trying to listen in. He was a professor from an American university. I drew a schematic of a propulsion system and asked Baev questions about it. The professor moved closer and peered over Baev's shoulder—another damn leech! I had run into them in Venice, Mar del Plata, Rome, Konstanz, and now in Marseille. No conference was immune to them! I wondered how many American scientists knew that their names were appearing on raw intelligence reports prepared by FTD, and how many persons like the Eagle and I had been placed on their enemies list. They were out to discredit me, and the meetings I was holding with the Russians could be listed on a dossier and sent secretly to Pratt & Whitney to justify easing me out the door.

Topchian invited Diane and me to join the Russians for lunch. He found an empty lunch table on the far side of the cafeteria, and we discussed politics, management, and life in Siberia. Half way through the meal, K. Scheller, the fat spook from Wright-Patterson Air Force Base who cross-examined Diane at the de Ville reception, sat at the end of our table without acknowledging us. For twenty minutes the engineer listened to the table discussion before getting up and rejoining his colleagues. Shortly after he left, a man from the University of Connecticut walked up to Topchian and said: "I'm interested in your paper. Where you go, I go!" Topchian completely ignored the man and continued showing us post cards of the Soviet Science City. The frustrated man walked away.

We returned to the lecture hall for the afternoon session, occupying the same seats we used in the morning sessions. This time, however, there was a larger concentration of certain Americans seated directly behind us. It would have been worthwhile for the KGB to chart the seating arrangement of the delegates throughout the week—the spooks were on the move.

When the sessions were over, Pazelsky said he wanted to see another cinema and invited us to join his delegation for the evening. We accepted his invitation and made arrangements to meet him on the corner of La Canebiere and Boulevard Garibaldi, a short distance from our hotel.

At 6:30 P.M. we were greeted by Pazelsky, Topchian, Mitrofanov, Baev, Smirnov, and Markov; this was roughly two-thirds of the Russian Marseille delegation. The Russians agreed to see the movie Pazelsky selected; he was the leader and his delegation showed him respect. Pazelsky looked like he could have been a ladies' man in his younger days, and from the remarks he made as we passed the movie billboards, he appeared to be looking for an X-rated film; the more flesh, the better. The Russians we met always regarded the sexual permissiveness of the West with more curiosity than anything else. They stopped at a billboard of a partially clad voluptuous girl. "We have no how-you-say topless women in Moscow," Pazelsky said. "We go here!" So here we were entering the K7 cinema building with two-thirds of the Russian delegation to see La Maison Jaune. The first "short" showed Bonanza star Lorne Greene in an old movie; if Greene knew that the film were being shown in Marseille, he probably would have been willing to pay millions to get his hands on it and have it destroyed. Several months earlier, Greene gave an outstanding performance in a television movie special entitled Destiny of a Spy, when he played a Russian KGB intelligence officer on assignment in Britain. Now, we were literally rubbing elbows with the KGB watching Greene in another cameo role.

Pazelsky said that he enjoyed movies, especially the James Bond movie, You Only Live Twice. He became confused with his English, however, and called the film, "He Only Live Twice." Having recently recovered from gland and throat problems in a sanitarium in Sochi, the experience gave him an appreciation for life.

When the films were over and the lights turned on, I glanced around the theater. I had a feeling that two-thirds of the Russian delegation would not be allowed to go to a movie in Marseille without being watched by someone. I saw a likely suspect, a young man, seated in the row behind us, two seats to Pazelsky's right. I had seen him somewhere before, but I couldn't place the face. We stepped out on La Canebiere and began walking toward our hotel. Pazelsky promised to send me literature for my book. I gave him my card. Examining the card, Topchian laughed and said, "Yes . . . it is impossible to have name like James Peter." I told the Russians that I did not want them to tell anyone at the conference that I was on a leave of absence from Pratt & Whitney Aircraft. Remembering K. Scheller's performance at the reception, they understood completely.

Pazelsky slipped the card into his wallet. We continued walking on La Canebiere among scores of Frenchmen. Markov, Smirnov, Baev, and Mitrovanov followed behind. As I was talking with Pazelsky—my eyes were on the pedestrian traffic approaching us—I saw a man about twenty feet away, looking very much like Rasputin, the vicious "holy man" who had hypnotic powers over Tsarina Alexandra, walking toward us. When he was but a few steps away, I recognized him. My God—it was Boris Mandrovsky, a supervisor with the Library of Congress. Wearing an Abraham Lincoln-type black beard and eye makeup to conceal dark circles under his eyes, the tall Mandrovsky slouched a bit as he approached. His beady eyes zeroed in on me. We'd never exchanged more than a sentence to each other in earlier years, but no disguise could change Mandrovsky's pronounced physical features. He passed by like an ordinary pedestrian. The surveillance was intensive, though crude. I continued listening to Pazelsky, acting as if nothing unusual had occurred. We were in the vicinity of the Astoria Hotel, where I had spotted another agent disguised as an indigent Frenchman earlier in the week. Was the Astoria Hotel the location of FTD's intelligence headquarters? Was Mitrofanov attuned to the surveillance? Who was the target: the Russians or us—or both? I lost sight of Mitrofanov. What the hell was Mandrovsky, of all men, doing on La Canebiere in Marseille? As the street light flashed red, the incidents in the past flashed through my mind; I tried to make some sense out of it:

• Boris Mandrovsky was in Lindau, Germany, in 1970; the Red Baron, the ex-Air Force officer who asked about our hotel reservations in Brussels, insisted that we join him for dinner in Lindau.

• Dr. S. A. Waiter of North American Rockwell was quite persistent when he invited us to the old port of Marseille for dinner or drinks the previous evening; twenty-four hours later I find Boris Mandrovsky masquerading on La Canebiere in a black beard.

• My CIA sources tipped me off that FTD was generating a massive dossier on Diane and me, starting with the Rome and Konstanz conferences; I could place Boris Mandrovsky in Konstanz.

I was not looking for Mandrovsky, yet I easily identified him. If the Russians had a dossier on him, and they probably did because he had written an analysis of the Soyuz spacecraft mission for the Library of Congress and he had attended the Madrid and Konstanz space conferences, then one of the six Russians may have recognized him. The amateur surveillance tactics could have led the Russians to conclude that I was setting them up for the super-team. An over-reaction by anyone in this potentially explosive situation could have triggered a violent clash between the KGB and the spooks on La Canebiere.

Pazelsky suggested that we have dinner. The senior member of the Russian delegation gave Mitrofanov orders, and Baev, Smirnov, Markov, and Mitrofanov left our group. Crossing La Canebiere, they headed back toward the university. We talked on the corner under heavy surveillance by the team. "Where should we look?" Pazelsky asked, taking the lead in search for a suitable restaurant. He crossed La Canebiere and headed toward the university, retracing the steps of Mitrofanov and his other colleagues. If Pazelsky knew about the surveillance, I couldn't tell. I was now bothered by the tip from a CIA source who indicated that FTD was trying to pin an indiscretion on me. Like the Eagle, they hoped either to coerce me to cooperate with them, or get me fired. There was no question they could easily trump up a good story, documented with names, times, and places. All circumstantial, but suspect. It was in Marseille that I began to feel the omnipotence of Uncle Sam and I didn't like it one bit.

Pazelsky saw a Middle Eastern nightclub on Garibaldi featuring belly dancers. A loud band played inside, ideal for carrying on a private conversation without having it monitored. I vetoed the idea because Diane was hungry. We walked further on Boulevard Garibaldi, following Pazelsky. The Russian suddenly turned around and retraced our steps all the way back to La Canebiere. Pazelsky was making it difficult for the surveillance teams in the area. It was an interesting move on his part: where was Mitrofanov? The outnumbered KGB agents were clearly challenging the spooks to make the first move. We crossed La Canebiere again. I looked up and down the street, trying to pick out other members of the surveillance team. As we passed the outdoor corner cafe, I talked the Russians into entering a small brightly lit restaurant called Le Petite Cadeau, just off La Canebiere, to defuse this situation.

It was midnight by the time we returned to the Hotel Noailles. There was no question that the conduct of U.S. government intelligence agents jeopardized the well-being of American scientists who were attending the Marseille conference for legitimate reasons. An immense intelligence force had converged on Marseille to spook a handful of Russians.

Diane and I went to sleep in anticipation of the morning excursion to Cassis, east of Marseille on the Mediterranean. I could not believe that the spooks would leave us alone.

Marseille, France, Wednesday, September 15, 1971: We dressed in casual Florida clothes and went to the university. Many of the delegates were dressed like they were going to a ball game. Markov and Mitrofanov were seated on a concrete ledge that circumscribed the nearby building complex. K. Scheller walked up to us and shouted, "Here come da celebrities! Let me take a pictcha of the beautiful lady!"

"No photographs," I said.

"Why no photographs?" he asked sarcastically.

"No photographs," I repeated, saying it in a low enough tone so that the Russians could not hear. I wanted no part of the man. Scheller approached Dr. Waiter and talked with his friend. Waiter walked over to us. "I'd like to take your picture."

"Save your film," I replied, trying to be diplomatic, but firm in front of Mitrofanov. Waiter laughed, stepped back, and snapped several pictures of Diane and me, making sure that Markov and Mitrofanov were in them as well.

A chartered bus discharged us at the dock before the ferryboat. As we were waiting to board, I turned and saw K. Scheller filming me with his movie camera. I snapped his picture before he could get the camera down in time. This was one picture that I intended personally to deliver to the CIA, along with a complaint: if Scheller's expenses were being paid by the U.S. government, and if he were in any way connected with a U.S. intelligence collection operation, or if he were dealing with the clandestine operatives in Marseille, I wanted the CIA to know that I was tired of the harassment and I intended to notify Congress that American citizens were being spied on by the military services both at home and abroad, and it was time someone looked into the reason why this authority had been granted and by whom. The bulging Scheller frowned after I snapped his picture, and walked away.

As Diane talked with Topchian and Pazelsky, Scheller confronted them and said, "How about yas linin' up and we'll take some pictchas?"

"Nyet," Diane replied.

"Why not?" he asked.

"Because I said no pictures!" The rotund spook from Wright-Patterson Air Force Base ranted on like a high-pressure used car salesman. Having been frustrated by the little girl from Palm Beach Shores, Florida, he gave his movie camera to Dr. Waiter, and the North American Rockwell Space Division scientist filmed Diane with the Russians. If the chief spook behind the Marseille operation returned with little useful intelligence, it was my guess that photographs of the Jameses with the Russians could be used to trump up an excuse that we tied up all the Russians all of the time, thus explaining their ineptness.

On the ferryboat a college-age American approached Diane and asked, "Where did you get that babushka pin? Were you in the Soviet Union?"

"It's not a babushka pin. It is called a Matryoshka."

"No it isn't. I have been to the Soviet Union and I speak Russian. It is called a babushka. Anyway, where did you get it?"

"From a friend." Diane walked away from him and joined me with Baev, as Topchian repaired an accordian given to him by the French hosts for the day. Several American combustion specialists took 35-mm pictures of us, while K. Scheller methodically filmed Baev, Topchian, Diane, and me. When a young man walked inadvertently in front of Scheller and with a cigar drooping from his mouth, the big American shouted: "Move outa da way, will ya?"

"Now we are movie stars," Diane said to Baev.

"Yes, but we will never see the cinema," he replied, quietly glaring at Scheller.

Topchian played the accordian and Scheller tried to strike up a conversation. The proud Armenian ignored him.

"Professor Topchian plays very well," Scheller said to Diane.

"I also play a little."

"Well, why don't ya play for us?"

"No thanks, I only play for myself."

"Yer really a discreet young lady, aren't ya? Ya don't wantcha pictcha taken, and ya won't play the accordian. Oh, look at the babushka. Where did ya get it?" he asked.

"It's not a babushka. It's a Matryoshka pin," she answered.

Scheller's young cohort said to Diane, "It looks like an unborn baby to me."

Both the young man and Scheller had interestingly made the same error about the pin, which suggested they had been talking about Diane when they were together earlier in the day.

After the ferry docked, Diane joined Topchian on the beach and listened to him play the accordian. Two university men from California accompanying Scheller passed by, yelling: "Should we throw her in? Maybe we should steal her purse." They were about as unprofessional as they could possibly be, and their arrogance had already offended some of the Europeans, who were by now probably saying, "Yankee, please go home."

Meanwhile, I was talking with Baev on the beach, when the bald man from the University of Connecticut approached and said he wanted to talk with me. The bizarre cross-examination began: "What is your full name? Who do you work for? Where do you live? What is your specialty? What school did you attend? What hotel are you staying in now? Where are you going after this conference?"

His third-rate interrogation lasted for five minutes. I was diplomatically evasive on all questions. How the New Englander had the nerve to cross-examine me in front of Baev was beyond my comprehension. I knew that Baev would certainly report the man's questions to Pazelsky.

We returned to the ferry with the Russians, as Topchian played Armenian songs and our requests. On the ferryboat, Topchian and Diane jointly played the accordian with Diane playing the keyboard and Topchian pulling the bellows and playing the bass. From my sitting position Diane was hidden behind the Russian and the accordian, and when she played *Anchors Away* and the Air Force theme song *Wild Blue Yonder* it amused the delegates aboard the ferry, because it appeared as if the hard-line Armenian from Siberia were playing American military songs. I talked with Baev about propulsion technology, Topchian played music from the Black Sea region, and Pazelsky danced Diane about the center of the ferry to the noticeable displeasure of the super-team.

More photographs of us with the Russians were taken and I began to get the feeling that the Pratt & Whitney managers in Florida would get to see Diane dancing with a member of the Presidium of the Siberian branch of the Academy of Sciences.

The bus dropped us in front of the university, and we welcomed Pazelsky's suggestion that we all rest for the evening. He looked weak and tired after the long bus ride, as if he should have rested another week in Sochi after his operation. We walked back by way of the St. Charles train station. It was dark, spooky, and the smell of urine was overpowering. About half way to the hotel, while passing an outdoor cafe to our right, I saw the disguised Boris Mandrovsky walking toward us. With a slight stoop and hands folded behind, the Library of Congress supervisor approached. Again he was wearing the Abraham Lincoln beard and makeup beneath the lower eye lids. Our eyes met when he was about five feet away, and I looked ahead, as if he were an ordinary Frenchman. This time he had overdone the makeup, and I suspect that most persons would have given him a double take for that reason alone. Mandrovsky passed by. Was he trying to satisfy himself that I did not recognize him? I felt uncomfortable: an American agent who was masquerading in a rough district of Marseille had us under surveillance, and there were others in Building 828 who knew that I was working on a book to expose them. We avoided the alleys and returned to the hotel. I wanted to move on to Brussels, but there was one area in my manuscript that I needed to double-check with the Russians. Besides, I wished to say good-bye and thank them again for their gifts and hospitality before leaving.

Marseille, France, Thursday, September 16, 1971: We lounged around the Noailles until 11:30 A.M. and joined Pazelsky and Topchian for lunch at the university. Diane told Topchian that we decided against staying for the remainder of the conference and we therefore would not attend the Friday evening banquet with them as he had requested. "I am disappointed," he said. "We look forward to your company for remainder of week."

We were joined by Baev, Markov, Mitrofanov, and Smirnov. The seat to Diane's right was empty, and she was already giving me the eye, as if to ask: "I wonder who is going to sit there?" The way things were going, we had several ideas. A Polish-American who had not spoken one word to us all week joined us, as Pazelsky outlined the organization of the Soviet research and development complex to me. Pazelsky's explanation and charts coincided with what I already knew to be true. While he was not disclosing government secrets, he was covering ground that was common knowledge to men of his caliber, but difficult to ascertain in the West. The Polish-American interrupted us to ask me where I lived and worked. I told him that I was on leave from the aerospace industry. Topchian stopped talking to Diane to listen. I was then cross-examined intermittently for ten minutes. Topchian smiled at Diane and took another sip of wine. I was amazed at the pressure being applied to me in front of the Russians. Pazelsky and Baev stopped eating to hear our exchange. "What is your full name?" he asked.

"It's not important," I replied. With Pazelsky and Topchian most certainly aware of security-related "do's" and "don'ts," they must have concluded that I was having security problems; this would not hurt my relationship with the Russians the least bit. In fact, it probably enhanced it.

When the Polish-American began another line of questioning, I said, "I'm sorry, sir, but you have interrupted my discussion with Professor Pazelsky and I must finish it. We can talk later." He knew that "later" meant "never," and he did not return my smile. I was not learning anything talking to this West Coast Sherlock Holmes, and he wasn't either, except that I was being evasive, and his colleagues knew this from the first day. Besides, I was not obligated to give him the time of day; I was paying my own way, and I didn't have the time to play charades in what was now becoming a worrisome three-ring circus.

Pazelsky invited Diane and me to his room so that we could discuss in private a possible invitation for me to visit the Soviet Science City in Siberia in 1972. Topchian joined us in Pazelsky's simple dormitory room. Both Russians talked guardedly, indicating that they thought the room was bugged. If it was, I didn't mind; bugs don't interrupt conversations. At the conclusion of the meeting, the Russians suggested that we meet them again at 9:00 P.M. for a farewell party. I agreed. The four of us took the elevator to the ground floor. In the lobby reading a newspaper was the man from the University of Connecticut who cross-examined me during the Cassis excursion. Why wasn't he attending the afternoon sessions like almost everyone else? The newspaper routine was getting old.

At 6:00 P.M. we stepped outside on La Canebiere. A slight haze permeated the cool evening air in the brightly lighted street. We window-shopped, bought French pastries for the morning's journey, ate at Le Petite Cadeau restaurant, and went to the university for the nine o'clock meeting. The elevator door opened onto the poorly lighted hallway. We approached Pazelsky's room and I heard Topchian's voice from within. The light crept into the hall from beneath the door. I knocked and Pazelsky opened the door with a big smile. "Come in!" On his bureau were bottles of Russian cognac and vodka. In a jovial two-hour farewell, highlighted by an exchange of gifts—birthday presents for Diane included a Russian record by Alexander Bertinsky and a bottle of perfume—Pazelsky insisted that they walk us back to the Noailles. In the dormitory lounge, the man from the University of Connecticut was watching television, but when he saw me, he rushed up and asked, "Did you move out of the Noailles?" I layed my notes on the table before him, exposing a New York publishing house envelope.

"No," I replied. His eyes caught the envelope and he gave it a second take. Yes, I said to myself; you'd better look at the envelope because you boys are playing with fire. I will write the book and no pawn or organization in the United States has the power or the authority to rescind the First Amendment to the Constitution.

"Where do you go after Marseille?" he asked.

"Paris and Denmark," I replied, following Topchian out the door. I was glad that on this occasion we had a KGB escort to our hotel. As we passed the St. Charles train station, Pazelsky exclaimed, "It is a conspiracy!"

"We go to the space conference in Brussels next," Diane said.

"That is very bad," Topchian replied. "I think Peter need mask. Maybe wig. You are wise to leave Marseille." We bid our Russian friends farewell; I knew that we would always relish our four days in Marseille, in spite of the hindrances. We said good-bye on La Canebiere, and as the two men walked away into the darkness, I wondered if we really would see them again.

This was the second of three conferences, and relative to past meetings it was the second clean sweep. Brussels, our last stop, was next; and this was what the trip was all about.

30

Friday, September 17, 1971: With the conference still in session we left Marseille early and drove north on the autoroute to Paris, where we spent the night before continuing to Brussels. We checked into the Hotel President on Boulevard Adolphe Max, but because of our past experiences in Dubrovnik and Marseille, and the Red Baron's efforts in the United States to determine which hotel we would select for the Brussels meeting, we checked out of the President on Sunday and arbitrarily chose the Amigo Hotel, hoping that the move would confuse Uncle Sam for at least another twenty-four hours. While waiting for the elevator at the Amigo, the door opened, and standing before us was Boris Mandrovsky, the tall Library of Congress agent from Marseille! This time he had no disguise and he was as shocked as we were. He quickly shifted his eyes and took a giant stride past Diane without giving us a sign of recognition. Because he wore no disguise, he should have said hello; it didn't work out that way. Alfred Hitchcock could not have planned his appearance in Brussels any better.

After the abrupt meeting with Mandrovsky at the elevator door, we went to the Congress Palace, where the Belgian authorities had permitted me to attend the Apollo 15 astronauts' press conference. I had just finished talking with Academician Jouli Khodarev of the USSR Academy of Sciences outside the press room when I was grabbed by the elbow. It was Mandrovsky! "How did you manage to get in and listen to the press conference? You're not with the press . . . are you?" he asked inquisitively. His beady eyes conveyed hatred; his question telegraphed fear that the press had learned about the surveillance of Americans abroad. With his hand clutching me above the elbow and his breath blowing in my face, Mandrovsky asked again, "How did you get in?"

"I walked in." He frowned. "It's the person who doesn't belong in the press room who could have difficulties," I said. It brought to mind something that Diane said: espionage agents analyze every word spoken to them, searching for that cryptic meaning. He was going through the analysis, trying to determine what I meant. "We've met before!" I exclaimed.

"Oh, and where might that have been?"

"Kennedy International in 1966, enroute to Madrid." Boris Mandrovsky was relieved. There was no need to mention that I had seen him masquerading among scores of Frenchmen on La Canebiere while Diane and I entertained the Russians—I hated to think that my tax dollars were supporting him, however. He gave me that "you dumb SOB" look and I impulsively said, "You've got the type of face people remember . . . Yes, it was at Kennedy." I terminated the conversation and joined Diane and Academician Ulanov.

Brussels, Belgium, Monday, September 20, 1971: We sat near the front-center of the auditorium for the opening ceremonies of the XXII International Astronautical Federation Congress. The auditorium was bustling with conversation and excitement because the ceremonies would be attended by King Baudouin of Belgium. Dr. Charles Stark Draper, the elderly president of the International Academy of Astronautics—he was in Marseille—was seated in the fourth row in front of us. Next to him was Dr. George Mueller, formerly associate administrator for Manned Space Flight at NASA. Directly behind him was Professor Jouli Khodarev, the most important Russian scientist attending. The three American astronauts—David Scott, James Irwin, and Alfred Worden— were on stage, and Soviet Cosmonaut Boris Yegorov was seated to their left. Unnoticed, in front of us on the aisle, was United States Ambassador to Belgium John Eisenhower, looking very much like his late father. When the king entered the auditorium, everyone rose and remained standing until he was seated. Some of the most prominent people in the world were in the Congress Palace, and as the international news media jockeyed for position amongst a throng of well over one thousand persons, behind the scenes was another group of men bent on spooking anyone they considered to be the enemy, and this included me, a CIA informant for six years. The Red Baron was in the Palace and he acted strangely cool toward us; was this the friendly man who took us out on Miami Beach, or was he a calculating agent whose job it was to find out about our Brussels plans?

By the end of the afternoon session, the FTD super-team made its presence known. Like bulls in the china shop, they spent the afternoon eavesdropping on my discussions with officials of the USSR Academy of Sciences and the State Committee for Science and Technology. One Russian, Valery Skatchkov, a liaison officer who had been in contact with Dr. Russell Drew of the Office of Science and Technology of the Executive Office of the President— Dr. Drew was one of the recipients of the second annual report on foreign technology I had authored—didn't care for the surveillance and hopped about from conference room to conference room; the spooks were always on his heels, however. Skatchkov was involved in the early discussions on the joint American-Russian spaceflight mission and for that reason, though I doubted that the spooks knew this, the surveillance should either have been called off or done professionally to avoid an international incident. The rule: *espionage agents should neither be seen nor bother third parties* applied doubly so in Skatchkov's case.

During my exchanges with Skatchkov, the conference leech who was assigned to monitor our discussions was the man Diane and I would refer to as *the homo,* because at a previous conference she had seen him walking off holding hands with a Moroccan waiter in the early morning hours. Whether he was a homosexual or not was his business, but this was our cryptic lingo to avoid mentioning his name in public because he appeared to be part of the super-team. Based on what had transpired in Dubrovnik, Marseille, and now Brussels, it appeared that FTD was going ahead with its efforts to trump up a charge that I was being indiscreet with the Soviets, to damage my credibility before I blew the whistle on Building 828.

Outside the Congress Palace, Diane and I rested on a bench in front of the gardens before returning to the Amigo. A stranger walked up, introduced himself as Mr. Beghin, a Belgian artist, and asked if he could take close-up pictures of Diane. In security briefings, one is cautioned about allowing strangers to take pictures of you because "the results might not be flattering." Realizing that the pictures would be useful for surveillance purposes, I was reluctant, but on the other hand, I had no evidence to indicate that

the Belgian was a spook. Diane consented, so the matter was resolved anyway. Beghin took three close-ups of her; he did not smile,
nor did he appear friendly. Now he had me thinking.

That evening, as Diane and I were getting into a taxi, the
bearded American that Victor Antonov had fingered in Dubrovnik
suddenly appeared and insisted on joining us for the ride to the
reception. The coincidences were adding up beyond belief. The
General Dynamics Company engineer cross-examined me and
was particularly interested in whether Pratt & Whitney Aircraft
was paying my expenses. I wanted to tell him that Pratt & Whitney
was funding my trip—this would have blown the roof off of Building
828—but I replied, "Diane and I are covering our own expenses; I'm
conducting research on a book."

The reception was wild. In a flippant mood, Cosmonaut Boris
Yegorov approached Diane and asked if he could keep her Konstanz
photographic album, and when she turned him down, he requested
that she mail him the photograph of Astronaut James McDivitt and
himself, with Diane in the middle. Yegorov officially introduced me
to G. S. Balayan, the scientific secretary of both the Russian delegation to the Congress and the Commission for the Exploration and
Use of Outer Space of the USSR Academy of Sciences. Balayan not
only looked like a KGB intelligence officer, but he was one. With
the Russians passing the photo album around, and mocking each
other for their sometimes hilarious poses, Boris Mandrovsky and
his colleagues stood along the perimeter of the reception hall in
much the same manner that a professional football scout observed
a game. Almost everyone who had attended the Konstanz conference—East and West alike—wanted to see it. Mandrovsky finally
got his chance. Flipping through each photograph like an intelligence officer, with Diane providing the commentary and identifying each Russian personality by his side, the irked Mandrovsky finally thrust the album into her hands without comment, realizing
that our contacts in Brussels included practically the entire Russian
delegation.

Brussels, Belgium, Tuesday, September 21, 1971: I promised
Balayan, the Russian scientific secretary, a written account of
what I needed for my book, so I began writing down my requirements using a coffee table in the Congress Palace as a desk. When
I was half way through, the homo, standing duckfooted and with
arms folded behind his back, walked by and stole a glance at the
write-up. Valery Skatchkov joined me, and as we talked, the
leech edged closer again. I found it impossible to carry on any
conversation without being overheard, and if I had to place money
on it, I would have bet that the leech was loaded down with elec-

tronic gear and miniature recorders; this was something the Eagle said the spooks used, and it was another reason why the costs for FTD to cover any meeting abroad were prohibitive. No scientist at an international meeting was immune to being bugged by FTD.

I gave Balayan my book requirements, mostly photographic requests of Russian launch vehicles, in full view of everyone, including two spooks who were leaning against a wall watching the action. No, I was not a spy passing the KGB American secrets. If I were, I wouldn't have been stupid enough to pass incriminating evidence to a Russian conference attendee in writing, knowing full well that FTD's fun and games included the pilfering of attendees' personal belongings. This was another thing FTD had going at both domestic and foreign conferences. In Building 828 I was shown the personal papers of Yuri Shmyglevskiy, a renowned Russian theoretician. The highly theoretical papers had been stolen by FTD agents covering a meeting in which Shmyglevskiy attended. By 1971, however, FTD had bought its way into a number of international conferences and its pawns were chairmen of technical sessions. Therefore, in some instances, FTD had control over the papers accepted at conferences, which meant that other pawns were guaranteed to get on the program. At the rate it was going, it was a matter of time before FTD silently sponsored its own international meetings and sent out invitations to the persons it hoped to spook.

As Balayan tucked my request in his jacket, the deadpan stares of the spooks watching the transaction conveyed a sense of helplessness because they had no legal authority to prevent Americans from talking with Russians or any other nationality group. Because FTD did not have complete control over the conduct of Americans abroad, this meant that the U.S. government did not have to rely exclusively on FTD's expert opinion, and that is what was bothering the spooks in Building 828 who were now drunk with power.

The KGB in Brussels responded to the heavy surveillance of their scientists by overprotecting them. As a result, legitimate scientists throughout the world were having difficulty striking any meaningful conversations with the Russians. If Marseille were a waste, Brussels was worse; the spooks were simply milling around looking for a reason to justify their expenses.

That evening Diane and I attended a reception in the fifteenth century Town Hall in the Grand'Place. In one of the smaller rooms of the classic Town Hall, G. R. Inger of the Virginia Polytechnic Institute accidentally bumped into us and called out, "How's the Marseille Mafia?" I had seen him in the Grand'Place when he first arrived in Brussels, and before that, in Marseille at the gasdynamics conference. I thought it was a strange greeting for someone who had meticulously avoided us in Brussels. Inger, who appeared to have trimmed his moustache, wore dark glasses during the day. In Marseille, he was polished, polite, and his conduct was entirely proper. But his comment, "How's the Marseille Mafia?" was food for thought.

While I was conversing with the Bulgarian delegation, someone grabbed Diane's arm as she was about to take a photograph for her Brussels album. It was Mandrovsky. "If you don't stop taking so many pictures, people will think you are an agent of the CIA," he said loudly.

"Maybe I am," she laughed.

"Ahh, I see. You're making it so obvious that no one will suspect you. Very clever." There were several Eastern bloc delegates standing nearby. Mandrovsky let her go and said, "You really get a kick out of the whole thing, don't you?"

She got away from him and walked across the room, but the Mar del Plata leech stopped her and bellowed: "You know, every year when the CIA comes to visit me, they ask, 'What are the Jameses doing?'" He too emphasized the letters C-I-A. The leech's companion then took pictures of Diane, holding his camera only a few feet from her face in the dimly lit room. Identifying her with the CIA in front of Eastern bloc delegates, especially when FTD knew that I had been cooperating with the CIA since 1965, was grossly negligent, as if FTD wanted the Russians to stay clear of us at any cost.

I met the Red Baron, who had done his best to avoid us in Brussels. On this evening he was exceptionally apprehensive. Why? The surveillance and eavesdropping of my conversations with the Russians continued until the lights in the Town Hall were dimmed. As Diane and I were walking down the stairs of the Town Hall, Peter Ryan, an Irish news correspondent who attended the previous year's Konstanz conference and looked as if he belonged in one of Charles Dickens' classics, asked us to join him for dinner. Peter Ryan and I had spent an evening with Cosmonaut Boris Yegorov in Konstanz, and when Peter met me at the astronauts' press conference in Brussels, he asked if I had seen Yegorov. "Boris will be joining Walter Sullivan [New York Times science writer] and me for dinner. You and Diane are welcome to join us," he said. I already had a standing invitation from Professor Georg Asparuchov, scientific secretary of the Bulgarian delegation, but I wanted to learn more about Soviet long-range space plans. I accepted, feeling that another meeting with the jovial Russian cosmonaut would be worthwhile. Diane and I followed Peter Ryan and Walter Sullivan out the doors of the fifteenth century building and we were joined, not by Cosmonaut *Boris* Yegorov, but *Boris* Mandrovsky! Peter introduced us to Mandrovsky's friend, Dr. Richard Lawton from General Electric. "And this is Boris Mandrovsky," Peter said.

"Yes, we've met," I replied. The six of us walked through the Grand'Place to the restaurant district, which reminded me of the Plaza Mayor in Madrid. I did not know Mandrovsky's friend, Richard Lawton, though I had seen the two together the previous evening. Mandrovsky and Lawton walked ahead whispering to each other, while Diane and I talked with Peter Ryan and Walter Sullivan. Was this to be the confrontation? I tried to maintain a conversation with Ryan, but my mind was on Mandrovsky.

In sizing up the situation, I had witnessed an inept attempt by FTD to spook the Russians from the shores of the Adriatic to the shores of Southern France to Brussels. We had been harassed and attempts had been made to discredit us before the Russians by implying that Diane and I were assisting the CIA. But the dinner invitation seemed to have deeper roots. I could have declined it as I had done in Konstanz in 1970 and more recently in Marseille, when strangers invited us to dinner, but I wanted to get at the heart of the conspiracy and determine how high up it went. I had to let them play out the scenario and find out under whose authority they were operating.

After rejecting four restaurant selections by Diane and me, Mandrovsky decided we would eat where both he and his friend Richard Lawton had eaten before. Unknown to me at the time, Mandrovsky shoved Diane and said, "Move." He selected a table in the crowded restaurant. The bearded man from Dubrovnik—the one fingered by Victor Antonov—was seated at the adjacent table to my right. I tried not to show it but my palms were wet. The tension was mounting.

"Diane can sit between Richard and me ... nice and cozy," Mandrovsky said sarcastically. I sat opposite Diane between Walter Sullivan, who had his share of drinks at the reception, and Peter Ryan. We ordered wine and dinner. With Sullivan's eyes beginning to close and form slits as the evening wore on, Boris Mandrovsky became more talkative. For the most part, Mandrovsky was addressing Sullivan, only occasionally casting a glance in my direction. Because I was writing a book on the FTD story, I paid particular attention to Mandrovsky's long-winded uninteresting stories, and essentially ignored the other men; Mandrovsky had something on his mind, and if he had something profound to say, I wanted it for the book. I was eating a filet when the first message came through. Mandrovsky talked about Maria Soukhanov, the petite daughter of Dr. Ivan Soukhanov, the Library of Congress supervisor I met in Rome and Konstanz, but Mandrovsky's physical description of the girl fit Diane. It was a neat cryptic way of getting a point across without alerting the very content Walter Sullivan. "She is spoiled!" he continued. "She thinks she is God's gift to men. Really, if the Russians and Americans did not make such fools of themselves over her ... that's what makes her that way." He glanced at Diane to see if she was listening. "If she would settle down and have a few children of her own, then she would know what doing a day's work is all about ... and it would give her responsibility. Then she'll know what it's like to wash dishes, and do all the things a housewife does. Besides, American men don't like her type anyway ... First of all, she is too plump ... Her legs are too muscular to be attractive." How to insult a CIA informant in one easy lesson. I let Mandrovsky ramble on; he seemed to be enjoying it.

Walter Sullivan scratched at his thumb nail as if he could care less about Mandrovsky's enlightening advice to "Maria Soukhanov." With Richard Lawton and Peter Ryan engrossed in their own conversation, Mandrovsky shifted his attack to newspapermen and the *Pentagon Papers*. Turning to me, he asked: "What do you think of Daniel Ellsberg?"

"It was good that the story got out," I said, "but I disagree with the way it was accomplished. It's a paradox. No one should be allowed to transmit classified documents to unauthorized personnel. From that standpoint Ellsberg was dead wrong. But it seems strange that almost all of the supposedly secret papers he gave to the press were in fact classified because of political reasons."

"Ellsberg was a damn do-gooder!" Mandrovsky said.

"Look, I'm not endorsing what he did. I totally disagree with his methods. You cannot accomplish anything if you allow the people you're trying to blow out of the water to put you in jail." Mandrovsky changed his position in the chair. Sullivan continued sipping his wine, oblivious to our exchange.

Mandrovsky took a giant bite of his filet and said, "Some people think they can scare the government by threatening to write a book!" An arrow meant for me. So, the book was the real issue; I always thought it was. "And if they don't get their way, or they're rejected, they'll threaten to cause trouble!" Mandrovsky shouted. So, here we were in a squeeze play in Brussels, and Mandrovsky was alluding to information privy to the operatives in Building 828 who wanted to keep me in line.

Mandrovsky sipped his wine and said, "I hate those people who don't get their way and then blackball someone for life." My God, I thought. FTD held me responsible for blackballing the Swimmer! Prior to my departure I was given the distinct impression by a CIA source that next to Ellsberg, I was number one on FTD's "hit parade." The Foreign Technology Division had gone to great lengths to recruit engineers within the United Aircraft Corporation complex for intelligence work and I had attempted to stymie its efforts. With the Fahrenheit 451 exercise and the Florida management's pro-FTD, anti-CIA policy, I was very much alone in the battle. The situation was worse than I suspected: FTD not only considered me to be a viable threat to its empire, but Mandrovsky appeared to be its hatchet man. I let him ramble and he began another long-winded story for Walter Sullivan. Diane, recognizing that something serious was developing on our side of the table, dropped her conversation with Lawton and listened in. Mandrovsky again called Ellsberg a "do-gooder." Turning to me he yelled, "I hate do-gooders!"

"Possibly you've misunderstood the problem," I said. "It seems to me that Ellsberg was motivated because of other considerations."

"I have a very good understanding of the problem," he retorted, tapping a knife on the edge of his wine glass, as if he had read the *James file.* "If *Uncle Sam* tells me to do a job, then by God, I'm going to do that job"—Mandrovsky looked me in the eye—"and nothing will stand in my way!" He took another bite of his filet. "And I can say that I have friends in the Mafia who can arrange an automobile accident. I'd be asked questions later"—Mandrovsky stuck his chin out and leaned toward Diane—"and I'd have a few difficulties, but they would be answered, and that would be the end of it."

There it was! And to think that Pratt & Whitney in Florida had crawled in bed and consumated its marriage with this crowd; men who believed that murder was justified under the guise of national security. Because I was writing a book, and FTD, Pratt & Whitney, and the spooks knew it, the threat also had grave implications: "Uncle Sam" was intimidating a private citizen of the United States who was exercising his rights of free speech and free press; and officials of Pratt & Whitney who were knowledgeable of FTD's questionable activities, at a period when the U.S. government was conducting inquiries, undertook measures to prevent me from notifying responsible government bodies of the problem.

As Mandrovsky poured himself another glass of wine and Walter Sullivan relaxed glassy-eyed in his chair, the meetings I had with FTD agents in the States flashed through my mind—Super

237

Smart: "If you don't work for us, protect yourself"; James Bartley: "The law doesn't mean much in this business"; and the Fox, who told me a frightening story about FTD's overseas operations. FTD agents in Germany, he said, suspected that one of their men was a double agent working for the East. "Executive Action" was ordered. The suspect was drugged, beaten, and left on the German autobahn to be hit by a car. The man awoke in time and the "accident" was never realized. The agent who was assigned the job of killing the alleged double agent was reprimanded by his superiors in the Operations Directorate with the remark, "What's the matter, can't you even kill a guy right?" Yes, it was believable that "Uncle Sam" had granted Mandrovsky the authority to arrange an automobile accident as he claimed. Surely the agents in Building 828 would understand. And, if "Uncle Sam" wished to cover up an incident, I knew it could. This is what really bothered me. If I had known that the dinner would turn into a cryptic battle of unilateral threats, I would never have accepted Peter Ryan's invitation to join him for dinner. And it made me wonder about Ryan.

Having heard Mandrovsky's Mafia threat, Diane searched my eyes as if to ask: "What do we do now?" I was in no position to assess Mandrovsky's worth to the intelligence community, but the threat appeared to be another FTD end run. I had reason to believe that I was caught in the middle of a conspiracy which had its roots in Building 828, had spread to the Florida Research and Development Center, and had transcended U.S. intelligence operations in the European theater. They had made a mockery of the U.S. Constitution, and I could see possible violations of federal statutes such as violating the civil rights of an American, conspiring to commit a felony, and misuse of government property (i.e., U.S. embassy secret communications facilities). I once thought that the surveillance and harassment antics by FTD pawns were tolerable, merely a sign of their ineptness. Coupled with the threat on our lives, it was a whole new ball game. We were now talking about indictable offenses, possibly prison terms.

As Mandrovsky began another story, I no longer felt safe in the crowded restaurant. I listened carefully and got the impression he was telling me that I could earn an easy $3,000 or $4,000 if I let him have my notes from the three conferences. To corroborate this interpretation, I said: "I took a few notes on this trip for my book; from Copenhagen to Greece, from Yugoslavia to Paris. Do you know anyone who could review them, to make a comparison [with FTD's intelligence] and to comment?"

Like a magician, Boris Mandrovsky quickly reached into his pocket and handed me his Library of Congress card. He pointed to the home address on the back and ordered, "Send them to this address!"

I was familiar with the "home address" technique used by FTD agents and I was pleased that he was giving me more evidence, another piece of the mosaic which congressional investigators could look into in addition to overseas operations.

Seeing that I tucked away his card without bothering to read it, Mandrovsky told Sullivan a boring story about a sea captain and the sailor whose body was dropped over the side, weighed down by concrete blocks.

"Well, it all depends on which side of the ship you're working on," I said, hoping that this master psychologist with the cryptic verse would cool it.

"Yes," he said, "that's very important. The side you work on is very important." Suddenly, an ear-piercing explosion, like that of a large air-filled paper bag popping, rocked our side of the restaurant. Diane jumped and Mandrovsky laughed. The bearded man from Dubrovnik, sitting with other men, appeared to have been the cause of the noise. I winked at Diane, telling her not to worry about it, and we both laughed. That calmed her down, but Mandrovsky did not like to see us in high spirits; after all, he was trying to make a point.

I had done my best to avoid FTD's spooks throughout the trip. They had sought me out; they had harassed me; they had intimidated me; they had derided my wife—and throughout I had turned the other cheek. Still they came. No, I was not going to let him intimidate us further. I wanted Boris Mandrovsky to know that there were many reasons why FTD was considered to be incompetent, and the reasons included him. I turned to Richard Lawton, knowing that Mandrovsky was listening, and said, "Say, some of those Russians are pretty smart cookies." Both Lawton and Peter Ryan dropped their conversation to listen. "When Diane and I were in Marseille, we went to the movies with the Russians. It seemed that no matter where we walked, there was this one Russian . . . his name was Mitrofanov. He was the watchdog. He always seemed to be on the lookout, as if watching over a flock of sheep." I paused. The table was void of noise. Mandrovsky had a tight grip on his wine glass. Diane sat rigidly with that frozen glare of hers which cried out, "Peter, don't do it!" I sipped my wine and decided against finishing the story. Lawton and Ryan went back to their discussion. Mandrovsky shifted himself about his chair. He was nervous, but he was not about to give himself away.

I had eaten four courses, yet I could not remember tasting the food; the conversation had engulfed everything. Suddenly, Mandrovsky snapped: "Some people never learn!" Diane gave me that "don't do it" look again.

"You know," I began, "getting back to Marseille, we had some pretty good weather. It was sunny." Mandrovsky leaned in my direction again, so I wouldn't have to raise my voice. Richard Lawton seemed equally as interested in what I had to say. I was hoping that someone was taping the conversation. If Mandrovsky had painted the picture that we were two incompetent kids having a fling at the conference, I wanted to set that thesis to rest at his expense. "There was one interesting guy—he looked like a Frenchman. He wore this ridiculous outfit in the evenings. I saw him wearing the outfit on two separate occasions. Anyway, Marseille is one thing. But you know, I saw another guy dressed just like that clown here in Brussels! Imagine seeing the same outfit in two different parts of Europe, and the climatic conditions are so different! That says a great deal about some people. You can spot those kinds of dressers anywhere. You'd think they'd have the brains to wear different clothes for different climatic conditions!" I looked Richard Lawton straight in the eye and I got the vibrations that he understood exactly what I was saying. Boris Mandrovsky moved about his chair like he had ants in his pants. I had played my trump card. Maybe I shouldn't have done it, but I did.

Mandrovsky turned to Walter Sullivan. "That reminds me about the story of the French winemaker." Mandrovsky was preparing his rebuttal, and he wasn't about to drag it out. He moved about like a wounded animal, gesticulating with his boney fingers. There was no telling what he would do or say. His eyes shifted rapidly back and forth, like they did when we met abruptly in the Amigo Hotel elevator. Both Diane and I listened carefully, as did Richard Lawton, but Walter Sullivan was completely bored. Mandrovsky concluded his story with ". . . and the French winemaker couldn't tell the difference between the Bordeaux and Burgundy wines." Mandrovsky appeared to be saying that Mitrovanov could not possibly have recognized him in Marseille on La Canebiere.

"That's interesting, but I doubt it," I replied. "I never heard of an experienced winemaker [espionage agent] who couldn't tell wines [agents] apart."

Mandrovsky turned to Walter Sullivan: "That's what's wrong with this new generation. They never believe their elders." He looked at me. "You'll never learn, will you?" Mandrovsky frowned, wrinkled his napkin, and threw it on the table. If Marseille meant anything, it indicated that Mandrovsky had command over a tremendous number of pawns who obeyed orders. The surveillance and questions directed at Diane and me during the two Brussels receptions and the photographs taken of us outside the Congress Palace served as further evidence that a covert FTD exploitation program was in operation and we were the targets. I had been warned in advance and I had been studying FTD's methods for several years, yet I had completely underestimated the extent that it would go to cover up its unethical activities and eliminate a thorn in its side; trying to get a man replaced or fired was one thing; threatening his life was another. I had fallen into this trap because I believed it couldn't happen; I was wrong.

Mandrovsky asked the waiter to prepare the bill. He tore the label off the Pouilly-Fuisse wine bottle. "Now we'll sign it on the back so Diane will remember this evening!" Mandrovsky announced sarcastically. Yes, the label was his calling card; he could produce three witnesses who would probably testify on his behalf that they heard no threat. Mandrovsky thrust the label before Walter Sullivan of the *New York Times*. The science writer slapped the label with the back of his hand.

"Sign it!" Mandrovsky said.

"Oh, no . . . no," Sullivan replied.

"Sign it!" Mandrovsky repeated.

"Oh, Boris . . . forget it."

Mandrovsky slid it before Sullivan. "Come on!" Walter Sullivan signed his name on the back of the label and dated it September 21, 1971. Mandrovsky affixed his signature and passed it on to Lawton; Diane and Peter Ryan followed. I picked up the label without signing it and tucked it in my pocket next to Mandrovsky's card. Again, Mandrovsky noted the businesslike manner in which I saved the evidence. The label was his way of mocking the rules of evidence. I didn't see it that way. Diane had also heard the threat and the label pinned down the fact that we were all together. All the years of my effort were coming to a climax and the conflict was between me and the Foreign Technology Division, not the Russians. Years ago my objective was to collect, analyze, and disseminate intelligence information vital to the national interest of the United States. I had accomplished this through my attendance at conferences, the transmittal of my notes to the CIA, and the preparation and distribution of two foreign technology reports, even though the last one had been censored. But I had stumbled across something that was even more important: FTD was involved in highly questionable domestic and foreign spy operations, its work could seriously affect our relations with foreign countries, it adversely influenced both the U.S. defense budget and the design characteristics of weapons systems, and it had set up a Big Brother spy complex which interfered with our traditional democratic beliefs, fundamental principles, and the free enterprise system. The embryo of a police state was taking hold in America and I felt as if the burden of exposing it were on my shoulders. Seated opposite me, however, was a tenacious beady-eyed representative of the U.S. government who referred to my book and claimed that he had the right to arrange an automobile accident if necessary. And my sanctuary was now 3,000 miles away.

As we left the restaurant and headed toward the Grand'Place, I whispered to Diane: "Get Boris' friends to pose with you in the Grand'Place, but stay the hell away from him." She did what I asked. I got one picture of Diane with Walter Sullivan and Peter Ryan, and one of her clowning with Richard Lawton, who adroitly shielded his face at the precise moment I snapped the picture— strange behavior for an ordinary American.

Mandrovsky suggested that we have a nightcap and he knew just the place—an old tavern in the Grand'Place. Peter Ryan and Walter Sullivan rejected the suggestion and bid us good-night. In the tavern, while Richard Lawton was in the men's room, Boris Mandrovsky talked about "the old days" and cryptically made the $3,000 offer for my notes again.

I tired of his games and said, "One of these days, I hope I can say that I played a part in having your organization's covert activities monitored by one chief, and that man will be a civilian. There are too many damn empires!"

"You just won't listen, will you?" he retorted, hot under the collar. We had reached an impasse. Mandrovsky wasn't going to try anything now, because there were too many witnesses who could testify that they had seen him with us. It was 3:00 A.M. by the time Diane and I returned to our room. I waited anxiously for Mandrovsky's next move.

31

Brussels, Belgium, Wednesday, September 22, 1971: Diane was moaning. It was 6:30 A.M. "What's the matter?" I cried.

"I don't feel well . . . I'm sick." She got out of bed and walked to the bathroom holding her stomach. By the time I got there she was vomiting.

"It's either your nerves, or those bums played around with our drinks. I feel the same way." We went back to bed, and rested for a couple of hours.

At 8:30 A.M. I made telephone arrangements to leave our Volkswagen with the Brussels Zaventem Airport Volkswagen representative. In the lobby I asked the concierge to have someone get our car in the Amigo garage. Suddenly, Boris Mandrovsky and Richard Lawton appeared from behind us. "Oh, I thought you'd be up working bright and early," Mandrovsky said sarcastically.

"I've been sick and don't feel well today," Diane replied.

"Oh, I feel responsible for that!"

"I've been so ill, I'm sure I won't gain any weight today. At least I'll look thin when I return home."

Mandrovsky addressed Lawton: "She's always trying to impress someone!"

As Diane talked with the desk clerk, Mandrovsky said to me,

"Look at her head. It keeps bobbing up and down. Do you really think she's paying attention? Look at her head. See it bob?"

The two men walked out of the lobby. After Diane finished with the desk clerk, we stepped outside. Across the street from the Amigo was a man wearing Air Force sunglasses attired in black slacks and a white turtleneck sweater. He was leaning comfortably against the grill of a black sedan reading a newspaper, but when he saw us, he began to stare noticeably. The roof of the sedan had the "taxi" emblem on it, and both the man and the polished car looked like they belonged on a Hollywood set. If we were under surveillance, he was making it obvious. I walked across the Amigo patio and stopped about forty feet from Diane. The man continued staring. To his left, up Rue des Violette, the street we had used leading to the Congress Palace, was a dark-complexioned man in a tan suit reading a newspaper. This man saw me, and as if on cue, he similarly lowered his paper and stared. I walked back toward Diane across the Real [Belgian] Lace Shop, watching the man in the tan suit from the corner of my eye; he stepped sideways to get an unobstructed view of us. He too was making it obvious. They had us covered by car and on foot. This was insane, especially after the threat. It was like compounding a felony. With my back to the men I talked with Diane for about a minute and then asked her: "That man behind me, leaning against the black sedan. Is he still looking our way?"

"Which one?" she asked excitedly.

"Take it easy. The guy behind me with the sunglasses."

Her eyes caught him. "Yes! Are they going to kill us?" she cried frantically.

"No, they're not. Just do as I say. I want to go back to our room. Let's go." I asked for the key to our room and cancelled our car order. Boris Mandrovsky and Richard Lawton did not just happen to bump into us. They sought us out. What was happening? Did I panic him by mentioning the La Canebiere incident? Was he really going to arrange an accident? Was he authorized to kill in the name of national security? Did they plan to abduct us on our way to the Congress Palace? Did they hope to scare us, just to make a point? One thought after another raced through my mind. I locked our room door and closed the curtains. "They've gone too far this time," I said. I examined the notes I had taken from the three conferences; the last entry mentioned Academician Boris Petrov's heart attack and next to that was Boris Mandrovsky's business card. I was supposed to send all of my notes to his home address, so they could be included in "his take" from the conference. No way. I wrote the following message:

244

> Boris, your message is clear. We are leaving early. I
> will send you my notes in several weeks. Room 239

I had no intention of giving him my intelligence notes, but I needed time; anything to appease him so he would call off the goons.

"Okay, Dear. Take your purse and any money you have." I grabbed our passports, airline tickets, and automobile papers and hid my intelligence notes in Diane's pantyhose in our luggage. "Let's go."

"Where are we going?"

"To the embassy."

"Which one?"

"Our own. We'll meet them head-on." We slipped out of the room and walked down the hall. A man in a gray suit waited before the elevator, but when it arrived, he glanced at us and left. We were fighting the clock and the super-team's communications network— inside and outside the hotel. In the lobby, I gave the desk clerk the key and the Mandrovsky message. Suddenly, Boris Mandrovsky entered the lobby from the patio. With the Library of Congress supervisor breathing down my neck, I turned to the desk clerk and said: "Give that message to this man. He'll know what to do with it!" The clerk handed the envelope to Mandrovsky. "Get me a cab. I'd like to go to the American Embassy! This is an emergency!" As if jolted by an electric shock, Mandrovsky, standing but four feet away, jerked his head, and with eyes the size of saucers, the tall supervisor made a quick beeline for the elevator. He stopped at the elevator with the envelope in his right hand and looked at us from the corner of his eye. We stepped outside. The man in the white turtleneck sweater lowered his newspaper and began staring again. His dark complectioned companion on the walkway followed suit. They were taken by surprise as our cab swung around the corner and swerved to the Amigo entrance coming to a screeching halt. I checked out the driver and we jumped in. "American Embassy!" I shouted. "Fast." Our driver gunned the engine and we were off to the embassy. Weaving through the narrow Brussels streets at breakneck speeds, I ordered Diane not to look back because she was upset, but she turned despite my warning. "Peter! They're following us!" she cried. The man with the white turtleneck sweater was seated in the passenger seat. His cab stayed with us through every turn.

"Just keep your head down," I said, fearing that the goon may have had orders to shoot if we tried to avoid pursuit. Our driver came to a sudden stop and pointed to our left. I saw only sidewalk construction.

"There's the [American] flag!" Diane said.

I paid the driver quickly. We jumped out hand in hand, hurdled the sidewalk construction, and ran through the front gate with our heads lowered. A girl was at the information desk. "My name is Peter James," I said, gasping for breath. "I'm a citizen of the United States . . . I hold a secret clearance . . . and I wish to speak to someone about a private and sensitive matter. This is an emergency."

"Everyone is out to lunch now, but I think Mr. Fletcher can help you," she said, picking up her telephone. Within seconds, Mr. Fletcher, a tall, light-haired man in a neatly pressed business suit came out and ushered us into a room.

After examining our passports, he asked: "What's the problem?"

"Mr. Fletcher, do you have a secret clearance?" Fletcher assured me that he had, as did most of the embassy personnel. "Last night my wife and I were threatened. The man who made the threat said he could arrange an automobile accident. This morning he appeared again, this time supported by other personnel who were assigned to follow us: one on foot and one in a car. We were followed to the embassy."

"Do you know who the man is?"

"Yes, I do."

Fletcher placed his pad on his lap. "What's his name?" I paused.

"Well, charity begins at home. For God's sake, your life has been threatened, what's his name?" Fletcher demanded.

"Boris Mandrovsky."

"Is he Russian?"

"No, I mean, yes . . . by ancestry, I suppose. But he's officially working for the Library of Congress."

"Mr. James, the person who should be handling this case is out to lunch now. I've got some looking around to do."

Fletcher escorted us into a small room on the street side of the embassy and introduced us to a marine guard named Adam. A few minutes later the office door opened and a heavyset woman entered and introduced herself: "I'm Alta Fowler, embassy consul," she said. Miss Fowler took off her coat and hung it up. She asked to see our passports as Adam, the marine guard, left the room. I summarized the threat for Miss Fowler.

"There are so many automobile accidents in Brussels," she said, "no one would bother to ask any questions."

"As she was taking notes, Fletcher entered the room. "Mandrovsky's not registered in the list of delegates. In fact, there is no record that you're registered either!"

"Call the Congress Palace," I said. "They should be able to confirm it. Better yet, call Professor Andre Jaumotte, president of the congress; he's the rector of the University of Brussels. He can give you a positive I.D."

"Oh, that won't be necessary," Miss Fowler said. Fletcher placed a call to the Congress Palace anyway and confirmed that we were indeed registered.

"Miss Fowler will handle your case from here on in," he said. "Good luck." With Consul Alta Fowler questioning Diane, a hefty man entered the room.

"Hello, Burley," she said.

"What's the problem?" Burley asked, looking in my direction.

"We've been threatened."

"He's the chief of security in the embassy, Mr. James. It's all right." Burley showed me his identification: United States Department of State.

"Who were you threatened by?"

"A member of the U.S. intelligence community."

"What branch?"

"I believe it was the military."

"Can you be more specific?"

"Air Force."

"Oh." Burley turned to Miss Fowler. "I'll take care of this."

Because of the "Venice fiasco," I knew about the agreement between Building 828 and the U.S. State Department whereby Air Force agents abroad could use American embassies as their base of operations. And since Burley was chief of security of the embassy, then he knew what I meant when I said, "Air Force." Burley listened to my story—I discussed the Marseille surveillance, the dinner table threat, and follow-up surveillance—and after I was through, he blurted out, "It's an unusual story! What's the man's name again?"

"Mandrovsky. Boris Mandrovsky."

Burley wrote the name on his pad. "And what was the name of the congress?" I could not believe that the chief of security in the United States embassy in Brussels did not know who Mandrovsky was, or the fact that Ambassador John Eisenhower et al. had attended the opening session of the XXII International Astronautical Federation Congress. When I first mentioned the Air Force, Burley reacted instinctively as if he knew exactly what I was talking about. Now, he was acting dumb.

"I'd like to take a lie detector test and be interrogated right now if you do not believe me."

"That won't be necessary. Now that you've brought us into the case, no one working in American intelligence would risk trying to kill you. I used to be in counterintelligence. In the old days they used to do things that way. Now it's different."

"I'd like to believe you, sir, but the man who threatened us really believes I'm a threat to his organization. What do we do now?" I was thinking about our luggage, other accommodations, airline reservations, and our Volkswagen, still parked in the Amigo garage. As Burley and Miss Fowler conversed, I thought of the memorandum in Pratt & Whitney's East Hartford headquarters in which it was spelled out in black and white that the military intelligence services' group activities were massive, and were perhaps more of a potential risk to American citizens and the company than Soviet agents. At the time I thought that the language used in the memo was strong. But now the evidence was there; I just couldn't believe it. Too much had happened during the past two years for me to take Mandrovsky's threats lightly. Miss Fowler asked to see our airline tickets and automobile papers as Burley excused himself from the office. She telephoned Sabena Airlines and made reservations for us to leave Brussels in the morning.

Burley reentered the room. "Could you please send a cable to Justin F. Gleichauf of the CIA Miami field office?" I asked the security chief. "I'd like him to know about the threat; I'd also like the CIA to meet us at JFK Airport when we arrive in the States." Gleichauf had once offered to have CIA men meet me at Washington National Airport—the CIA had wanted to talk to me about my foreign technology report, but I never made the trip because of political pressure in Pratt & Whitney—so my request was not out of the ordinary. Burley shook his head and appeared visibly disturbed.

"You've already told us about the problem!" he said.

"I intend to document this incident in detail with the CIA." He apparently believed that since I had notified the Department of State, I would not pursue the matter through other government channels. There was something about his expression which bothered me. Because he seemed hesitant, I added, "Before we leave Brussels, I'd like to receive confirmation from the CIA whether they'll meet us at JFK. Miss Fowler has the flight information."

"I'll include your request in the cable," he finally said.

"Now we've got to get your luggage," Miss Fowler said. "I'll take you in my car." Diane looked at her in bewilderment. We were both thinking the same thing:

"Miss Fowler, I suspect they might still be at the Amigo. They could be going through my notes in the room right now."

"If you like," she said, "Adam can come with us."

"Yes," I replied. "I would like that very much. And Diane stays here." Miss Fowler picked up her coat, and Adam his black attaché case. I followed them past the reception desk and toward the main entrance. I scanned the outside area and saw nothing unusual. With Miss Fowler leading the way to her car, Adam walked with me stride for stride. At the gate a man in a gray suit and hat was walking briskly toward me. With the man only five feet away, Adam yelled, "Hello, John!"* The man turned into the gate and walked into the embassy.

"Thanks," I said, "for letting me know you knew him." My nerves were on edge; everything seemed suspect. This was the first time anyone had threatened my life. With diplomatic tags on her car Miss Fowler approached the hotel by way of Rue des Violette— neither the man in the white turtleneck sweater nor his friend in the tan suit were there—and she parked on a side street next to the Amigo. The three of us entered the hotel and took the elevator to the second floor. As I inserted the key into the door, Miss Fowler braced herself dramatically against the wall, as if expecting an explosion. I gave the door a shove and nothing happened.

I settled my account with the cashier at 4:10 P.M. and asked about the parking fees for the car. "If the car is wired," I whispered to Miss Fowler, "then the garage attendant is in danger."

"Oh . . . yes, tell the desk clerk not to move the car." Oh no, I thought. On one hand she braced herself against the wall as if expecting an atomic explosion, while on the other she hesitated to alert the hotel staff that the car may have been wired. This was highly inconsistent, and it led me to conclude that either the consul did not believe I was in any danger, and she therefore had to humor me until I left Brussels, or worse, she may have been briefed and instructed to follow orders on a delicate "national security" matter. That made sense since at first she seemed anxious to drive me to the Amigo to pick up our luggage without a bodyguard.

It was 4:35 P.M. when we arrived back at the embassy. Diane was still in Miss Fowler's office, looking a bit more relaxed. Another man whom I did not recognize was seated at a desk next to Miss Fowler's. "You can stay at my place for the night," Miss Fowler said.

Still worried, Diane replied, "I'd rather stay in the embassy until we leave. We'll even sleep on the floor if we have to."

Miss Fowler smiled and answered, "My flat is out of the way and you'll be safe. We don't accommodate overnight guests in the embassy."

"What about Burley's cable?" Did the CIA respond yet?" I asked.

---

*The actual name of the man Adam called to escapes me, and I failed to record it in my notes.

"Not yet. We expect a reply in the morning. Shall we go?" she asked.

We had to trust someone. In this case, it was Miss Alta Fowler, consul of the United States embassy, Brussels.

"Okay."

"Good. I'll call and have the room ready for you."

As we were leaving the embassy, the man in Miss Fowler's office told me: "I wouldn't tell anyone in the States what happened, if I were you."

"Why?" I asked.

"Because they probably won't believe you."

I took a deep breath and followed Miss Fowler to her car. As she backed out of her parking space, she said, "Peter, when we returned to the embassy from the hotel, I was told two men—one carrying a camera—entered the embassy. When our receptionist and one of the guards approached them, both men fled. No one got their identities." What the hell was she telling me this story for? Here, my wife had gone through a traumatic experience—it still wasn't over—and she was implanting an unnecessary incident in her mind.

I turned sideways in my seat to look out the back window. "Don't worry about being followed, Peter. I'm going to make a turn and take a different road to my place. No one will be able to tail us!" She veered sharply to the right onto a small side street, lined with parked cars on both sides. After making another turn, hitting forty miles an hour through the snake-like streets, I was satisfied that no one had followed us. She pulled into her quarters, a four-story building resembling the apartments in the Cherry Hill, New Jersey, area.

"I'll get the garage door," I said, thinking that it would be best to unload the luggage inside the building.

"No, that won't be necessary. I'll be leaving again. Put your luggage inside the garage." Diane and Miss Fowler entered the building. I looked about for anything out of the ordinary. Two men in their late forties approached on my side of the sidewalk. Both wore business suits and were walking briskly in step, as if in a military parade. Here we go again, I thought. I placed a bag on the ground and watched as they passed. The man closest to me looked familiar. I had seen him somewhere before; perhaps at the conference or in a meeting room in Building 828. Suddenly, as if a drill instructor had shouted "about-face!" they turned around and walked toward me in step. The man nearest me, wearing a blue suit, looked at the partially exposed passport in my breast pocket. He practically brushed against my side; I was certain we hadn't been followed, yet these men were waiting for us at Miss Fowler's flat. Were we really safe?

If I considered the leeches who monitored my conversations with the Russians; the Belgian who took Diane's picture in the Congress Palace gardens; the man who greeted us in the Town Hall with "How's the Marseille Mafia"; the Mar del Plata leech who mentioned the CIA to Diane in front of Eastern bloc delegates; Boris Mandrovsky and his dinner companions; the man with the white turtleneck sweater who followed us to the embassy; his dark complexioned companion in front of the Amigo; the two men in front of Miss Fowler's flat; the team that harassed us in Marseille; and the men fingered by the young Russian in Dubrovnik—even if I were wrong about some of those people, it still was obvious that we were being intimidated by "Uncle Sam" and this was by no means a small-scale operation. How they could muster the manpower and resources and justify this operation was beyond me. The cost had to be astronomical. Was this authorized by the chief of European operations for the "Air Force"? Or did it go higher? What about the embassy personnel?

I loaded the luggage in the garage and took the elevator to the fourth floor; our room faced the street. Miss Fowler closed the curtains and admonished Diane: "Stay away from the windows." The quaint room with wooden floors had two single beds, an end table with a lamp and paperback books, and a small sink in the far corner with two towels hanging from a rack. "I must return to the embassy," she said. "I'll be back later. I told my maid not to open the door for anyone."

Having had little food and about three hours sleep in the previous thirty-six hours, Diane was in tears again. Fortunately, she didn't know about the two men outside. Another interesting situation: the people who threatened us had two men outside and we were left alone. I doubted that they would try to kill us; at least I didn't think they would, but they were still applying pressure, as if obsessed with a fanatical, sick desire to impress me with the power and resources at their disposal. I never questioned it. Putting a stop to it was my objective.

The hate and anger for the individuals responsible for our predicament built up in me. I rested in the bed, staring at the ceiling, trying to sift out our remaining options. I had never dreamed that FTD's innocuous proposal in 1968, soliciting Pratt & Whitney's assistance to evaluate technical publications for the "Air Force," would end up in a Brussels flat with espionage agents parading beneath our window, following up a threat on our lives by a third-rate agent. The floor boards outside our door creaked. I watched the knob turn slowly and the door opened. Miss Fowler, carrying a tray of snacks and drinks, entered.

"What is it? Nerves?" Miss Fowler asked. Diane nodded.

She left the tray behind. With Miss Fowler at the door, Diane gasped for breath. "Oh . . . Peter, I don't feel well." I glanced at Miss Fowler—her back was to Diane—and I saw an unforgettable smile cross her face just as she left the room.

I picked up the paperback books on the end table. The titles of the books read: *One Life; Poisoned; Blood . . .; Execution.* Another book showed a series of Andy Capp cartoons. On the cover, one character said, "Buzz Off!" The books were fairly worn, as if used before.

More pieces to the puzzle fell into place: in July 1969 in Building 828, James Bartley once described how FTD used "hot surveillance" on U.S. scientists in Europe to keep them away from Russian scientists. The technique was to put a few goons on the American scientists—make the surveillance obvious—and shortly thereafter the American "targets" usually split. I now realized why it was so successful. *Almost all of the Americans who were intimidated naturally assumed that the surveillance came from members of the Eastern bloc;* those who reported anything to a U.S. embassy felt there was no reason to file a complaint elsewhere, since what could be more official than a United States embassy? Most, if not all, of these complaints probably ended up in the circular file in the "national interest" to protect FTD. The mosaic was now almost complete, and the picture was not pleasant. When Diane and I were tailed in Venice in 1969 after the Europa Hotel reception, I similarly thought we were being tailed by the KGB. What I didn't know at the time was that James Bartley, Fred Meisetz, et al. were in Venice coordinating the U.S. government intelligence collection effort in an obscure hotel room. Why didn't I comprehend the significance of their surveillance tactics in 1969? When the Jews were marched off to concentration camps, how many Germans tolerated the pogrom because it didn't involve them directly? Why didn't I take decisive action when James Bartley admitted to me that FTD used goons to intimidate Americans? I had erred by remaining silent; my secret statements to Leo Faucher behind closed doors were a far cry compared to what had to be done. The full FTD story had to be told to both congressional investigators *and* the American people, and I had to name names.

32

Brussels, Belgium, Thursday, September 23, 1971: Daylight pushed through the curtains. Diane's eyes were bloodshot and her lids swollen. I felt stomach pains; nerves and hunger. I walked to the window and looked onto the street; the early morning skies were gray and overcast. I snapped a picture through Miss Fowler's window to prove I was there. Our plane was scheduled to depart at 11:00 A.M., but Miss Fowler was adamant that we leave at 9:30 sharp. She showed us through her spacious apartment, as the Armed Forces Radio blared from a stereo, and asked us to be seated in the kitchen while she prepared breakfast. I scanned the gourmet cookbooks propped up near a windowsill. Diane gave me two quick shifts of her eyes, telling me to look at the table. Lying face up before Diane was a paperback book. Its title read: *Murder.* I rolled my eyes, conveying to her that she was right in her assumption— seventy-five cookbooks and one book on murder lying on the table before us. Miss Fowler didn't strike me as the type of person who read trashy paperback books. And to think we weren't allowed sanctuary in our own embassy, where we could at least have had some peace of mind in our own solitude.

Miss Fowler promised to drop our car off at a Brussels Volkswagen dealer for shipment to the States. "We'll shake it down before delivery to the dealers," she said. I paid her for the extra shipping charges—the Mandrovsky threat took care of our plans to drive the car to Emden, Germany, after the conference for shipment—and I gave her our Friday night banquet tickets.

"One of your [FTD] attachés might be able to use them," I said. At exactly 9:30 A.M. we got into her car and were off to the airport. "Did the Agency confirm they would have someone waiting for us at JFK?" I asked.

"They never responded," she replied. In my six years of association with the CIA, I had received a response to every one of my queries. Now, Miss Fowler was telling me that the CIA didn't respond. Did the embassy ever send the cable? Who would meet us at JFK?

Since there were a number of spooks involved in the "James case," I suspected they would have someone follow us to the airport. With that in mind, I purposely didn't look out the rear window; I didn't want to give them that satisfaction. She drove past the tree-lined streets of a residential section and after five minutes, as we were talking about the preceding events, Miss Fowler said, "Look at that cute MG behind us." I couldn't justify ignoring her, so to satisfy the consul, I turned and saw a white MG with its left blinker on. Suddenly, Miss Fowler swerved into the right lane and made a turn. The MG also turned right, but its left blinker remained on. Miss Fowler made more turns enroute to the airport, and the MG, with its left blinker still on, stayed with us. Again, they were making it obvious.

The MG followed us all the way to the short access road to the terminal building, before veering off. Within seconds we were at the international departures terminal. If the MG had taken the final turn, the driver would have been trapped in a small driver's circle, with no passenger to discharge.

I thanked Miss Fowler for her "assistance," and as I closed the car door, I said: "Miss Fowler, it's good to know that American citizens can depend on their embassy." She smiled and drove off. If she had known my side of the story, I wondered whether she would have blindly followed orders and executed her task so perfectly. Even if she didn't know my side of the story, it seemed to me that the physical and mental well-being of any American walking into a United States embassy should always be the first order of priority without qualification. In the terminal building, as I talked with the Sabena ticket agent, a man in a cashmere topcoat was reading a newspaper, but his eyes shifted repeatedly to the side, as if he were trying to look at me from the corner of his eye. The check-in clerk placed the New York tags on our luggage and the man stepped to the counter and looked at the tags. The clerk stamped our tickets and gave me the gate instructions as the man eavesdropped. What would he have done if the tags read "Budapest"?

At 11:35 A.M. our Boeing 747 taxied down the runway. I gazed out the window at the observation deck. The nightmare was almost over. It seemed that the only people who knew about the problem were the military intelligence services and a handful of embassy officials whom I didn't trust. Even the man in Miss Fowler's office told me that it wasn't worth telling anyone in the States about the threat, because no one would believe us. What else were they up to? The threat, the agents in front of Fowler's flat, the paperback books, the MG, and the cashmere topcoat; what guarantee did I have that we would have no problems in New York? Miss Fowler told us she could guarantee our safety in Brussels, but not in New York. Why would she even bother to make a point of this?

Would we be intercepted at the airport and in the name of "national security" be hustled off by FTD agents to a secret hideaway? Would they panic and order Executive Action because I had enough to launch a congressional investigation into their activities, and I had not yet signalled that I would acquiesce to their Mafia-like tactics?

I asked Diane to watch my notes spread over the serving trays, so I could get a good look at the passengers. On the aisle was a man from the conference; he was middle-aged and had short gray hair like the men at the air base. Was he a delegate who had left Brussels early, or was he tied up with the spooks? I asked the stewardess for two pillows and a blanket and walked across the back row of seats and up the right side aisle. I recognized two more men, again from the conference.

Diane and I tried to sleep on the flight, but it was impossible. The stewardess announced that the plane would arrive in New York in less than two hours. I tried to reevaluate our possible options. If we were going to be picked up in New York by FTD, I wanted either the CIA or the FBI involved, to ensure that our rights were not violated. I summoned the stewardess. "Miss, my wife and I have a serious problem. I would like to talk with the chief steward."

She probably wondered whether this was the making of a hijack attempt. "One moment, I'll get him."

The chief steward, a man in his late forties, pushed aside the curtain that separated the first and tourist class cabins. "May I help you?" he asked.

"Sir, when my wife and I were in Brussels, our lives were threatened. We expect to have the same problem in New York. I would like to have someone meet us at the airport. Preferably, the United States Federal Bureau of Investigation—the FBI."

The steward looked around. "Are you in any danger now?"

"I don't think so. I'm worried about New York, though."

"What is your name?"

"Peter James . . . and this is my wife, Diane." He wrote our names down in a palm-sized pad.

"Are we in any danger?" Diane cried.

"Not any more. Burley was right about one thing. If you bring in another organization, you've got less to worry about." We waited for the steward. The curtain moved and he popped his head through.

"I'm sorry, Mr. James. The captain said he could not send the message."

"Why?" I retorted indignantly. I could not understand it—similar messages had been transmitted before.

"Perhaps, Mr. James, you could contact the police at the airport when you arrive."

"No, it could be too late." Just then, a man entered the tourist class section from the first class cabin on the other side of the aisle; it was one of the men from the conference! He looked our way and walked down the aisle. What was he doing in the first class section? Had he interceded, possibly showing his United States government credentials to the steward or the captain? All sorts of wild thoughts raced through my mind. "I understand that I could receive protection from the New York City police, but I have been threatened by people who are affiliated with the United States government. The problem is sensitive." I knew this was my last chance to convince him that the message had to be sent. "It's important that other organizations within my government be made aware of the problem. As a citizen of the United States, I'm entitled to talk with agents from the Federal Bureau of Investigation. If you have been approached by someone from my government, asking you not to deliver the message, I beg of you to listen to my argument. No U.S. government representative, if his intentions are honorable, would ever object to having the FBI brought into the case, unless he had something else to hide—something that he is not telling you!"

My heart was pounding. The steward kept leaning over, trying to read my eyes. He pursed his lips. The seconds seemed like hours. "Very well, Mr. James. I will talk to the captain." He left, closing the curtain behind him. I glanced toward the man who entered the tourist class section. He was now seated about six seats over and two rows behind us, and still looking in our direction. I had to keep my cool; I could only conjecture at this point, but it appeared that an attempt was being made to keep the Brussels incident under wraps, at least until we arrived in New York. I felt that a reception party would be waiting with more threats, so that I would never reveal what had transpired in Brussels and never again work on the book.

The curtain moved again. The steward popped his head through. "Mr. James," he said smiling, "the captain wants me to tell you he is sending the message now." I was relieved.

"We appreciate your efforts."

"Is there anything else I can do?"

"Yes, I'd like writing paper and an envelope. If I write a letter, can you mail it for me?"

"Yes, Mr. James. I'll get it for you." For the first time since we left the embassy, I felt like I was getting control of the situation again. The steward returned and gave me the stationery and envelope.

"Who are you writing to?" Diane asked.

"I don't expect any complications, but I want Gleichauf to know about the Brussels incident." This was a precautionary measure in the event something went wrong at JFK. I drafted a two-page letter, addressed to both Gleichauf, who was probably no longer in Miami, and his replacement, Jack Hennessey, whom I had yet to meet. I gave the envelope to Diane, remembering that she had a few stamps. As she affixed a stamp to it, I had the uncomfortable feeling that someone was behind me. I turned, and leaning over us was a man looking out the window from behind Diane's seat; his eyes drifted to the envelope, resting on the portable serving tray on her lap. I quickly flipped over the envelope. The Peeping Tom returned to his seat across the aisle next to the gray-haired man from the conference. The incident could have been harmless, but I doubted it.

I gave the letter to the steward. "Mr. James," he said, "when we land, no one will be allowed to deplane until you are safely off."

The Boeing 747 descended and made a perfect landing, employing the reverse thrusters of the Pratt & Whitney Aircraft JT9D turbofan engines; the company was the furthest thing from my mind. The boarding ramp was lowered . . . we waited . . .

"What's the problem here?" an excited voice shot out from behind the curtain. It was pulled back by the steward and he pointed to us. Two serious, well-dressed men in their early thirties ran towards us.

"Are you with the FBI?" I asked.

"Yes, what's the problem?" the taller of the two asked.

"I'm sorry, but I must see your identification." He scowled and fumbled with his wallet. I read it carefully: Federal Bureau of Investigation.

257

"Our lives have been threatened."

"By someone on the plane?" he asked, looking at the passengers behind us.

"No, it's an involved story. May we talk in private?"

The FBI agent turned to his colleague. "Where can we talk?" The steward pointed toward the spiral staircase, leading to the first class section.

"Okay," he replied. "Follow me. Let's go." We walked up the staircase. The FBI agent signalled that it was all right to empty the aircraft. I identified myself, showed my passport, and told them that we had been threatened by U.S. intelligence agents.

"How do you know they are intelligence agents?" the tall one asked. "I work in the FBI and I don't know any intelligence agents."

"It's a rather involved story, but they were intelligence agents. I suggest that you call Justin F. Gleichauf of the CIA. The men at his office know me."

"Are you a CIA agent?"

"No, I'm only a citizen of the United States."

"Are you employed by the CIA?"

"No, I am not."

"Then how do you know them?"

"The CIA is authorized by law to approach any U.S. citizen who has had contact with the Eastern bloc. I was first contacted by the CIA in 1965, after attending a conference in Greece. Since then, I've attended other conferences and have cooperated with them. I've voluntarily prepared intelligence reports for them. They've always been grateful. We've had a good relationship."

"The people who threatened you. Do they know that you're helping the CIA?"

"Yes, they very definitely do. And that's part of the problem. During the last two years I chose to cooperate with the CIA only."

"I can't believe an agent from our government would threaten you if he knew you were helping the CIA."

"Neither can I, but it's true. Believe me, it's a very involved story."

"Why did you call us?"

"Because I have reason to believe that the group responsible for the threat in Brussels intends to follow through, in one form or another, while we're in the States, possibly at this airport. I wanted your organization to know of the problem. Up to this time, I had no guarantee that anyone, except the people who threatened us, and a few others, knew of the threat."

"Let's talk about this in our office. You have all of your bags?" I nodded. "Let's go." I thanked the steward, who wished us luck and said my letter was in the Sabena mailbag; he admonished me for using a postage stamp! We deplaned.

"If you question anything I'm saying, I'll be glad to take a lie detector test." The taller agent went ahead and arranged for another passport control booth to be opened.

Within seconds we were through passport control and on our way to customs. With the shorter agent at my side, I got a hurried glimpse of the carry-on luggage owned by the gray-haired man aboard the flight. The destination tag read "Detroit." He had a striking resemblance to a man whom I had seen with Boris Mandrovsky during the 1970 Konstanz conference. With mob rule dominating the scene at the luggage arrivals counter, a shouting lady with a barking poodle shoved her way between me and the gray-haired man from Detroit, and when I got my bearings, he was gone.

"Who's custody am I in now?" I asked.

"You're in my hands now," the agent answered, standing like defensive linebacker Sam Huff, looking to his left and right, as if expecting someone to jump me. I packed the last bag on the cart and wheeled it quickly to the customs booth. Diane and the taller agent were talking with a Federal Aviation Agency (FAA) official and the chief of the customs department. The FAA got into the act because the control tower received the captain's call requesting the FBI. "Please expedite these people as soon as possible," the taller agent ordered the customs chief.

"Now dammit, wait a minute!" the customs chief shouted. "We're not going to expedite anyone until I get through with them!"

"I'm sorry," the taller agent said, "I didn't mean to interfere with your job."

"Well you are interfering!" The chief turned to his man behind the counter and pointed a finger at him. "Do your job! And don't let anyone interfere!" It was pandemonium. We spread our luggage and personal belongings on the counter. The customs man searched every case, feeling the side pockets of the larger cases, and looking for false bottoms in the smaller ones. While Diane read off our list of purchases and declarations, I studied the faces of the curious onlookers at the arrivals observation deck, wondering whether an FTD reception committee was quietly watching the action. When the search was over, the chief ordered me to step into a nearby room. His assistant and another man followed us. "Mr. James," the chief said, in a determined voice, "have you declared everything?"

"I believe I have."

"Now you told me you did!" his assistant interrupted, holding up our declaration forms. "You told me you did!"

"Okay, I have declared everything I want to declare. Get on with it."

"Mr. James," the chief said, "we're going to ask you to place everything in your pockets on the table . . . everything!" I emptied my pockets. The chief examined the comb and other material on the desk, as his assistant frisked me. "Where in France have you been?"

"We've been to Marseille, if that's what you're wondering."

"What's the problem?"

"My life was threatened."

"Now you're in my custody. I want to know by whom?"

"It's a sensitive matter."

"You're in my custody now! I want to know by whom?" His voice was strained and overbearing.

"By a member of the United States intelligence community." He looked at my business card.

"Is this an ordinary business card?"

"Yes, it is."

"So, it's an ordinary business card."

"Yes." His assistant transcribed the information on the card to his pad.

"You got everything?" the chief asked his assistant. "Okay, Mr. James. We're done." I joined Diane and the FBI agents.

"Mr. James," the tall agent said, holding a slip of paper. "Please follow me into the office. . . . we've been in touch with the CIA headquarters. They assured us that they are aware of the situation. They asked us to tell you not to worry. They want you to proceed to Florida and give the Agency a call when you arrive.

"Did you talk with Gleichauf?"

"No."

"How about Mr. John Hennessey?" I asked impatiently.

"They don't have a record of him. Anyway, Gleichauf has not been transferred yet." I was thoroughly confused; the embassy sent the telegram after all. I joined Diane. "Mrs. James," the FBI agent said. "We'd like a word with you." I picked up our bags, as Diane went into the room with the FBI men. The events didn't make sense. She finally came out with a worrisome countenance.

"Peter, they asked me if you are all right."

"What do you mean, all right?" She pointed to her temple. "Did they ask you that?"

"They really did not ask . . . they asked if you had been under a mental strain."

"Oh . . . no! The damn embassy sent a message all right—one that would discredit us. That's what that guy in Fowler's office meant when he said no one would believe us! He knew." A massive cover-up was in the works. They knew that a number of persons were indictable, and the whole thing was about to blow sky high. Their only hope was to destroy my credibility.

33

Palm Beach Shores, Florida, Monday, September 27, 1971: The drive to Palm Beach Shores was tiresome and uneventful. At 8:30 A.M. our telephone rang. It was the Eagle! "Pete!" he exclaimed. "I'm surprised to hear your voice. I thought that you'd be locked up in a padded cell by now!"

"So you heard about it?"

"Heard about it? My friends tell me the wires were hot all last week . . . James this and James that. What the hell was going on in Brussels?"

"It's a long story. I'm interested in the padded cell routine. What's the latest you've heard?"

"The clowns [FTD] are trying to trump up a story that you are both in need of psychiatric help . . . Pete, this is no laughing matter. Get yourself F. Lee Bailey. You're going to need him. I don't think this is over."

"Thanks for the info. I don't want to contact any lawyers yet. Let them play their hand."

At 9:00 A.M. I telephoned the CIA Miami field office and asked for Gleichauf. "I'm sorry Mr. James. Mr. Gleichauf is no longer with this office. Perhaps Mr. Hennessey could help you." I was confused; the FBI said that Gleichauf had not been replaced. A man answered on the other end.

"Hello?"

"Hello. This is Peter James . . ."

"Peter, this is Jack Hennessey. Where are you calling from?"

"I'm in Palm Beach Shores. We arrived from New York last Saturday. We had problems in Brussels and I'd like to get them cleared up. May I get in touch with Mr. Gleichauf?"

"Mr. Gleichauf is no longer with us. I'm taking over your case. The only way we can get together is through the corporation. Mr. Gleichauf made that clear before he left."

"Is there any way I can get in touch with him," I asked, feeling that I needed the help of the man who knew me since 1965.

"No, we have your file."

"I return to work on the fourth of October, but I'd like to get this matter cleared up before then."

He paused. I could hear conversation in the background. "There is no other way we can get together, Peter. I'd like to get more on your case. Let me call you in a couple of days. Anything said now might damage your case."

We hung up. What the hell did he mean: ". . . anything said now might damage your case." Why didn't they want to bring Gleichauf into it? If there was one government organization that knew what this was all about, it was the CIA.

But if they wanted to, they could wash their hands of the affair and leave me on my own.

"Peter," Diane cried from the mail box, "you've got a letter." It was from a friend—a CIA source—who had heard about the Brussels incident. His letter read:

> . . . Your most recent trip—excluding one final incident—is the kind of vacation I would like to take sometime, or all the time. I recommend that you retain a good lawyer. This monkey business of character assassination, denunciation, and trumped-up phoney stories of misconduct and unreliable conduct is not something to be handled on a do-it-yourself basis. You must put up a massive defense of your personal integrity, and the ethics of the campaign apparently directed at you are such that you must have counter efforts to offset the fabrication and cover up. Don't mess around, get a lawyer, file a large counter suit, and claim for personal damages—pain, suffering, etc.
>
> I don't think many people are aware of the persistence, lack of ethics, and type of tactics that the clowns use to attempt to accomplish a goal. They are a cancer always trying to penetrate

an organization, and spook up the joint. A complaint to the Chief Executive Office and Senate is called for.

I can recommend the drugstore at Riviera Beach for good quality, reasonably priced aspirin. Best wishes for the hurricane season.

Word of the Brussels incident was leaking out. I was grateful that some people already suspected that there was more to it than the secret embassy cablegram must have implied. But I was confused by his advice to "file a large counter suit," What was that all about?

Tuesday, September 28, 1971: Hennessey of the CIA called and said it was the CIA's position that it could not see me unless the corporation approved. "Under the circumstances," I said, "I feel that it is in my best interest to request a meeting to include your organization, the FBI, the military, and my security department. I want to be interrogated and I want to take a lie detector test. And I think other people should be made to take the test. I want this matter cleared up now, privately or publicly."

"You would be willing to take a lie detector test?"

"Yes, I would. I made this known at the embassy in Brussels, and with the FBI in New York. You can check the records on that. I've got nothing to hide." He paused again, as if talking to someone in his office.

"Peter, let me get back with you in a couple of minutes." We hung up. I doubted that the CIA would risk getting involved in any joint meeting unless it had all the facts beforehand. And until the CIA talked with me, it had only one side of the story. I waited by the telephone and it finally rang. "Peter, I've talked with our chief, and he agreed we should get together before we hold any joint meetings. So, if it's okay with you, I'll call Mr. Faucher [security chief of the Pratt & Whitney Florida division] and tell him you want to talk with us. I have your letter [the letter mailed by Sabena] mentioning the incident and your book. If I get permission, I'll call back." Jack Hennessey called fifteen minutes later and we agreed to meet in the Palm Beach Gardens Holiday Inn at 9:30 in the morning.

Later in the day our phone rang again. "Hi, Pete. This is Lowell [Ruby]. How was your vacation?"

"Hi, Lowell, it was great. We covered quite a bit of ground."

"The reason why I'm calling . . . what's this I hear about your book?" So he was calling about the book. I could still remember H. Norm Cotter's declaration: *And no book!* "Do you have a publisher?" Ruby asked.

"No. I'd rather talk about the book at work." We hung up.

263

Wednesday, September 29, 1971: At 9:15 A.M. Hennessey called. We drove to the Holiday Inn, parked, and knocked twice on his door. It opened and a man in his late thirties, well built, and wearing a white shirt and tie, welcomed us in. He showed his identification: John F. Hennessey, United States Central Intelligence Agency. He appeared well-organized with pen and note pad on his lap and a tape recorder at his side. "Jay [Gleichauf] always spoke highly of you. I'm glad to meet you both in person. Tell me your side of the story." In a six-hour tape-recorded session—Hennessey stopped the recorder occasionally to inject his own off-the-record comments—I recapped the Brussels incident and named Boris Mandrovsky in my indictment of FTD et al. The most important point I made was that when Mandrovsky made the automobile threat, he claimed to be operating under carte blanche authority on behalf of "Uncle Sam." The reason why I emphasized this point with Hennessey was that I wanted the CIA to determine who had given Mandrovsky this authority, and why.

Hennessey said that the Brussels embassy notified CIA headquarters that we would arrive in the United States at Miami International Airport. The CIA therefore alerted its Miami field office to meet us at the airport. That was shocking since Alta Fowler had booked us on the Sabena flight 541 for New York, and she knew when and where we were arriving, and that we were driving, not flying to Florida! Why didn't the embassy give the CIA our flight number? Why didn't it send my message asking the CIA to meet us at JFK? As Hennessey was putting the recorder away, he said, "Your side of the story will be presented to the proper authorities. After spending the day with both of you, I can tell you're not in need of psychiatric help. If you need my assistance in court, I'd be happy to testify on your behalf."

"By the way," I said, "I have no intention of sending Mandrovsky my notes. If I don't send them, will I have any problems?"

"No, you won't," he said firmly. "If you do, call me . . . You promised them to him under duress."

"What do you think about the affair?" I asked.

"It's bizarre. When this came in at headquarters no one believed it. It was weird. Then one of our girls ran across Mandrovsky's name. She said: 'If Mandrovsky's involved, I believe it!' He's got a reputation for the out-of-the-ordinary."

"Have you ever met him?" I asked.

"I was involved in a quarterback operation once. Our people [CIA] couldn't get near the Sovs [Russians] because Mandrovsky closeted them. Yeah. . . . I know about him."

"Well, I really couldn't take any action against him in Brussels.

264

I didn't know whether he was considered to be one of our top agents —the James Bond of the United States—or a clown."

Hennessey laughed. "He's no James Bond, believe me."

Monday, October 4, 1971: I drove to the Florida Research and Development Center, parked the car in the west lot, and walked toward the entrance, recognizing only a handful of people on the way in. The recently promoted Swimmer flashed by me like a whirlwind and literally ran into his office with reports in one hand and a comb in the other. I felt like a stranger on the second floor, like I no longer belonged there. It was 8:15 A.M. when I found Lowell Ruby talking to H. Norm Cotter. "Norm, let's get together in your office, so we can talk in private." Their smiles vanished. "I want you both to know," I said, closing the door to his office, "that I attended three international conferences and I intend to finish my book." H. Norm Cotter gulped. Ruby stared in awe. "The memorandum you had me sign [prior to the trip] is unconstitutional—an extension of your no book, no travel decree last year. My discussions with foreign scientists and engineers were necessary for me to complete the book. If the company wishes to fire me because I exercised my constitutional rights, then so be it. I stand on my record. Let the chips fall where they may." For all practical purposes, the Fahrenheit 451 exercise and threats of dismissal to keep me in line had been in vain. The die was cast.

"Why did you have to tell us anything?" Cotter asked curiously.

"Because I've always leveled with you in the past and I don't intend to stop now."

"We'll get together with you on this later, Pete." Ruby glared at the floor like a mannequin in a spellbound trance, as if the roof were about to cave in.

I walked down to the security office to sign the foreign travel security debriefing form, to abide by Defense Department security regulations. With security chief Leo Faucher as the witness, I signed the form which stated that no attempts had been made by foreign agents to intimidate or coerce me. Under the circumstances, the form had something missing: there were no blanks for American scientists to indicate whether they had been intimidated by the Foreign Technology Division.

At exactly 2:10 P.M. I received a call from George in the Payroll and Retirement section. "Peter, I hear you're leaving us!" he shouted.

How strange; they didn't even have the guts to tell me officially. George and I talked about the company's "retirement program." Since I had "elected not to stay" with the company, I would receive a rebate on my retirement savings. I hung up and walked down to the security office. I could not help but notice the solemn expression on Lucille Hoagland's face as I entered her boss's office. The termination form was on Leo Faucher's desk, waiting for my signature. Like a good soldier, Faucher explained the purpose of the form. I listened to the dry monologue and then heard the words ". . . and your resignation . . ."

So that was it! If the FTD bag of worms blew open, the company wanted to be able to produce a signed document which would prove that I had left the company voluntarily; not under duress. It had taken them five hours to hatch this scheme up. Did they really believe I would sign a piece of paper which would in effect absolve the company of coercive acts in return for its promise that I could go through life with an "unblemished" Pratt & Whitney record? No, I was not that vain. "Leo, I have no intention of resigning! If the company wants me out the door, you'll have to fire me." That explained why George in the payroll department called me, and why no one had asked for my resignation or announced that my services were no longer needed. It was a legal maneuver; another "brilliant" move by management.

"Haven't you spoken with Cotter?" the security chief asked innocently.

"No, I haven't."

"You'd better see Cotter," he said.

I entered H. Norm Cotter's office. Two supervisors were standing before him. To capitulate and resign was to sweep it all under the rug. What would an "unblemished" name be worth if I failed to stand by my principles? I now was confronted with a moral obligation, independent of the FTD problem: I wanted no wide-eyed college graduate to sign the bottom line of a Pratt & Whitney Aircraft Florida division employment application without first having read about the James case. I wanted no company engineer in the Florida division to risk his career by needlessly making statements in confidence to the security department about alleged unethical or illegal activities concerning either company or government employees without knowing the details of the company's secret records.

"I was in Leo's office," I said to Cotter. "He said something about me resigning. I don't plan to resign!"

"Well, in that case, this will be your last day," Cotter replied. The supervisor on my left shook my hand and started out the door.

"Pardon me," I said, facing the executive, "I'm afraid I don't even know your name."

The man turned, and in a businesslike fashion said, "I'm Jim Peed" [General Manager W. L. Gorton's assistant]. John Worley, the other supervisor, was befuddled, as if he weren't sure why I was being fired, though it was his duty to participate in the scenario.

"What do you plan to do?" Cotter asked.

"I'll finish the book. I've still got a ways to go."

"Ha, I thought it was at the publishers by now."

"No, there are a few more chapters that need writing."

I returned to Faucher's office to sign the Defense Department termination forms. As I was affixing my signature to the paper, Faucher said, "If you mention your termination in the book, you should mention that the company gave you the option to resign."

"You can be assured of that," I replied.

I walked back to the engineering department and spent an hour cleaning out my desk. . . . The plaque of St. Basil's Cathedral in the Kremlin, given to me by a Russian during the 1969 Paris Air Show; a colored photograph of Diane in the Piazza della Repubblica in Rome; photographs of Russian agents; and other small mementos, mostly conference-related. Carrying a large cardboard box of personal belongings and memoranda I had written, I allowed bewildered Les Harrell, my administrative supervisor, to search its contents, before I walked out to my car. I turned and looked at the facility for the last time.

My first day at the Florida Research and Development Center was July 3, 1962: how things had changed. There was both sadness and relief in my heart. I drove to the gate and held out my badge for the guard. "This is my last day. Here's my badge."

"Who's your supervisor?" he asked.

"Harrell . . . Les Harrell."

The guard wrote Harrell's name down on the clipboard and wished me luck. I drove home and was greeted by Diane.

"How did it go?" she asked.

"Dear, there's no more job." I took a deep breath. "What do you say we finish the book?"

34

At 1:30 P.M. on October 6, 1971—two days after I was fired—Pratt & Whitney security chief Leo Faucher, dressed in a dashing gray suit, visited us in our apartment. He had with him a seven-page statement which the company wanted me to sign. Six of the seven pages concerned a legitimate national security item which I had already volunteered to the FBI and CIA, but Diane was first to note that part of the remaining page concerned management's alleged directives prior to my European departure. If I signed this page, I would have absolved the company of any coercive acts or attempts to intimidate me prior to my termination.

"What happens if I don't sign this statement, Leo?"

"I'd indicate you volunteered this to me and it would be filed as such." In theory, the security chief could give me a bad security rating if I didn't cooperate, thereby fixing my chances of employment elsewhere, but it appeared that both the company and FTD had already taken care of that matter.

"I won't sign anything that states I wasn't intimidated by the company. Let's change the statement to read that I was not intimidated by you during my employment. I can't say that about other persons in the Center. I'd also like a copy of what I do sign."

"We'll send one to you," he replied. I made the changes and Faucher left with a partially signed, watered-down statement. As it turned out, both Faucher and the company refused to send me a copy of the revised statement I had signed—another chapter in Pratt & Whitney's secret diplomacy.

Because FTD was bent on destroying my credibility and it apparently was still challenging my loyalty before other branches of the government, I felt compelled to lend the CIA portions of my previously undisclosed papers, prepared exclusively for my book. This included notes from the Rome, Konstanz, Dubrovnik, Marseille, and Brussels conferences. I did not believe that Jack Hennessey of the CIA was coercing me when he asked for the notes and more photographs of the Russians. But with FTD making strong charges behind the scenes, it would have been imprudent for me not to cooperate with the CIA at that time. And it was abundantly clear that the CIA revered its own interests more than the truth, and like FTD, it also feared congressional investigations. If I had to do it all over again, I would have told both FTD and the CIA where to go. I was opposed to secret organizations which made puppets of men and hid from the truth in secret hideaways under the pretense that they were acting in the national interest. The intelligence establishment was supposed to serve the nation, but somehow the roles had been reversed.

I went behind closed doors and began organizing my files for what I knew would be the greatest challenge of my life—getting the story out. Meanwhile, Pratt & Whitney managers in the Florida division were busy themselves. My colleagues were told that I had been fired for "violating company rules," and because the company refused to elaborate, unabated rumors abounded, including a slanderous story that circulated in North Palm Beach—I had been fired because of security reasons. This version was bought by both persons who had seen our foreign conference slides and the red-necks on the second floor of the center who, according to Diane's former boss, had her pegged as a "pinko" because of our 1967 Yugoslav trip.

With the success of the Brussels operation under FTD's belt, I feared that an overzealous FTD agent might find it justifiable to break into our apartment with the hopes of absconding with my files. I had to buy time to get organized. Accordingly, I approached *Palm Beach Post* staff writer James Quinlan and gave him a rundown on my firing and the company's anti-book position, but I made no mention of my intelligence background or the FTD problem. I kept my fingers crossed and hoped that press coverage of my firing would keep the spooks in Building 828 at arm's length. Quinlan rose to the occasion and on October 20, 1971, the *Palm Beach Post* ran a fantastic front-page spread followed by three more pages covering my dealings with Russians in Paris, Mar del Plata, and Konstanz. As I expected, the company steadfastly refused to comment on my charges that Pratt & Whitney management had attempted to muzzle me. The Quinlan story focused on the constitutional issue of free speech and the book I planned to write on the Russian strategic threat. The key to my intentions, however, which I directed at the FTD spooks, was a cryptic passage in the Quinlan article that read: "The common man, the taxpayer, James said, should know his government was encouraging procurement of high-cost, inferior products and weapons systems, and supporting non-cost-effective programs."

It didn't take long for the underground war to get heated up: on October 27, 1971, at 5:30 P.M. a mysterious Air Force colonel who refused to give his name called to announce that he was "alarmed" over the Quinlan article. The next day a frantic neighbor telephoned me. "Pete, a man stepped out of a Volkswagen and he's taking pictures of your car!" I grabbed my camera and rushed outside. He was gone. "Uncle Sam" was on the move again. I reported the incident to the FBI office in West Palm Beach, but after the JFK International Airport episode, I doubted that it would take any action.

I was overcome by an indescribable feeling of helplessness. By late 1971 the government had set up the secret machinery to intimidate any private citizen it wished, and there wasn't much a citizen could do about it. When men in government deny their fellow man basic human rights, when they conduct their business in secret for fear of public reaction or because it is outrightly illegal, then there could be no other interpretation: they were looking for the ultimate in power. No, this was not a *Seven Days in May* affair—at least not yet—but "Uncle Sam" was operating under a general mandate that had singled out for intimidation any citizen who challenged the policies of the Executive Branch of government. The press was my only hope, but the time was not ripe to blow open the FTD story because Pratt & Whitney could still distort my charges and challenge my credibility, using the prestige of a multi-million dollar corporation. I had to get the company either to tell the truth or lie publicly.

With the CIA sitting on the sidelines trying to stay out of the crossfire, I applied for unemployment compensation. On November 8, 1971, the claims examiner for the State of Florida Department of Commerce ruled that I was eligible. In a move which did not surprise me, W. T. Dwyer, director of personnel for Pratt & Whitney, acted swiftly and filed an appeal with the Florida Department of

Commerce Industrial Relations Commission. A private closed-door hearing was set for 4:00 P.M. on December 13, 1971. Representing the company was none other than Leo Faucher, the security chief. The appeals referee for the Industrial Relations Commission was Mr. D. W. Hall, Jr. I represented myself. After Hall outlined the ground rules of the hearing—outsiders were barred from the proceedings—he asked Faucher, "Why was Mr. James dismissed?"

Answering under oath, the confident security chief replied: "Mr. James was dismissed for violating company rules."

"What rules did he violate?" the appeals referee asked.

"He attended conferences attended by foreign scientists." To imply that this was a company rule was to stretch the truth beyond belief. In 1970 company engineers H. Tiedemann, H. Stetson, and my department head H. Norm Cotter were among those who had attended conferences attended by foreign scientists; in 1971 I had attended three such meetings; and as I was to learn subsequent to this hearing, in 1972 my former boss Lowell Ruby, R. Frazier, C. Joslin, W. Dunham, and G. Garrison had attended a conference attended by foreign scientists, and in 1973 S. A. Mosier, another company engineer, had similarly attended a conference attended by foreign scientists. The "company rules," as Faucher called them, had never been posted for other employees to read, but that apparently didn't matter; Pratt & Whitney had to overturn the State of Florida's ruling in my favor, because to lose this decision was to invite a crescendo of follow-on unfavorable rulings that would eventually lead investigators to the second floor of the Florida Research and Development Center and ultimately to Building 828 in Dayton, Ohio.

In the colloquy with Hall, I began to get the feeling that the constitutionality of the "company rules" was not the issue; *Florida State law was concerned with whether I had obeyed the orders of my superiors.* To buttress the company's position, Faucher moved in for the kill and submitted as evidence my May 12, 1971, memorandum, which stated that the company could fire me if I met with foreign scientists or provided various branches of the U.S. government with information as a result of this or future trips. The company was willing to submit this memorandum as evidence behind closed doors knowing full well that the proceedings were not subject to public scrutiny. This was America, but I felt as if I were participating in one of Stalin's secret purge trials.

"Why are you representing the company?" Hall asked the security chief. "Was security a factor in Mr. James' termination?"

"No, security was not a factor," Faucher replied.

"How did the company learn Mr. James attended the international meetings?"

"He volunteered the information to me." Faucher glanced at

my briefcase, perhaps wondering how many worms I had in it. I had enough ammunition to turn the State of Florida unemployment compensation hearing into a private three-ring circus but this would have served no useful purpose. I just wanted to open the door and let the fresh air in.

On January 21, 1972, Hall reached his decision:

> Given due consideration to the facts in this case, it must be found that the claimant's discharge was for misconduct connected with his work within the meaning of the Unemployment Compensation Law. . . . Misconduct connected with work as the term is used in this law has been defined as a deliberate act or course of conduct in violation of the worker's duties which is tantamount to an intentional disregard of the employer's interest.

I filed an appeal with the Industrial Relations Commission in Tallahassee, Florida, but again, I made no mention of the CIA or the FTD problem. In a two to one decision, the three-member panel of the Industrial Relations Commission upheld Hall's ruling. Whereas the company had thwarted me from collecting about $1,100 in unemployment compensation, its "victory" had been achieved at the cost of submitting the May 12, 1971, memorandum into the record. This meant that Pratt & Whitney was now locked in officially as to why I had been fired.

On April 2, 1972, the *Miami Herald* carried my article on the NASA space shuttle program. The most significant point of the *Herald* story was that science writer Richard Pothier mentioned that I had authored an 800-page secret report on foreign technology—no reference was made to FTD, however—and after battling with Larry Rogers, the company's public relations director, he extracted a carefully prepared statement from Pratt & Whitney management concerning my firing. Pothier wrote: "Pratt & Whitney officials at first declined to comment on James' charges [about being fired for conducting research on a book]. Then, a company official said: 'There is absolutely no connection between the reason Mr. James is no longer employed by Pratt & Whitney and his announced intention to write a book.'" It was like pulling teeth, but the company was now on record that the book was not the issue, in spite of H. Norm Cotter's anti-book declarations and Lowell Ruby's "what's this I hear about your book?" telephone call to my home before I was fired.

May 5, 1972: Our door bell rang. Standing at the front door with the coconut palms swaying behind him was the Red Baron!

"Peter . . . Diane," he said, "so good to see you again. I'm driving to Bal Harbour and I thought I'd drop by and say hello." Diane invited him in as I put our barking hounds into the bedroom. "Can you have dinner with me? We have so much to talk about. I'm sorry we didn't get together in Brussels."

"Yes," I said, "we'd be delighted to have dinner." My article in the *Miami Herald* the previous month may have prompted the visit because I had alluded to the second annual foreign technology report for FTD, and my public statements were getting dangerously close to Building 828. I knew the Red Baron well, and his air of renewed warmth was coated with a chilling tinge of frosty insincerity. Spooking an American in his own home was on par with FTD's latest bag of tricks, and we played him along. Diane showed the Baron the *Palm Beach Post* story about the firing.

"How's the book coming along?" he asked.

"Very well. I hope it's read by everyone."

"Make it vicious! Don't you agree? That sells books!"

"I suppose the truth is sometimes vicious." We talked for half an hour and I pumped him up with enough information to confuse the agents in Building 828.

"I'll get dressed for dinner," Diane said.

"Oh, come to think of it," the Red Baron said, looking at his watch, "I'd better get on down to Bal Harbour. Maybe we'll meet again." Since he had learned what he came for, having dinner with the Jameses would have been senseless.

When he was at the door, I unloaded the bomb. "Oh, by the way, when you see Boris Mandrovsky at the next conference, please give him our regards."

The wide-eyed pawn backed out the front door and left. The fuse was getting shorter.

The following Monday Jack Hennessey of the CIA telephoned. He asked about my book. "Well, have you determined whether we're [CIA] in it or not?"

"Yes, you're in it," I replied.

"Oh oh . . . How about FTD? Are you grinding them in?"

"They're going to be in it too."

"How about your travels in Europe this past summer [i.e., Brussels]?"

"I'm putting that in too."

"Ah ha . . . okay."

By early July 1972, the draft of my typewritten notes numbered 1,300 pages, and I had signed a contract with Arlington House Publishers to write *Soviet Conquest From Space,* the book on the Russian strategic threat. While I intended to introduce the FTD problem in this book, my main efforts were still behind the scenes.

July 28, 1972: I wrote a four-page letter to Richard M. Helms, director of the Central Intelligence Agency, objecting to the illegal undercover operations of the Foreign Technology Division. Excerpts from this letter are shown below:

Dear Mr. Helms:

This letter is to inform you that personnel affiliated with the Air Force Foreign Technology Division [FTD] have repeatedly intimidated private citizens of the United States, and particularly those persons employed by aerospace corporations who have prepared intelligence assessments on Russian aerospace technology that differ from those "finished intelligence" assessments prepared by the military intelligence services. I am one of the private citizens that was targeted.

... I reject allowing my tax dollars to be used to subsidize intelligence operations overseas that are directed at U.S. citizens, particularly when the antagonists know that these citizens desire contact with your organization only. I charge that the military intelligence services exceeded their authority in Brussels. ... I believe that scientists, engineers, members of the press, and authors should have the right to participate at international meetings without being intimidated by agents of the U.S. military intelligence services and I strongly suggest that the cost-effectiveness of their operations abroad be investigated.

I addressed carbon copies of the letter to FBI agent James Janney of the West Palm Beach office and Senator John McClellan.

August 11, 1972: A disturbed Jack Hennessey telephoned me. Senator McClellan received his copy of the letter earlier in the week, and transmitted it to the liaison man responsible for handling intelligence queries between Congress and the intelligence services. McClellan reportedly asked: "What the hell is going on?" There was some confusion because Helms did not receive his copy until several days later. Hennessey said that the CIA director had read the letter and asked his deputy to follow it up. Accordingly, Hennessey was directed by CIA headquarters to give me its reply in person.

Monday, August 14, 1972: Hennessey visited us. He appeared noticeably upset because I did not channel my correspondence to Helms through his office. In a very formal atmosphere, Hennessey made it clear that the Air Force Foreign Technology Division was not a member of the United States Intelligence Board, which includes the heads of the Central Intelligence Agency, Defense Intelligence Agency, National Security Agency, and Federal Bureau of Investigation. As Director of Central Intelligence and head of the

Intelligence Board, Richard Helms had no authority to monitor the activities of FTD. Furthermore, while the CIA could give me a guarantee that Diane and I would not be harassed by CIA agents, it could not give me a blanket guarantee which included FTD agents.

"I thought President Nixon recently gave Helms control over all of the intelligence agencies," I said. "That's what my other sources told me."

"Those were the President's wishes," Hennessey replied, "but the legal mechanism to do so does not exist. If you want action on your case, we suggest you take it to another branch of the government."

I was left with the impression that the organization of the U.S. intelligence community left much to be desired, and there was friction between the President and CIA Director Richard Helms.

August 15, 1972: I transmitted a letter to Hennessey and sent copies to the FBI and Senator McClellan.

Dear Mr. Hennessey:

Thank you for personally summarizing the "four-point" position of your organization in response to my letter of July 28 to the director. . . . The "four-point" summary again demonstrates that our country needs one director for all operations. If the head of the USIB [United States Intelligence Board] cannot assume the responsibility for the Brussels incident or control the actions of the group in question [FTD], it is clear to me that Congressional action is required to define divisions of authority and responsibility.

With regard to the Brussels incident, I have done everything possible to have the matter investigated, and this included notifying the Department of State, the FBI, and your organization. Rather than tie up government personnel listening to recording tapes of my version of the incident, it would certainly be very cost-effective to simply ask Mr. Mandrovsky and Miss Fowler to consent to a polygraph examination. *I will gladly delete the Brussels incident from the book (about 50 pages) if the polygraph tests show that I have erred.* I believe that this is a fair proposal and is consistent with the late Allen Dulles' position on the usefulness of the polygraph. Naturally, I would also consent to an examination.

It was time for a trial balloon. I wrote to Mr. Larry Jinks, executive editor of the *Miami Herald*, and informed him that I was putting together an exposé on the U.S. intelligence community. Within days I was contacted by Rose Allegato, his assistant, and told that the *Herald* was interested in the story. She assigned reporter Rob Elder to the job. Elder visited us in our Palm Beach Shores apartment and I laid out the FTD story on the line. I gave him rough draft excerpts of the Brussels incident from my manuscript and a detailed listing of all our travels, dates, places, purpose of each visit, and names of American contacts; this included Boris Mandrovsky, and Justin Gleichauf and Jack Hennessey of the CIA.

Having made my first significant move to get the story out, I began conducting inquiries into Pratt & Whitney's relationship with FTD since my firing. I met company employees in local taverns and I telephoned others at their homes. One source sent me the following cryptic message:

> . . . Continuing chummy clandestine footsie game between [the Swimmer] and the Dayton Devils [FTD]. Cotter [H. Norm Cotter] was nearly a picture of Hitler just before the Third Reich collapsed because some FRDC [Florida Research and Development Center] employees were talking to you. Lowell Ruby puts on the most unbelievable dumb act. Equally dumb is the conduct of the two Hals [company project engineers]. Cotter is boiling mad since he knows full well that there is a good possibility of a future messy explosion.

Following up on this message, Diane and I drove to New Orleans in late November 1972 to attend a propulsion specialists conference. In the Jung Hotel innocently having breakfast was the Snake—the FTD spook whom I met in 1968 in the Falcon Motel in Fairborn, Ohio, and the man who contacted the Swimmer to spy for FTD. Seated next to him was the chief of the Air Force secret facility. And representing Pratt & Whitney Aircraft in Florida at this meeting *attended by foreign scientists* was none other than my former boss, Lowell Ruby!

During the conference sessions the Snake was as busy as ever, making new contacts with managers from other aerospace companies. FTD's operations were still in high gear. I finally cornered the Snake at a reception and told him about the Brussels incident.

"You're kidding!" he exclaimed.

"Pratt & Whitney fired me. I suppose you've heard about that too."

"Why no . . . no," he replied, shaking his head in complete innocence with palms up. "I don't know a thing about it, Pete, really."

"Well, when you go back to [Building] 828, I'd like you to deliver a message."

"No, no . . . you'd better send it to them directly."

"No, I'm telling you, and you can deliver it!" The Snake shook his head and nervously shuffled his feet. "You tell the gang that I'm going to the press, Congress, and other branches of our government with the Brussels incident. And when I'm through, they [Building 828] won't know what hit them. What happened to Diane and me will never happen to another American again—at least not by your crowd. You guys are through!"

Diane similarly cornered an engineer who was moonlighting for the Defense Intelligence Agency; he had attended the reception in the Town Hall in Brussels in 1971. When she related what happened in Brussels, the horrified agent backpeddled and cried: "Oh, no!"

"Yes," she said. "And Peter is going to Congress with the problem."

"Oh please. I've got a wife and family. Don't bring me into it. I don't know a thing about it."

Meanwhile, I cornered another engineer who had attended the Town Hall reception in Brussels, and he too pleaded ignorance. "I've changed jobs since then," he said. "I'm no longer in the [intelligence] business." As I suspected, the spooks and collaborators who placed us under surveillance in Brussels were following orders. How many, if any, knew that Mandrovsky had threatened our lives? How strong they were in numbers; how weak they were alone.

Also in New Orleans were three spooks from the 1969 Venice conference, and a Dayton, Ohio, engineer who heard the scuttlebutt that I was making strong charges against FTD.

"Where'd you hear this?" I asked the engineer.

"Word gets around. Why're you interested in the Mafia?"

"What do you mean, the Mafia?"

"Hey man, haven't you heard? They're known in private circles as the Air Force Mafia."

"No, I never heard that, but it makes sense . . . a great deal of sense, now that you mention it."

"They're the black sheep of the Air Force, you know."

"What's your connection with FTD?" I asked.

"I knew people who worked for them. They've got quite a reputation for their underhanded operations."

"For instance?"

"Getting promotions and travel benefits for fixing intelligence assessments."

"You know about this? Why didn't you do anything?"

"Fight the Mafia? Hell no. Are you really taking them on?"

"I'm writing a book on them."

"Hey look, buddy, you're crazy. Forget I said anything. Don't quote me, will ya?"

"Not by name."

"Look, I don't want them abolished. Just some changes have to be made. Don't throw my name around, will ya?"

"Don't worry." The engineer took off.

And finally, before leaving New Orleans, I had an encounter with Lowell Ruby. The gray-haired Ruby still had a deep tan that distinguished him from the other executives. Ruby apologetically explained how he tried to salvage my job by personally appealing to General Manager W. L. Gorton. "But," he reflected, "when Gorton gets his dander up . . ." He didn't finish the sentence. It was academic anyway.

Rob Elder of the *Miami Herald* visited us in Palm Beach Shores again and indicated that the *Herald* would indeed publish the story with the understanding that it was theirs exclusively. In preliminary telephone interviews with Pratt & Whitney, Elder told us that Lowell Ruby had said that I was "highly imaginative" and assistant to the general manager A. R. Weldon reported that I was "just an average engineer." The ground tread by Elder was important to me personally because it confirmed that my book on FTD would have to name names and reference documentation to back up both my competence and story. The fact that Ruby and Weldon held important positions in the company was independent of the fact that the company was covering up its involvement with FTD, and the reasons did not include national security. Besides, what they chose to tell the news media couldn't change what had transpired.

Several weeks later in January 1973, Elder wrote to me and said that after talking with Boris Mandrovsky and checking his own sources, he could not in good faith write a story which would advance my cause—to have the operations of the FTD investigated— and he had no desire to write anything which would damage me, so he elected to write nothing! Because Elder was known in the Miami area as an advocate of the polygraph machine—he was investigating a police sniper case and he had written a two-page story on the merits of the polygraph—I telephoned him and volunteered to undergo a polygraph examination for the *Herald*.

"In your case, I doubt if it would help," Elder answered. He could have corroborated my side of the story by simply asking either Boris Mandrovsky or Miss Alta Fowler to take a lie detector test, but he admitted he had made no such request.

"Rob," I said, "you're welcome to review the documents in my safety deposit box if you would like to verify my charges against FTD."

"No . . . that won't be necessary," he replied, as if the decision not to run the story had already been made.

"You still have a responsibility to your readers. I have absolutely no objections to what you say about me, no matter how damaging you feel it might be. The truth will eventually come out. I've got nothing to hide."

"I can't write the story," he reiterated. The matter was closed. I was willing to show the *Herald* documentation to back up my charges of FTD's intimidation of the Eagle and myself, yet he would have no part of it. Why?

I received more feedback on the maneuverings in the Pratt & Whitney Florida division. One cryptic message read as follows:

> Several weeks ago the Miami [*Herald*] newspaper fellow [Rob Elder] called. I hope I did no harm. Yet I detected that old B & G [Blood and Guts: code name for a company manager] and his equally untrustworthy friends have mounted an overkill attack to discredit many [of your] items. B & G sure sold you out. This is a consistent trait. He tried similar stunts on others, however, these others . . . have seen through the thin veneer and side-stepped in time.

The *Herald's* queries about Pratt & Whitney's involvement with FTD set off another panic, even though Elder didn't follow through. A message to me dated February 26, 1973, read:

> B & G [Blood and Guts] again displayed his true colors. *Fahrenheit 451 may repeat on small scale.*

And again, on April 16, 1973, I received the following query and message from a friend:

> Nom de plume or alias of the threatening torpedoes who applied the muscle in BRU [Brussels] and NY? Because arm-waving wonder boys [the Swimmer and the Designer] continue to play games with their under the table pals, and despite Weldon's [general manager W. L. Gorton's assistant] public relations cover stories of complete innocence . . . their wonder boys field reputation is sinking to a record low level, contributions of B & G [Blood and Guts] and others.

The Rob Elder episode convinced me that my approach to the press was wrong. In studying the case histories of muckrakers such as Daniel Ellsberg and Patrick Fitzgerald, the man who exposed the Air Force C-5A military transport cost overruns, I concluded that I had to step forward and personally launch the attack using all available means of communication—the press, radio, and TV—and the power of the legislative branch of our government. By granting one reporter the exclusive right to the story, I was in effect restricting

279

myself to his interpretation of the facts, and I still left myself open to being destroyed by the very people I sought to expose. My draft of *The Air Force Mafia* was completed, but the story was not complete. I had to expose the cover-up and get the culpable parties to deny my charges both publicly and under oath. There was no other way. I had to blow open the FTD story in Pratt & Whitney's backyard —the Palm Beaches.

In the spring of 1973, names like Daniel Ellsberg and Watergate had become household words, and the public was shown documented evidence that some high-level government officials in Washington couldn't be trusted. The White House was implicated in a cover-up of the Watergate break-in, but as the sordid details of what would later be called "the White House horrors" came to light, it became apparent that Watergate was the tip of the iceberg, and President Nixon had personally approved a broad top-secret plan for spying on American citizens. The so-called Huston Plan was put into effect in July 1970—this was about two months before we attended the Rome and Konstanz conferences—and it allowed undercover agents to tap the phones of U.S. citizens, open their mail, burglarize their homes, intercept telephone calls and telegrams made by U.S. citizens to persons overseas *and increase surveillance on Americans abroad.* This explained why in September 1970, FTD spooked just about any American who was seen with a Russian. In December 1970 I had unknowingly documented the surveillance aspects of a Huston-type plan to Pratt & Whitney security chief Leo Faucher, but the company sat on the information. Thus, when the President claimed that he had rescinded it on July 28, 1970, and the plan never really got off the ground, I wondered whether that was the case. The files in Pratt & Whitney, Building 828, and other units of the Executive Branch, as well as the testimonies of Americans who were targeted, prove that a Huston-type plan was executed by FTD agents. The question yet to be answered was whether there was a connection between the agents in Building 828 and members of the Executive Office.

By May 1973, the never-ending Watergate revelations and the Brussels incident indicated to me that in 1971 an Executive Order had been given to stop by any means all "security leaks" prejudicial to the Nixon Administration, and the cover to be used was "national security." Boris Mandrovsky had orchestrated this theme in Brussels when he made it clear that he had the backing of "Uncle Sam" to *commit murder* if necessary to keep me in line. Interestingly enough, Mandrovsky's performance occurred only three weeks after other members of the Executive Branch—the White House plumbers—had burglarized the office of Daniel Ellsberg's psychiatrist.

I saw the Air Force Mafia as an independent silent partner in the Executive Office's attempt to evade the Constitution by using Gestapo-like tactics to stifle opposition to the administration's policies and its own operations. And I thought there was just cause to investigate the Executive Office's secret role with the U.S. military intelligence services in relation to the surveillance and harassment of American citizens.

Accordingly, on May 22, 1973—after James McCord completed his testimony to the Senate Watergate Committee—I sent a registered letter to Senator Sam Ervin and attached copies of pertinent letters I had written to CIA director Richard Helms and other parties.

Dear Senator Ervin:

The attached letter to the American ambassador in Brussels appears to be related to your Watergate-Ellsberg investigation. I suggest that your committee ask members of the Executive Office the following:

1. Did the U.S. Department of State receive directives from the Executive Office to assist intelligence agents from the Air Force Foreign Technology Division and the Defense Intelligence Agency on matters concerning the "national security"—to include the illegal harassment and intimidation of U.S. citizens travelling in Europe?

2. Did the Executive Office give the U.S. military intelligence services or agents blanket authority to use whatever means at their disposal—legal or illegal—to keep the Daniel Ellsberg types in line?

. . . I am writing a book on this subject and a national scandal which involves the Air Force Foreign Technology Division and the Defense Intelligence Agency.

Very truly yours,
Peter N. James

In June 1973 I went to Washington and talked with William H. Hogan, Jr., counsel of the House Armed Services Committee. I outlined my charges against FTD and he recommended that I send a summary to the chairman of the committee, Rep. F. Edward Hebert (D.-La.).

Senator Ervin thanked me for the material I sent him and he asked for more documentation. Representative Hebert later acknowledged that he was making inquiries into my charges.

On July 16, 1973, I sent a three-page letter to the new general manager of the Pratt & Whitney Aircraft Florida division, Edmund V. Marshall, and asked him to investigate the irregularities which led to my dismissal. I also wrote to Faucher and asked him to protect my files at the Center from being destroyed; a copy of this letter went to the FBI.

General Manager Marshall wrote back and said that he had investigated my termination and he was also responding for Faucher: "It is our practice," he wrote, "to retain the files and records of our employees, and I can assure you that we are following that practice in your case. Reports, memoranda, or other product data which you generated during your time with Pratt & Whitney will be retained, as long as the data remain pertinent to the company's operations, or as required under our contract with the customers."

Marshall made no mention whether I could review my company files, as I had requested. In a follow-on letter to Marshall, I detailed my experiences with the Air Force and CIA in relation to Pratt & Whitney and told him that my company files contained information pertinent to ongoing Congressional investigations. Excerpts from this five-page letter dated August 2, 1973, read as follows:

> . . . 4D. My company files during 1970-1971 contain memorandums, handwritten notes, and private records—in some cases acquired at my own expense—which document the improper activities of certain undercover agents (and an intelligence group) who were operating with carte blanche authority without supervision or control from responsible government bodies. Some members of this group harassed me in Brussels; the agent who threatened to kill me (he was also in Marseille wearing a disguise) stated that "Uncle Sam" had given him the authority to take whatever measures he deemed necessary to keep the Daniel Ellsberg "types" in line—this included murder. If the information in my December 1970 statement to Mr. Faucher, which was transcribed by his secretary Ms. Lucille Hoagland, and other files were disclosed in 1970 or early 1971 to appropriate government officials, it is possible that an ensuing investigation would have blown the whistle on—or curtailed the scope of—the illegal activities of these agents, and possibly the 1971 "horrors." In this regard, FRDC [Florida Research and Development Center] management must be held accountable for withholding vital information concerning improper activities of U.S. undercover agents from responsible U.S. government officials.
>
> 5. I cannot accept your decision that material I generated or received during my employment with Pratt & Whitney "will be retained, as long as the data remain pertinent to the company's operations, or as required under our contract with our customers." . . . Your letter of July 26, 1973, clearly invites another "Fahrenheit 451" exercise unless definitive action is taken, and I therefore

respectfully submit that the existing company policy is unacceptable and not in the national interest. . . . Pursuant to my letter of July 16, 1973, I have yet to receive a definitive position from Pratt & Whitney Aircraft as to whether (a) I will be given access to my December 1970 statement to Mr. Faucher and (b) I will be extended the courtesy to review my company files. I am preparing a statement and "road map" for use by Congressional investigators and a written response from you on the Pratt & Whitney official position on my request would be helpful.

General Manager Marshall ignored this letter.

Friday, August 10, 1973: Things began to move. A lieutenant colonel from the Air Force Office of Special Investigations in Washington telephoned and requested a meeting with me to follow up on queries from Representative Hebert. The following Monday Lt. Col. Richard Bellinger and Major Thomas Nelson of the Air Force Office of Special Investigations flew into the Palm Beaches and in five days of discussions, in which both the Air Force and I taped the question and answer sessions, we prepared a twenty-nine page statement which I signed under oath; I named names, gave dates, places and documentation, and on page 28 of the statement I made it clear that I would consent to a polygraph examination concerning anything we discussed in the five days of recorded conversations.

With the Air Force investigators out of the way, I reached an agreement with managing editor Tom Kelly of the *Palm Beach Post* to write an exposé on the Air Force Mafia in a copyrighted series for the *Post*. The Dayton *Daily News* learned that a story was being written on the Air Force Foreign Technology Division and it kept its pulse on the *Palm Beach Post* wires. Meanwhile, a *Palm Beach Post* reporter sent queries to Pratt & Whitney, giving the company the opportunity to respond to my charges, so its rebuttal could be presented to the public when my series hit the press. Similarly, the *Dayton Daily News* telephoned the company and Air Force headquarters for a response. Pratt & Whitney would accept only written questions, and it responded with a carefully worded statement of its own. Apparently believing that the press would be carrying a small column containing vague unsubstantiated charges by me, Pratt & Whitney took the giant step and responded as follows:

"In past years we have performed analytical work under contract to the Air Force Foreign Technology Division. But we know of no threats or coercive actions against either the company or Mr. James by anyone in the Air Force.

"Mr. James was dismissed by Pratt & Whitney Aircraft on

Oct. 4, 1971, for violation of company rules and not for any security reasons.

"Because a point-by-point rebuttal would require us to divulge classified or proprietary information we cannot respond to your other questions."

There it was. The company was now denying publicly what it knew privately to be true—the Foreign Technology Division had indeed intimidated both the company and its employees, and this was the subject of numerous private memoranda in both East Hartford and Florida and verbal and written statements I had made to the security chief Leo Faucher. Yet, the party line to the public was ". . . But we know of no threats or coercive actions against either the company or Mr. James by anyone in the Air Force." That was another lie to destroy my credibility.

Palm Beach Post editor Ray Mariotti read my story one last time. Flopping it on his desk, he looked up at me and said, "Okay, we run it this Sunday!"

Sunday, September 30, 1973, front page—Dayton Daily News:

In Building 828 of Wright-Patterson Air Force Base near Dayton, Ohio, there exists a hush-hush operation of spies who answer to no one but the Air Force, who spy on their fellow citizens, and whose operations are so illegal and unethical that they are known privately as the "Air Force Mafia."

"That is how Peter James kicks off in today's *Palm Beach Post* a five-part series of copyrighted articles containing accusations against the Air Force's Foreign Technology Division, headquartered at Wright-Patterson. . . .

In a daily front-page barrage—Sunday, Monday, Tuesday, Wednesday, and Thursday—the *Palm Beach Post* carried the exposé of FTD's operations. Supported with documentation, including Super Smart's February 11, 1970, memorandum intimidating East Hartford, I outlined the company's sordid involvement with FTD's spy operations and how it had succumbed to pressure by the "Air Force." And, of course, the *Post* carried the company's denial. With Pratt & Whitney employees secretly reading the exposé in their automobiles during the lunch-hour breaks and some high-level managers in the design department passing the newspaper around in sealed inter-office correspondence folders, as if the exposé were Solzhenitsyn's *Gulag Archipelago,* I began getting positive readings from employees who learned for the first time that I had been assisting the CIA since 1965 and I had not been fired for security reasons as most believed. Meanwhile, Air Force officers from Patrick Air Force Base near Cape Kennedy were picking up three copies of the *Palm Beach Post* throughout the duration of the five-part series for delivery to the shell-shocked agents in Building 828, who by now could see the temple walls crumbling. When asked to comment on my charges by the *Dayton Daily News,* one high-level Air Force official who did not wish to be identified doubted that there was anything to it, and he dismissed my charges as those of a "disgruntled employee."

With FTD still reeling from the assault, I quickly dispatched the five-part series to Senator William Proxmire's office and asked for an investigation of FTD's activities. Senator Proxmire wrote back and said that he would give the matter his careful and prompt attention, and he appreciated receiving any further documentation that I had. In a subsequent exchange of letters, I sent the senior senator from Wisconsin the Sam Ervin package, my 29-page statement under oath, and other documents to support my charges against FTD. In a response to Senator Proxmire's queries, Mr. Joseph J. F. Clark of the Department of the Air Force notified the senator in a memorandum dated December 11, 1973, that the Air Force had investigated my charges. Clark wrote:

> This matter has been investigated by the Air Force Office of Special Investigations (AFOSI). As you are aware, Mr. Peter N. James, who made the allegations, provided AFOSI with a lengthy sworn statement, supported by numerous documentary exhibits which he believes lend credence to his allegations. Based on this sworn statement, numerous military and civilian FTD employees and officials named by Mr. James, or who were identified as having been familiar with the many facets of the allegations, were interviewed. These interviews support Mr. James' facts insofar as dates of international meetings, identities of FTD attendees, etc., are concerned. The interviews do not, however, appear to substantiate his allegations against FTD of improper administrative conduct, intelligence collection malpractice, threats or harassment. The investigation did not reveal any evidence, other than Mr. James' statement, to substantiate his claim of an alleged FTD-inspired conspiracy to threaten or harass Mr. James and his wife in Brussels, Belgium, in September 1971. Various personnel specifically identified by Mr. James as having been present at that time were interviewed. All denied any knowledge of alleged threats of harassment.

I regretted Clark's response. It meant that some parties had lied to government investigators, which is a felony, and I knew that I would have to throw in everything including the kitchen sink into the book to prove my charges against FTD. With Pratt & Whitney

Aircraft and FTD marshalling their forces to counter the next assault—I was now applying pressure on FTD by speaking before college audiences and appearing on talk shows—the *Washington Post* carried a front-page story on March 14, 1974, by Laurence Stern blowing open nationally Senator Proxmire's involvement in the FTD matter. Stern wrote:

> After investigating the James affair, contained in a 29-page sworn statement plus exhibits given to the Air Force Office of Special Investigations, Sen. William Proxmire (D.-Wis.) called yesterday for abolition of the Foreign Technology Division.*

With Diane handling telephone calls from CBS and *L'Express*, the Paris-based paper, and with the Associated Press, *Dayton Daily News*, *Miami Herald*, and *Palm Beach Post* having picked up the scenario that followed, the previously unknown Foreign Technology Division was put on the worldwide scoreboard. The news media kept me abreast of the fast-moving action in Washington. In a colloquy between Senator Proxmire and Secretary of Defense James Schlesinger in hearings before the Joint Economic Committee, Proxmire raised the FTD question and the defense secretary said he would look into it. In a follow-on Sunday front-page story by the *Dayton Daily News*, it was reported that the Pentagon had signalled to Senator Proxmire a willingness to restrict severely the overseas collection activities of FTD's worldwide spy apparatus.

Feeling that the Pentagon would not curtail the activities of the Air Force Mafia until the full story was told and the legislative branch of government conducted a wide-sweeping investigation (a CIA source informed me that the Air Force Mafia would not be deterred from the international conference circuit in spite of Proxmire's pronouncement), Diane and I spent a week in Washington in April 1974 and met with the staffs of four Senate and House committees. On Capitol Hill, I was told that the Pentagon had prepared a classified report on "the Jameses"—the battle was far from over. We made tentative arrangements to transmit my files to Congress

---

*Justin F. Gleichauf, my former CIA contact and an asset to any organization, retired in 1973 after a quarter of a century service with the CIA and joined the Wackenhut Corporation, the nationally known detective agency. In Laurence Stern's March 14, 1974, *Washington Post* article concerning my role as a CIA informant and Senator Proxmire's pronouncement that FTD should be abolished, Stern wrote:

> On the other hand James had been reporting regularly to the CIA through the then-chief of its Miami field office, Justin F. Gleichauf, since 1965. Gleichauf, now retired from the agency and an employee of Wackenhut in Miami, warmly praised James for his services in a Dec. 18, 1969 letter.

Very shortly after the *Washington Post* story was published, Gleichauf was notified by Wackenhut that his services were no longer needed.

after I was done with them. And, of course, they would be sent advance copies of *The Air Force Mafia* from the publisher to tie the pieces together.

The visit was worthwhile to me personally because in a tape recorded session with a staff member of the Senate Foreign Relations Committee, I learned that congressional investigators were hot on the trail of CIA agents who had conducted questionable domestic spy operations against American citizens. (A covert spy program adroitly blown open in December 1974 by Seymour M. Hersh of *The New York Times*.) This explained why in September 1971 an agent of the CIA New York field office had privately asked an FBI agent not to file a report on the JFK International Airport incident and my allegations concerning FTD, the Brussels threat and surveillance (the FBI filed it anyway); why CIA agents had approached Justin F. Gleichauf, former chief of the CIA Miami field office, and asked him to discredit me (which he would not do); and why CIA headquarters reported that John F. Hennessey's Holiday Inn tape recordings covering my charges of intensive surveillance and harassment by U.S. government agents had been "routinely erased" when I asked the agency to make the tapes available to Senator William Proxmire. The CIA was involved in a massive coverup of its own, and this further explained why during 1971-72 a CIA agent "routinely" called me at home to check on the status of the book and particularly the name of my publisher.

Walking down the steps of the Capitol I could not help but notice the cherry blossoms which contrasted sharply against the dark clouds that hung over the White House. I had seen the embryo of a police state take hold in America, nurtured by pawns who obeyed orders without questioning the moral implications of their orders, corporate executives who forsook their fellow man and our American heritage to "move up" in the world, and people who believed that the end justified any means and that the masses were too ignorant to understand what was best for them. That was the mentality of men who wrought Nazi Germany and led to the genocide of millions of Jews.

No, mine was not a sour grapes affair, for the battle lines had been drawn well before I was fired. And no, this was not a personal vendetta, for more was at stake than personalities. When historians look back at the Watergate era, they will record that the U.S. government was corrupted at its very highest levels, and they will find the remains of a nascent police state. This will be a sad chapter in our nation's history. But they will also record that many Americans cared, and that they did something about it.

Epilogue

On September 19, 1974, Senator Howard Baker (R.-Tenn., and past vice chairman of the Select Committee on Presidential Campaign Activities—the Senate Watergate Committee) introduced a broadly supported bipartisan bill (S. 4019) to create within the Congress a Joint Committee on Intelligence Oversight. The purpose of the Baker-Weicker legislation is to establish a 14-member joint House-Senate committee responsible for overseeing the operations of the Central Intelligence Agency (CIA), Federal Bureau of Investigation (FBI), Secret Service, Defense Intelligence Agency (DIA), National Security Agency (NSA), and other federal agencies having intelligence jurisdiction. Similarly, Congressman Michael J. Harrington (D.-Mass.), the congressman who disclosed publicly that the CIA had secretly funneled millions of dollars into Chile to support the anti-Allende forces, introduced legislation (H.R. 1231) in the House of Representatives to create a standing House intelligence oversight committee which would meet regularly and, among other things, would also oversee Air Force intelligence operations.

Senators William Proxmire (D.-Wis.) and Howard Baker (R.-Tenn.), and Congressman Michael Harrington (D.-Mass.), along with Senators Lowell Weicker (R.-Conn.), Walter Mondale (D.-

Minn.), Philip Hart (D.-Mich.), Frank Church (D.-Idaho), Mike Mansfield (D.-Mont.), Hubert Humphrey (D.-Minn.), Alan Cranston (D.-Calif.) Joseph Montoya (D.-N. Mex.), Daniel Inouye (D.-Hawaii), Edward Brooke (R.-Mass.), James Pearson (R.-Kans.), and Jacob Javits (R.-N.Y.), are accepting information that would be useful to the Legislative Branch of the United States Government for controlling and monitoring the activities of the United States intelligence establishment; all persons wishing to cooperate with Congress on this matter are advised to abide by federal, state, and local statutes when transmitting material or documents.

On September 26, 1974, the Florida law firm of Lloyd Herold, P.A., and Evan I. Fetterman, Esquire, filed a 6.2 million dollar law suit on my behalf in United States District Court for the Southern District of Florida (West Palm Beach, Fla.) naming Pratt & Whitney Aircraft, a division of United Aircraft Corporation, as the defendant. Among the eight causes of action cited in the suit, both Pratt & Whitney Aircraft and the Air Force Foreign Technology Division are charged with conspiracy to violate my constitutional rights and to prevent me from writing this book. Action on this case is now pending.*

*All persons wishing to provide additional information on Pratt & Whitney Aircraft and/or the Air Force's involvement in the case (or related incidents) are respectfully asked to contact me (send information to Peter N. James, Project Red Dog, P.O. Box 9661, Riviera Beach, Florida 33404). Be sure to abide by federal, state, and local statutes when transmitting material or documents; anonymous tips are also being accepted.

Appendix 1

Commands of the United States Air Force

In mid-1974 the United States Air Force numbered about 933,000 civilian and military persons. About 97 percent of all Air Force personnel are assigned to fifteen Commands and about three-quarters of them are assigned to 108 air bases in the United States. Within this massive complex is Building 828 of Wright-Patterson Air Force Base, the hush-hush worldwide headquarters of the Air Force Foreign Technology Division, a division of the Air Force Systems Command.

Aerospace Defense Command (ADC)
Air Force Communications Service (AFCS)
Air Force Logistics Command (AFLC)
Air Force Systems Command (AFSC)
Air Training Command (ATC)
Air University (AU)
Alaskan Air Command (AAC)
Headquarters Command, USAF (HQ COMD USAF)
Military Airlift Command (MAC)
Pacific Air Forces (PACAF)

Strategic Air Command (SAC)
Tactical Air Command (TAC)
United States Air Forces in Europe (USAFE)
USAF Security Service (USAFSS)
USAF Southern Command (USAFSO)

Appendix 2

Corroborating Photographs
and Memoranda

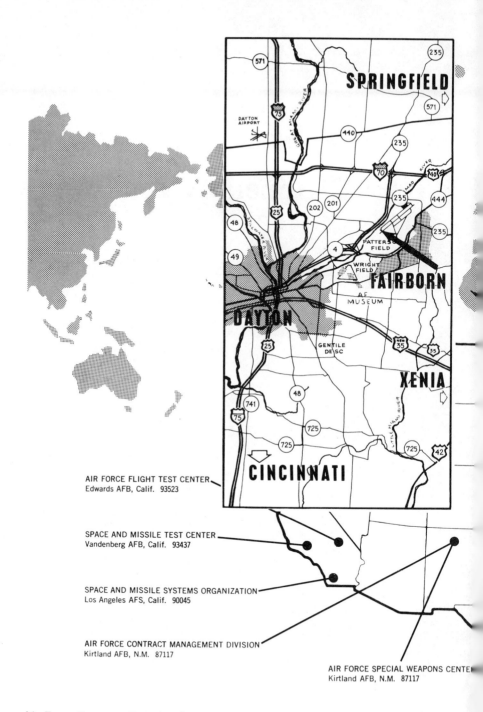

AIR FORCE FLIGHT TEST CENTER
Edwards AFB, Calif. 93523

SPACE AND MISSILE TEST CENTER
Vandenberg AFB, Calif. 93437

SPACE AND MISSILE SYSTEMS ORGANIZATION
Los Angeles AFS, Calif. 90045

AIR FORCE CONTRACT MANAGEMENT DIVISION
Kirtland AFB, N.M. 87117

AIR FORCE SPECIAL WEAPONS CENTER
Kirtland AFB, N.M. 87117

Air Force Systems Command

294

AIR FORCE SYSTEMS COMMAND

WORLDWIDE RESPONSIBILITIES

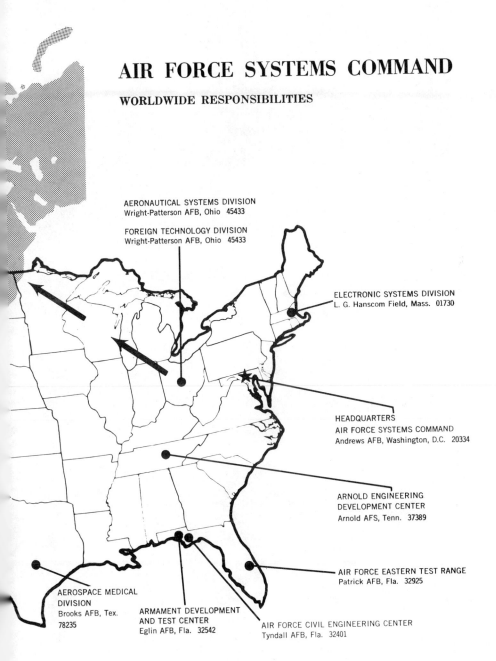

AERONAUTICAL SYSTEMS DIVISION
Wright-Patterson AFB, Ohio 45433

FOREIGN TECHNOLOGY DIVISION
Wright-Patterson AFB, Ohio 45433

ELECTRONIC SYSTEMS DIVISION
L. G. Hanscom Field, Mass. 01730

HEADQUARTERS
AIR FORCE SYSTEMS COMMAND
Andrews AFB, Washington, D.C. 20334

ARNOLD ENGINEERING
DEVELOPMENT CENTER
Arnold AFS, Tenn. 37389

AIR FORCE EASTERN TEST RANGE
Patrick AFB, Fla. 32925

AEROSPACE MEDICAL
DIVISION
Brooks AFB, Tex.
78235

ARMAMENT DEVELOPMENT
AND TEST CENTER
Eglin AFB, Fla. 32542

AIR FORCE CIVIL ENGINEERING CENTER
Tyndall AFB, Fla. 32401

Building 828, Wright-Patterson Air Force Base (Headquarters of USAF Foreign Technology Division) (photo credit: Ed Roberts, *Dayton Daily News*)

Gray Clouds Hang Over Pratt & Whitney Aircraft Florida Research and Development Center (photo credit: *Palm Beach Post*)

Col. George R. Weinbrenner, Commander of the Air Force Foreign Technology Division

"In the councils of government, we must guard against the acquisition of unwarranted influence, whether sought or unsought, by the military-industrial complex. The potential for the disastrous rise of misplaced power exists and will persist. We must never let the weight of this combination endanger our liberties or democratic processes. We should take nothing for granted."

PRESIDENT DWIGHT D. EISENHOWER
January 17, 1961

W. L. Gorton, Former General Manager of the Pratt & Whitney Aircraft Florida Research and Development Center

(photo credit: *Palm Beach Post*)

298

Leo J. Faucher, Chief of Plant Security of the Pratt & Whitney Aircraft Florida Research and Development Center
(photo credit: *Palm Beach Post*)

DEPARTMENT OF THE AIR FORCE
HEADQUARTERS FOREIGN TECHNOLOGY DIVISION (AFSC)
WRIGHT-PATTERSON AIR FORCE BASE. OHIO 45433

REPLY TO
ATTN OF: TDPTA-5

SUBJECT: Participation in the Foreign Technology Program

FEB 1 1969

TO: Mr. Frederick C. Polhemus, Jr.
Field Representative
Pratt & Whitney Aircraft Division
United Aircraft Corporation
Suite 1311, Talbot Tower
Dayton, Ohio 45401

1. In reference to your previous conversation with Major William F. Morris and Captain Harold W. Gale of this headquarters, we propose that your Florida Research and Development Center participate in an exchange of information with FTD.

2. We propose to furnish Pratt & Whitney with translations and abstracts of foreign technical literature, including texts, journal articles, patents and other publications pertinent to advanced liquid rocket engine technology.

3. In addition, under contract AF 04/611-68-C-0002, "Advanced Development Program to Demonstrate a High Performance Reusable O_2/H_2 Rocket Engine," monitored by Capt E. D. Braunchweig, Air Force Rocket Propulsion Laboratory, we have initiated action to establish a need-to-know so that we can furnish you classified technical intelligence pertinent to advanced liquid rocket propulsion research and development.

4. We would like to establish an information requirement profile of pertinent topic tags under our mechanized Central Information Reference and Control System (CIRC). It will be necessary to consult with a member of your Florida R&D Center to establish this profile. Once the profile is established, we will forward the resultant information as it is received. Classified material will be accounted for as required by your contract with AFRPL.

5. In return for furnishing information on foreign rocket research, we would like to have your expert opinion on the foreign work. The opinions we would like to have would answer the following questions:

   a. How does the particular foreign work differ from the U.S. approach to similar technical problems?

   b. What level of capability does the particular work indicate or what limitation does it impose on capability? (For example, what maximum heat flux handling capability would a particular research indicate?)

   c. How does the particular work compare to U.S. state-of-the-art?

6. We would appreciate it if you could furnish us an annual report, the date to be mutually agreeable, on your opinion of the information furnished during the year.

7. We believe that we can furnish foreign technical information which will assist you in your own research and development work, and we would value your opinion in assessing the foreign capabilities. We think that this arrangement could be mutually very beneficial.

NICHOLAS POST, Acting Chief
Aerospace Technologies Division
Directorate of Production

Copy to:
AFRPL (RPI)
AFRPL (RPR)

300

REPLY TO
ATTN OF: TDPTA-5/Capt Gale

SUBJECT: Letter of Appreciation

APR 2 3 1969

TO: AFRPL/RPI (Lt. Col. W. Trigg)
RPRZ (Capt Braunschweigh)
IN TURN

1. Please convey our appreciation to Pratt & Whitney Aircraft, for their fine assistance to FTD during FY69. We have a letter agreement based on the need-to-know per Air Force Rocket Propulsion Laboratory contract F04-611-68-C-0002, titled Air Force Reusable Rocket Engine Program.

2. The Florida Research and Development Center of Pratt & Whitney Aircraft Division of United Aircraft Corporation, has prepared an excellent report after one year of association technology with FTD. The report was an independent summary and analysis of foreign liquid propellant rocket technology. It was comprehensive and timely; portions of the report were used within days of its arrival. We express our appreciation for the efforts on the part of Pratt & Whitney Aircraft, particulary, Mr. Ruby and Mr. P. James. We look forward to a continuing association under the letter of agreement.

HAROLD W. GALE, Capt, USAF
Group Leader, Propulsion Group

RECORDED

MAY 2 1969

GOVERNMENT MAIL CONTROL
PRATT & WHITNEY AIRCRAFT
FLORIDA RES. & DEV. CENTER

Letter of Appreciation by Capt. Harold W. Gale (FTD)

← How It All All Began

DEPARTMENT OF THE AIR FORCE
AIR FORCE ROCKET PROPULSION LABORATORY (AFSC)
EDWARDS, CALIFORNIA 93523

REPLY TO
ATTN OF: RPI

29 April 1969

SUBJECT: Letter of Appreciation

TO: Pratt & Whitney
ATTN: W. L. Gorton
Vice President and Gen. Manager
Florida Research & Development Center
P.O. Box 2691
West Palm Beach, Fla 33602

Dear Mr. Gorton

I am enclosing a letter of appreciation from Capt Harold W. Gale,
Foreign Technology Division, Wright-Patterson AFB for the outstanding
summary and analysis of foreign liquid propellant rocket technology
prepared by Mr. Ruby and Mr. James. Such independent work is of
great value to the Air Force Rocket Propulsion Laboratory by giving
us a better understanding of our primary competitors.

We hope to present a new Foreign Technology Briefing this summer so
don't be surprised if some of your own words are fed back to you.

Please convey the Rocket Propulsion Laboratory's appreciation to those
members of your division who have and are contributing to the Foreign
Technology Division's rocket propulsion analysis efforts.

Respectfully

WILLIAM J. TRIGG, Lt Colonel, USAF
Chief, Foreign Technology Division

1 Atch
Letter of Appreciation

RECORDED

MAY 2 1969

GOVERNMENT MAIL CONTROL
PRATT & WHITNEY AIRCRAFT
FLORIDA RES. & DEV. CENTER

INFORMATION COPY

ACTION COPY ROUTED TO:
W. L. GORTON
INFORMATION COPIES TO:
R.J. COAR   R.A. SCHMIDTKE
R.C. MULREADY   R.R. ATHERTON
L.E. RUBY   P. JAMES
GOVERNMENT MAIL TECHNICAL PUBLICATIONS

Letter of Appreciation by Lt. Col. William Trigg (Air Force Rocket Propulsion Laboratory)

Belgrade, Yugoslavia (1967)

MAY 1969

SMIRNOV

SARYCHEV

DIANE WITH RUSSIANS

Venice, Italy (1969)

304

ZHIVOTOVSKIY

(ASSISTANT TO DEPUTY PREMIER USSR)

ISTOMIN

(KGB-ATTACHE)

KGB COL. BELOUSSOV

(KEELER SEX SCANDAL)

(KGB WATCHDOG)

SMIRNOV

ZHIVOTOVSKIY

RUSSIAN SPOOKS AND ENGINEERS

AT LE BOURGET FIELD

COSMONAUT
VLADIMIR SHATALOV

DIANE

PHOTOGRAPH TAKEN BY CIA AGENT CATCHES ME ABOUT TO
SNAP A PICTURE OF THE RUSSIAN ROCKET ENGINE DISPLAY
AT LE BOURGET FIELD

Paris, France (1969)

306

Dayton, Ohio 45424

Mr. Pete James
112 Bravado Lane
Palm Beach Shores, Fla.

Hi *Pete,*

Last summer in a conversation the possibility of a spring vacation
in Southern Europe was mentioned. To get funding for the trip, it's
always nice to be giving a paper at a conference in the tour area. I
just happened to hear about a conference in Rome that might be of
interest to you. Just for my own entertainment, I wrote up an abstract
that might be accepted by the meeting sponsors. Feel free to re-write
into your own words. The abstracts should arrive at the address below
by 30 November 1969.

10th International Technical Scientific Meeting
on Space

Secretariat of
RASSEGNA INTERNAZIONALE ELETTRONICA
NUCLEARE E TELERADIOCINEMATOGRAFICA
Via Crescenzio, 9 - 00193 ROMA, Italia
Tel. 656.93.43/44/45 - Cable Address: ROMATOM, Roma

Be sure to make your corporate affiliation clear in the abstract
submission letter. I'll be able to help with the actual paper later if
you so desire.

Your friend,

████████████████

How FTD Secretly Recruits Spies

Mar del Plata, Argentina (1969)

DIMENTIEV BELOTSERKOVSKIY ZAVERNAEV

ZHIVOTOVSKIY DIANE

This one is worse than any report ever received by us, no-cost or otherwise. I prefer to attribute the contents to the author, rather than the corporation since I have met many fine people in Florida. We terminated relations with the originators of the previous worst report, which this surpasses, but prefer not to do so here, if possible. If Mr. ████ is not replaced as the corporation representative, we will have little recourse except to consider that Pratt & Whitney does not desire further association with us. Interestingly, this is occurring as the excellent relations with their competitors improve.

Specific Comments on the Report:

Page 1, paragraph 5: The lag of 8 to 12 years cited here is contradicted by the next paragraph and in subsequent portions of the report. The identity of Soviet and P&W practices lead to an inference that P&W is 8 to 12 years behind Mr. ████ notion of the general US capability. We have a higher opinion of P&W.

Page 1, last paragraph: Mr. ████ is not using the latest information which I personally provided to him.

Page 2, paragraph 2: Useless assessment: "Engines will get better."

Page 2, last paragraph: Complete nonsense contradicting the opinion of specialists from competing groups and factual data supplied to Mr. ████.

Page 3, paragraph 2: Here Mr. ████ demands access to foreign developments whose contempories in the US are not accessible to either of us.

Page 3, paragraph 2: Mr. ████ demands operational data on engine use. Such data is being reported but Mr. ████ ignores it.

Page 4, paragraph 2: Mr. ████ refuses to accept Soviet data as a basis for assessing Soviet capability. In other places he refuses to accept data from other sources.

Page 4, paragraph 3; etc: Here Mr. ████ repudiates his earlier statements one by one, until none are left.

Summary: The report evinces a commitment to preconceived notions arrived at years ago. The author has chosen to avoid use of factual data that contradicts his views and has substituted a diatribe that is not even consistent from paragraph to paragraph. If this were a personal contract we would terminate relations post-haste; since it is not, we will attempt to salvage the relationship. I refuse to believe, at this time, that Mr. ████ is typical of P&W technical competence.

How FTD Intimidates a Government Contractor

P M James   70.1007

DEPARTMENT OF THE AIR FORCE
HEADQUARTERS FOREIGN TECHNOLOGY DIVISION (AFSC)
WRIGHT-PATTERSON AIR FORCE BASE, OHIO 45433

REPLY TO
ATTN OF: TDP
                                              AUG 6 1970

SUBJECT: Letter of Appreciation

TO: Pratt and Whitney Aircraft
     Attn: Mr. W. L. Gorton, General Manager
     Florida Research & Development Center
     Division of United Aircraft Corporation
     West Palm Beach, Florida

     1. The Commander and I wish to extend our gratitude and appreciation
     to Pratt and Whitney Aircraft Division for your foreign technology
     effort and in particular for your outstanding study on Soviet liquid
     propellant rocket technology and its applications. This study was both
     comprehensive and timely.

     2. Your responsiveness in foreign technology support to the AFRPL
     Contract Nr. F04-611-68-C-000Z, entitled, "Air Force Reusable Rocket
     Engine Program," demonstrated high competence on the part of your
     personnel. Personnel of AFRPL provided the necessary guidance. In
     this respect, Mr. L. Ruby and Mr. P. James of your organization, and
     Capt Robert Probst, the contract monitor of AFRPL, are to be commended
     for their outstanding performance in connection with the study.

     3. Again, I wish to thank you for your contribution and trust that
     your interest and participation will continue as part of the total
     national effort.

     Benjamin Smotherman

     BENJAMIN F. SMOTHERMAN, Colonel, USAF
     Director of Production

ACTION COPY ROUTED TO:
    W/O H/E G. L. Gorton
INFORMATION COPIES TO:
    W. L. Gorton
    H. M. Cotter
    R. R. Atherton

Letter of Appreciation by Col. Benjamin F. Smotherman (FTD)

TDPTA-5/Capt Pfeifle/70151/jom/1 Sept 70

Pratt & Whitney Aircraft - Annual Report on Foreign
Rocket Technology (U)

AFRPL (RPRE/Capt Probst)

1. On 15 July 1970, the Pratt and Whitney Florida Research and
Development Center published its second, "Annual Report on Foreign
Rocket Technology." The expertise with which topics of interest
were covered and the information content in general, make it
desirable that Pratt and Whitney be permitted to give the report
wide dissemination in the research and development community. The
report should be of particular interest to major aerospace
contractors.

2. It is requested that AFRPL (RPRE) assist Pratt and Whitney in
determining those organizations to receive this report, and act as
a monitor for report distribution. This is a continuation of the
access monitorship provided in accordance with the security
requirements of contract F04611-68-C0002, "Advanced Development
Program to Demonstrate a High Performance Reusable O_2/H_2 Rocket
Engine."

3. In addition, it is requested that a listing of tentative
recipients be provided this office prior to final distribution of
the documents.

FOR THE COMMANDER

/s/ Halstead

WARREN W. HALSTEAD, Colonel, USAF
Chief, Aerospace Technologies Division
Production Directorate

Directive by Col. Warren W. Halstead (FTD)

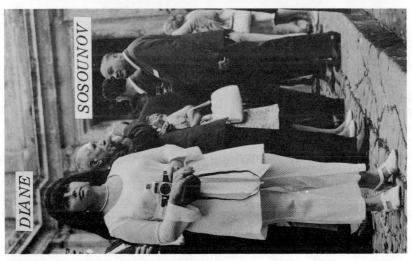

Rome, Italy (1970)

Konstanz, Germany (1970)

SMONAUT BORIS YEGOROV

DIVITT YEGOROV

SEVASTYANOV YEGOROV

COSMONAUT SEVASTYANOV YEGOROV

ADAMOVICH

315

Pratt & Whitney Aircraft
FLORIDA RESEARCH AND DEVELOPMENT CENTER

To _____ L. E. Ruby/H. N. Cotter _____   Date _____ October 27, 1970 _____

From _____ P. N. James _____ Ext _____ 753 _____

Subject _____ Foreign Technology _____

1. I wish to phase out my activities with the Foreign Technology Division at WPAFB because of personal reasons.

2. I recommend that FRDC also phase out its direct affiliation with FTD for the following reasons:

   (a) We have already achieved our objective during the past two years and currently enjoy a healthy relationship with the Air Force.

   (b) Continued association with FTD could worsen our relationship with the Air Force:

      1. We will never provide FTD with as much coverage in the future as was done in this year's report.

      2. FTD is interested in splitting PWA-FRDC/PWA-EH.

   (c) Experience has shown that FTD has nothing to offer that is technically or financially beneficial to the company.

   (d) Company resources and contacts are better than those of FTD.

   (e) The Defense Intelligence Agency (i.e., FTD) was criticized by the Blue Ribbons Defense Panel for poor work. Its principle problems were summarized as, "...too many jobs and too many masters." FTD has already undergone two major cutbacks in personnel and is scheduled for a 20% cutback during the next 2 months.

   (f) FTD is not currently in favor with anyone.

   (g) Numerous FTD-DIA personnel are trying to salvage their jobs by pinning indiscretions on each other and private industry. An attempt is currently being made to pin an indiscretion on personnel at East Hartford. We don't need these kind of friends.

3. I recommend that we maintain an informal-friendly-no paperwork relationship with AFRPL, ASD, and the Aeropropulsion Laboratory instead. These people count.

P. N. James

P. N. James

PNJ/ljt

PWA FRDC SIA REVISED 6-67

Breaking Relations With FTD

PRATT & WHITNEY AIRCRAFT ENGINES
FLORIDA OPERATIONS

To A. L. Harrell, Jr.   Date 12 May 1971

From P. N. James   cc: H. N. Cotter

Subject Leave Of Absence

I have scheduled my vacation for the last two weeks in July and request a leave of absence without pay during August and September so that I can visit my relatives in Greece.

I understand that if I participate in any technical activities (i.e., international conferences, discussions with foreign scientists or engineers, etc.) my employment with FRDC could be terminated. I am very much aware of the corporate position regarding the conduct of its employees while travelling abroad and have made it perfectly clear to various government organizations that they can expect nothing from me as a result of this or future trips.

I believe that the company's records will show that I have not taken any sick leave in almost 2 years and have complied with the security department's directions and regulations regarding previous foreign travel. Approval of my request to take a 2 month leave without pay would be greatly appreciated.

P. M. James

P. N. James

PNJ:vsm

"Company Rules"—Trying to Keep the Lid on

WITH VICTOR ANTONOV IN THE
ADRIATIC HOTEL

DIANE

SOKOLOV

Dubrovnik, Yugoslavia (1971)

318

OPCHIAN

PAZELSKY

DIANE

MITROFANOV

BAEV

PAZELSKY

Marseilles, France (1971)

Marseilles, France (1971)

AFTER QUESTIONING AND PHOTOGRAPHING DIANE, K. SCHELLER OF WRIGHT - PATTERSON AIR FORCE BASE TURNS HIS MOVIE CAMERA ON ME

SEPT. 15, 1971

PAZELSKY

WAITER

SCHELLER

In the Name of National Security—Marseilles, France (1971)

322

AFTER PHOTOGRAPHING US AT THE UNIVERSITY DR. S.A. WAITER OF THE (NORTH AMERICAN) ROCKWELL INTERNATIONAL SPACE DIVISION PREPARES TO SNAP A PICTURE OF DIANE *(not shown)* WITH THE RUSSIANS.

TOPCHIAN

SEPT. 15, 1971

BAEV

WAITER

SOLOUKHIN

BAEV

TOPCHIAN

BALAYAN   KHODAREV

ADAMOVICH   DIANE

324

GRAND'PLACE

VIEW FROM EMBASSY CONSUL ALTA FOWLER'S
FLAT (AFTER THREAT AND SURVEILLANCE
SEPT. 23, 1971)

Brussels, Belgium (1971)

SKATCHKOV (SEPT. 21, 1971)
DIANE
DUBOSCHINE

ULANOV

BRUSSELS, BELGIUM
JAMES
SKATCHKOV
DUBOSCHINE

WITH BULGARIANS IN TOWN HALL

ASPARUCHOV

KONDRATYEV

COSMONAUT BORIS YEGOROV

KHODAREV

Brussels, Belgium (1971)

327

GUESS WHO'S COMING TO DINNER

BORIS MANDROVSKY, SUPERVISOR
WITH THE LIBRARY OF CONGRESS

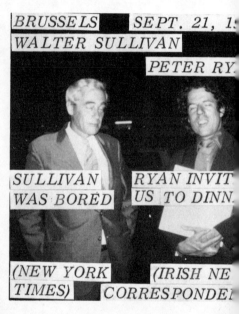

BRUSSELS   SEPT. 21, 1~
WALTER SULLIVAN
                 PETER RY.

SULLIVAN   RYAN INVIT
WAS BORED   US TO DINN.

(NEW YORK   (IRISH NE
TIMES)   CORRESPONDE

IN MARSEILLE, FRANCE DURING SEPT. 14-~
1971, BORIS MANDROVSKY WAS DISGUISED I
A BLACK BEARD WHEN HE HAD US UNDER
SURVEILLANCE. IN BRUSSELS, BELGIUM ON
SEPT.   21, 1971, MANDROVSKY ALLUDED
MY BOOK AND SAID HE HAD FRIENDS IN THI
MAFIA WHO COULD ARRANGE AN AUTOMOB
ACCIDENT. HE IS SHOWN HERE (WITHOUT A
DISGUISE) AS HE APPEARED IN LINDAU, GEI
MANY ON OCT. 7, 1970. CIA AGENTS CLAIM
THAT MANDROVSKY AND HIS COHORTS HAV.
A REPUTATION FOR DOING THINGS "OUT OI
THE ORDINARY."

For "Uncle Sam" of Course—Brussels, Belgium (1971)

CONFERENCE EXCURSION TO LOPUD, YUGOSLAVIA ON SEPT. 8, 1971

THE KGB FINGERED SUBJECTS "A" AND "B" AND TIPPED ME OFF THAT DIANE AND I WERE UNDER SURVEILLANCE

BRUSSELS, BELGIUM (SEPT. 20, 1971)

ASTRONAUT DAVID SCOTT

SUBJECT "B" LATER SHOWED UP IN BRUSSELS WITH HIS BEARD TRIMMED. ON SEPT. 20, 1971 SUBJECT "B" CROSS-EXAMINED ME DURING A TAXI CAB RIDE TO A RECEPTION.

MARSEILLE, FRANCE (SEPT. 15, 1971)

G. R. INGER, VIRGINIA POLYTECHNIC INSTITUTE AND STATE UNIVERSITY, PRESENTS PAPERS AT INTERNATIONAL MEETINGS. HIS RESEARCH WORK IS SUPPORTED BY THE UNITED STATES AIR FORCE.

BRUSSELS, BELGIUM (SEPT. 21, 1971)

DIANE

Palm Beach Shores, Florida
(Place)

August 17, 1973
(Date)

I, Peter Nicholas James , hereby state that
Richard Bellinger has identified himself to me
as Special Agent AFOSI USAF.
(Special Agent AFOSI, Security Police, Other-Specify)

I do hereby voluntarily and of my own free will make the following statement without having been subjected to any coercion, unlawful influence or unlawful inducement.

To place this statement in the proper context, the following background information would be helpful. I earned a bachelor of science degree from Case Institute of Technology in Cleveland, Ohio in 1962 (refer to exhibit 1) and joined Pratt & Whitney Aircraft's (P&WA) Florida Research and Development Center (FRDC) on July 3, 1962. During 1962 - October 4, 1971 I was employed in the FRDC Applied Research, Advanced Propulsion, and Systems Analysis Departments (refer to exhibit 2). After representing FRDC at an international space conference in Athens, Greece in 1965, I was contacted by Mr. Justin F. Gleichauf, Chief of the CIA Miami Field Office, via the FRDC security office. Thereafter, I voluntarily covered meetings for the CIA with the knowledge of FRDC management and security office in the following cities: Athens, Greece (1965); Madrid, Spain (1966); Belgrade, Yugoslavia (1967); Venice, Italy (1969); Paris, France (1969); Mar del Plata, Argentina (1969); Rome, Italy (1970); Konstanz, Germany (1970); Dubrovnik, Yugoslavia (1971); Marseille, France (1971); Brussels, Belgium (1971); *Miami, Florida (1972).

My work was regarded highly by the CIA as shown by exhibits 3 through 5. In 1968 FRDC entered into an agreement with the Air Force Foreign Technology Division (FTD) and I was selected to coordinate this program. In 1969 and 1970 I wrote two voluminous reports on Russian rocket technology. The Air Force and FRDC response to this effort was very favorable as shown by exhibits 6-12.

I learned of improper FTD activities during 1969-1970 and reported much of what I learned to my superiors. Management took no action on my written and verbal charges, allegedly because it was the FRDC policy not to upset the Air Force. However, by early 1970 at least one FRDC manager had privately entered into an agreement with FTD without the knowledge of the Company's Security Department, and I was aware of FTD's continuing desire to penetrate the FRDC organization and recruit spies. When FTD's improper activities caused an internal rift with Pratt & Whitney Aircraft (P&WA) -- the P&WA division in Connecticut would not capitulate to FTD's improper demands, while the P&WA division in Florida was very accommodating -- I no longer wanted any part of any dealings with FTD, and thus on October 27, 1970 I wrote a formal memorandum to my superiors and asked to be phased out of the Company's program with FTD and I recommended that the Company do likewise. See exhibit 13. FTD's infiltration into FRDC continued -- more managers were privately approached.

*No longer affiliated with FRDC

AF FORM 1169

Page 1 of 29 Pages
PNJ

Opening Page From My Statement to the Air Force Office of Special Investigations (August 17, 1973)

Staff Photo by Judy Morohovich

Peter James

He proposes
to document
for the nation
what he calls
'its greatest
moral challenge'

Peter's Principle: Precision

By JIM QUINLAN
A Commentary
Post Staff Writer

If you think the astronauts as a group are the epi-tome of the clean, scrubbed, all-American type then you haven't met Peter James.

Peter James, meticulous, soft-spoken, deliberate, makes by comparison the band of space voyagers we have been admiring for a dozen years appear a little sloppy.

It isn't appearance alone that gives this young man an aura of self-assurance and poise.

Peter James' confidence and drive come, it appears, from some marriage of mind with reality. He is a care-ful, conservative talker. If five different people all wit-nessed the same pig running across a street, Peter James would be the only one after the fact to have a precise memory of the scene.

Article From the Palm Beach Post (Sunday, September 30, 1973)

"A pig, white with a black spot over the right front shoulder, weighing approximately 28 pounds, walked eight feet then began to run in a northeasterly direction across U.S.1," Peter James would probably say.

So, it was this Peter James whom I first met in October of 1971, two weeks after he had been fired by Pratt and Whitney.

The affair at P&W was bizarre. Peter James then 31, was in his ninth year with the rocket builders. He was trained in physics and working on advanced rocket mission analysis. It was all highly secret stuff but if the letters of praise from superiors were any proof, Peter James was one competent man.

Where Peter James went wrong was his insistence on letting America know of waste and danger in the space program.

For his effort Peter James was fired.

The average man who lost his job with virtually no chance of resuming his career anywhere in the country would be downhearted.

But not Peter James, at least not outwardly. His cool, analytical mind appeared to be hard at work as he adjusted during those days following his firing.

He and his wife Diane plunged into writing a book about the space age and the involvement of big business.

One of his fun projects was tinkering with a method of programing pro football teams. His analysis and predictions of an earlier Cleveland Browns-Baltimore Colts game had come to the attention of New York Jets coach Weeb Eubank.

Eubank, like any coach, would probably love to take the fun out of football and know his opponent's next play. Although James's little avocation was no guarantee, Weeb thought it was worth a close look.

But there was a final, serious phase to James' evolving awareness. Like many scientific people he had been ignorant of the dark side of business, politics and government ethics. He had painfully learned that a business may approve many questionable acts to gain a "sale" and that a believing public may unknowingly defend a government's any means to an end philosophy.

With characteristic precision Peter James gathered his materials and prepared to document for the American people what he termed "its greatest moral challenge."

PWA FR-**3195**
MAY 1969
VOLUME I

(UNCLASSIFIED TITLE)

ANNUAL REPORT ON FOREIGN
ROCKET TECHNOLOGY (U)

1968-1969

Approved By: L. E. Ruby

Pratt & Whitney Aircraft DIVISION OF UNITED AIRCRAFT CORPORATION

FLORIDA RESEARCH AND DEVELOPMENT CENTER
BOX 2691, WEST PALM BEACH, FLORIDA 33402

Artist's Reproduction of the Title Pages of My Three Annual Reports on
Foreign Technology—the May 1969 report was the first to state that the
Russians were developing reusable ICBM launch silos

PWA FR-3760
15 JULY 1970
VOLUME I

(UNCLASSIFIED TITLE)

ANNUAL REPORT ON FOREIGN ROCKET TECHNOLOGY (U)

(1969-1970)

Prepared By: P. James

Approved By: L. E. Ruby

Pratt & Whitney Aircraft DIVISION OF UNITED AIRCRAFT CORPORATION
FLORIDA RESEARCH AND DEVELOPMENT CENTER
BOX 2691, WEST PALM BEACH, FLORIDA 33402

SECRET
NOFORN

(THIS PAGE UNCLASSIFIED)

NOFORN

SECRET

PWA FR-3760A
1 SEPTEMBER 1970
VOLUME I

(UNCLASSIFIED TITLE)

ANNUAL REPORT ON FOREIGN ROCKET TECHNOLOGY (U)

(1969-1970)

Prepared By: P. James

Approved By: L. E. Ruby

GROUP 1
EXCLUDED FROM AUTOMATIC DOWNGRADING
AND DECLASSIFICATION

AFFECTING THE
WITHIN THE
18 U. S. C.
OR THE
MANNER TO
BY LAW

NOFORN

FOREIGN NATIONAL EMPLOYEES OF THE CONTRACTOR OR
SUBCONTRACTOR(S) INCLUDING THOSE POSSESSING
CANADIAN OR UNITED KINGDOM RECIPROCAL CLEARANCE
ARE NOT AUTHORIZED ACCESS TO CLASSIFIED INFORMA-
TION RESULTING FROM OR USED IN THE PERFORMANCE
OF THIS CONTRACT UNLESS AUTHORIZED IN WRITING BY
THE PROCURING CONTRACTING OFFICER.

Aircraft DIVISION OF UNITED AIRCRAFT CORPORATION
FLORIDA RESEARCH AND DEVELOPMENT CENTER
BOX 2691, WEST PALM BEACH, FLORIDA 33402

SECRET
NOFORN

WARREN G. MAGNUSON, WASH., CHAIRMAN

JOHN O. PASTORE, R.I.   NORRIS COTTON, N.H.
VANCE HARTKE, IND.   JAMES B. PEARSON, KANS.
PHILIP A. HART, MICH.   ROBERT P. GRIFFIN, MICH.
HOWARD W. CANNON, NEV.   HOWARD H. BAKER, JR., TENN.
RUSSELL B. LONG, LA.   MARLOW W. COOK, KY.
FRANK E. MOSS, UTAH   TED STEVENS, ALASKA
ERNEST F. HOLLINGS, S.C.   J. GLENN BEALL, JR., MD.
DANIEL K. INOUYE, HAWAII
JOHN V. TUNNEY, CALIF.
ADLAI E. STEVENSON III, ILL.

FREDERICK J. LORDAN, STAFF DIRECTOR
MICHAEL PERTSCHUK, CHIEF COUNSEL

United States Senate

COMMITTEE ON COMMERCE
WASHINGTON, D.C. 20510

October 3, 1974

Mr. Peter N. James
██████████████████████████████

Dear Mr. James:

I appreciate the receipt of your letter of September 20 regarding your forthcoming book, The Air Force Mafia.

I believe that a copy of your book would be useful and informative as we attempt to develop background information supportive of my proposal for the creation of a Joint Committee on Intelligence Oversight. Consequently, if possible, I wish to accept your generous offer of a pre-publication copy of The Air Force Mafia.

I have taken the liberty of enclosing a reprint of the legislation which I introduced, together with my introductory remarks. I believe that the broad jurisdictional provisions of the bill would encompass jurisdiction over intelligence activities conducted by the Air Force Foreign Technology Division, or any other such activities conducted by any agency or department of the United States Government.

Sincerely,

Howard H. Baker, Jr.

HHBJr:gdt

Enclosures

336

October 9, 1974

Mr. Peter N. James
███████████████████
███████████████████

Dear Mr. James:

Thank you for your letter concerning the Air Force Foreign
Technology Division. I would certainly appreciate a copy of
your forthcoming book, "The Air Force Mafia", as I expect
it will be the only widely available source of information on
the Air Force intelligence activities.

As far as Congressional oversight of intelligence activities,
I have introduced House Resolution 1231, to create a standing
House oversight committee which must meet regularly, keep
records, and include members of the Foreign Affairs Committee. The resolution specifically provides that Air Force
intelligence will be subject to the jurisdiction of the committee.
S. 4091, the Baker-Weicker Intelligence Oversight bill, also
creates an intelligence oversight committee that would have
jurisdiction over the Air Force intelligence activities.

Thank you for taking the time to write. Please do not hesitate to continue correspondence on this or any other matter.

Yours sincerely,

Michael J. Harrington

MJH:srs

𝔘𝔫𝔦𝔱𝔢𝔡 𝔖𝔱𝔞𝔱𝔢𝔰 𝔖𝔢𝔫𝔞𝔱𝔢
WASHINGTON, D.C. 20510

November 7, 1974

Mr. Peter N. James
███████████████
██████████████████████

Dear Mr. James:

I very much appreciate your letter concerning
the question of Congressional oversight of the intelligence community, and would welcome the opportunity
to examine your book. Thank you for your very generous
offer.

As you may know, I am hoping to hold hearings
in November on CIA oversight. It is clear to me that
Congress must reform oversight procedures in connection with the intelligence community. I am sure
your personal experiences with F.T.D. would provide
helpful additional input in determining the scope of
existing intelligence activities.

With every good wish, I am

Sincerely,

Edmund S. Muskie
United States Senator

Appendix 3

The SALT Connection

Both the Air Force Mafia and the past administrations have attempted to formulate foreign and domestic policies by conducting their business in secret and lying to the American people and Congress. There is an aspect of the Air Force Mafia-Pratt & Whitney story which must be publicized because it contributed to the Nixon Administration's efforts to steamroll the SALT I Treaty through Congress during a political year, even though it was known that the Soviets would subvert the intent of SALT I. My letter to Senator Henry Jackson dated October 5, 1972, and excerpts from an address I gave at Hillsdale College on February 3, 1974, summarize the problem.

Dear Senator Jackson:

I am contracted by Arlington House Publishers to write a book entitled *Soviet Conquest From Space.* Your position on the SALT Agreement is very sound and I hope to bring forth information for the man-on-the-street to place this and other agreements that we might reach in proper perspective. I wish to quote some of your positions on this agreement and would appreciate receiving material from your hearings on the Soviets. . . .

PLEASE NOTE: One point that I am making in the book is that the public and Senate have been deluded into believing that the agreement freezes the number of Soviet land-based ICBM's to about 1,600. That is not so. The agreement essentially freezes the number of *silos*, which we can monitor with our satellites, *but the Soviets have developed the capability to reuse these silos, so that more than one ICBM can be launched from the same silo.* This is important for a first strike capability. I am speaking from a background of nine years in the aerospace field, an intelligence analyst for four years, and I have talked with the heads of the Soviet space and defense establishment and some of their intelligence personnel.

Good luck.

Sincerely yours,
Peter N. James

My Hillsdale Address:

. . . There is another disturbing aspect of the SALT agreement which must be made public at this time. When President Nixon signed the SALT agreement in St. Vladimir Hall, the Executive Office and the U.S. intelligence community were aware that the Soviets were designing their land-based ICBM launch silos so that they could be used over again. The public and United States senators, however, were never informed of this fact, and the illusion was created during this political year that SALT represented a slowdown in the Soviet arms build-up, when there was nothing further from the truth. Compared to the U.S. land-based ICBM force of 1,054, designed on the basis of one ICBM per launcher, the Soviets are expected to have up to 4,000 operational land-based ICBM's by the late 1970's and these missiles can be launched from the 1,618 launchers which are permissible under the SALT agreement. With the reusable launchers and a MIRV capability, the Soviets will be able to deliver well over 10,000 nuclear warheads to U.S. targets—a reign of terror more deadly than the *Gulag Archipelago* described by Solzhenitsyn. Compared to U.S. missiles, by the end of this decade, Russian ICBM's will be capable of carrying still larger warheads, more MIRV's, and more decoys to foil U.S. defenses and more on-board protective shielding to prevent them from being destroyed. And this can be achieved without violating the terms of the SALT agreement.

The secret record shows that the Executive Office and the U.S. intelligence community were aware of Soviet work on reusable ICBM launchers by 1970 at the latest. As Pratt & Whitney Aircraft's foreign technology expert, my intelligence assessments were distributed to the CIA, Executive Office of the President, Department of Defense, National Aeronautics and Space Administration, and other branches of the U.S. government. In a secret document I authored entitled "Annual Report on Foreign Rocket Technology (1968-1969)" (report identification number PWA-FR-3195; the report was released to the CIA and Air Force intelligence units during May 1969), it was stated in the strategic threat summary that the Soviets were designing reusable ICBM launch silos. As the Soviets were engaged in a massive clandestine ICBM arms build-up during this period, I prepared an eight hundred-page two-volume secret document the following year. The first version (report number PWA-FR-3760, dated July 15, 1970) was released to the Air Force and CIA. Again, in the strategic threat summary, I stated that the Soviets were designing reusable ICBM launchers. Because the report was political dynamite—the trends indicated that our political leaders were misleading the country and the U.S. military-industrial complex was squandering our tax monies because of poor planning at the highest levels—Pratt & Whitney Aircraft management ordered me to delete the strategic threat section entirely, or I would not be permitted to distribute the report outside the U.S. intelligence community. I therefore rewrote the report, but I still included a summary section covering the reusable Soviet ICBM launchers. Two copies of this document, report number PWA-FR-3760A, dated September 1, 1970, were sent to the Executive Office of the President on October 29, 1970. Similarly, other U.S. government documents correctly assessed Soviet intentions regarding reusable launchers. In other words, the SALT agreement was signed with the knowledge that a loophole existed for the Soviets to subvert the intent of the agreement, but this was never announced publicly.

By early 1971 Pratt & Whitney Aircraft suddenly rejected requests by bona fide government agencies to receive the censored version of the secret report; organizations such as the prestigious Hudson Institute, which performs special studies on national security issues, were flatly rejected access to the report on the grounds that "all available copies have been distributed," when a number of copies existed in the company's files. The documents were subsequently destroyed by the company because they were political dynamite.

In a tumultous series of events, I learned from a reliable intelligence source that President Nixon became involved in a foreign technology problem concerning Pratt & Whitney. By this time management threatened to fire me if I attempted to write my planned book on the Soviets. During a two and one-half months leave of absence from the company in 1971 without pay, I conducted research on my book in Europe. When I returned to work, I was fired by Pratt & Whitney Aircraft management. Seven months later President Nixon signed the SALT agreement in Moscow, culminating years of secret negotiations with the Soviets. If the public had been told the truth of the Soviet capability and the Nixon Administration had disclosed beforehand the scope of U.S. concessions to the U.S. Senate and defense specialists, the SALT agreement would never have been ratified. . .

(NOTE: My intelligence reports during 1969-1970 and letter to Senator Jackson in October 1972 preceded the public announcements of 1973-1974 that the Soviets were in fact developing reusable ICBM silos.)

Plate 29 is an artist's reproduction of the title page of my first annual report on foreign rocket technology. This document, which stated that the Soviets were developing the capability to reuse their ICBM launch silos, was distributed to both FTD and the CIA during the spring of 1969. The mysterious negotiations which led to the SALT Treaty of May 1972 should be investigated in relation to what the Air Force Mafia and CIA knew at the time and what the Executive Office conceded secretly to the Soviet government without telling the American people.

In conclusion, on the basis of the material presented within, it is my belief that the national security of the United States and the individual rights of Americans can be better protected if the Air Force Foreign Technology Division is abolished and the more qualified analysts and agents be absorbed by either the Defense Intelligence Agency or the Central Intelligence Agency. Furthermore, I recommend a massive closed-door congressional investigation of the U.S. intelligence establishment to weed out the unethical secret empires which have yet to be uncovered and to ensure that the establishment serves the best interests of the American people and the Free World—not vice versa.

Peter N. James
October 4, 1974

Index

344

Gleichauf, Justin F., 40, 51, 66-67, 82, 83, 90, 98, 107, 122-25, 131, 147, 161-62, 189-90, 191-93, 203, 204, 287
Glickstein, Marv, 58, 128-29
Gorton, W. L., 82, 83, 114, 117, 144, 148, 157, 168-69, 175, 194
Goudz, Boris, 150
Grodzovskiy, 123-37
Grumman Aerospace Corporation, 31

Hall, D. W., Jr., 271
Harrell, Les, 170, 194, 196, 267
Harrington, Sen. Michael, 289
Hart, Sen. Philip, 290
Hassen, Grant, 115
Hebert, Congressman F. Edward, 34, 281
Helms, Richard, 112, 273-74, 275
Hennessy, John, 262, 263, 264, 274, 287
Herold, Sen. Lloyd, 290
Hersh, Seymour M., 287
Hillsdale College, 17
Hillsdale Daily News, 16
Hogan, William H., Jr., 281
Hoggland, Lucille, 164-65, 166, 191
House Judiciary Committee, 24
Howmet Corporation, 31
Hudson Institute, 171
Hughes, Michael, 140-42, 143
HUMINT, 134, 137-38, 139
Humphrey, Sen. Hubert, 290

IBM Corporation, 174
Illinois Institute of Technology, 31
Inger, G. R., 233-34
Inouye, Sen. Daniel, 290
Institute of Space Research (in Moscow), 61, 137
International Business Machines Corporation, 31
Israili Six-Day War (1967), 91
Istomin, 80, 150, 151

Javits, Sen. Jacob, 290
Jaworski, Leon, 24

Jinks, Larry, 275

Keldysh, Mstislav, 151
Keldysh, V. V. (Miss), 151
Kelly, Tom, 283
Khodarev, Jouli, 137, 207, 230
Kiefer, Eugene, 111, 113
King, Bill, 171, 172
Kirillin, Vladimir, 204
Korobeinikor, 220
Kosygin, Aleksei, 161
Kreuser, Edward, 204

Laird, Melvin, 133, 144
Lawton, Dr. Richard, 235-42, 243
Library of Congress, 18, 150, 155, 179
Lockheed Aircraft Corporation, 31
Los Angeles Herald-Examiner, 18
Losers, The, 90

Mahan, Charles, 163, 164, 166, 167, 169
Mandrovsky, 22, 226, 229, 230, 232, 234, 235-40, 241, 242
Mansfield, Sen. Mike, 290
Marchetti, Victor, 32
Mariotti, Ray, 284
Markov, 221-23, 224
Marks, John, 32
Marquardt Corporation, 31, 152
Marshall, Edmund, 281-83
Matthews, Charles, 171, 172
Maykapar, Prof. Georgiy, 123, 151
McAbee, Frank, 156, 159
McAllister, 134-35, 140
McClellan, Senator, 274
McCracken, Betty, 85
McDermott, Jack, 116-17
McDonnell Douglas Corporation, 26, 27, 31, 54, 92, 102-03, 106, 171, 172
McGarvy, Patrick, 32
McGraw-Hill, 48
Meisetz, Fred, 122-24, 140
Miami Herald, 13, 272, 275
Mikeladze, Prof. V. G., 150, 153
MiG 25, 26, 27